Ursula Ferrigno's
Complete Italian Cookery Course

Ursula Ferrigno's
Complete Italian Cookery Course

Photography by
Jason Lowe & Francesca Yorke

MITCHELL BEAZLEY

Ursula Ferrigno's Complete Italian Cookery Course
Ursula Ferrigno

First published in Great Britain in 2006 by Mitchell Beazley, an imprint of
Octopus Publishing Group Limited, 2–4 Heron Quays, London E14 4JP.
© Octopus Publishing Group Limited 2006
Text © Ursula Ferrigno 2006

A CIP catalogue record for this book is available from the British Library.

ISBN 10: 1-845331-92-3
ISBN 13: 978-1-845331-92-3

While all reasonable care has been taken during the preparation of this
edition, neither the publisher, editors nor the author can accept
responsibility for any consequences arising from the use thereof or from
the information contained therein.

Commissioning Editor: Rebecca Spry
Executive Art Editor: Nicola Collings
Design: Lizzie Ballantyne and Nicola Collings
Editor: Susan Fleming
Photography: Jason Lowe and Francesca Yorke
Home economy: Fizz Collins and Pippa Cuthbert
Production: Angela Couchman
Index: John Noble

Printed and bound by Toppan Printing Company in China
Typeset in American Garamond and Trade Gothic

contents

introduction

I have been cooking, demonstrating cooking and writing about cooking for my entire professional life. I have been teaching classes in Italian cooking for 15 years, and I can honestly say that each year I enjoy it more and more. Telling other people how to combine ingredients, how to savour and flavour, how to master techniques and share my enthusiasms, has given me a pleasure no other job possibly could. For me, cooking is play, a time of total relaxation. I may usually cook for other people, but that in itself is enjoyable – being a means of giving pleasure and joy to friends and family. But cooking with other people brings its own unique satisfaction. We all know eating is about sharing, but cooking can be too and, as a teacher, sharing my knowledge with a group of fellow enthusiasts is one of the most rewarding ways possible of spending my time – and of earning a living!

And that is what this book has been designed to do: to commit to print the lessons I have been giving over the last few years. The book may not be able to capture the sense of camaraderie an actual class engenders, or make you literally 'feel' the correct texture of a pasta dough, but it will take you a large part of the way. People go to cookery classes for a number of reasons, whether to learn from scratch, to hone existing skills, or to perfect a particular technique. It's usually to do with acquiring confidence, though, and I hope that the workshops here will instil that essential sense of confidence. They range from details of Italian ingredients, to making the perfect risotto, *crespella* (pancake), custard or sponge, to segmenting a chicken or cutting scallopine of veal, chicken or pork. For once you have grasped the basics of a technique or a dish, next time you will approach that technique or dish in a subtly different way. It won't daunt you any more, and you will gain speed, which in turn inspires confidence and makes the whole process of cooking far more enjoyable.

When I am teaching, I find I am also learning at the same time. The questions I am asked by my students are one of the most important aspects of my work.

Recognising what people don't know or don't understand helps me to assess what I am doing, and whether I am doing it right. Questions – and indeed feedback – help me to keep to the right track and to hit the right notes in my presentation. And this again is what I have done here, in this book. I have distilled all the knowledge I have gained from my students in the workshops, and in theory every question that you might have should have been anticipated.

This book will, I hope, introduce you to the whole palette of Italian food and cooking; it will guide you, give you confidence, hold your hand and answer questions that you might have had burning in your mind. You may not have known before how to deal with that uniquely Italian vegetable, the globe artichoke, but you will learn it here. You may be uncertain about bread-making, but Italian breads are some of the tastiest in the world, and my guidelines and related recipes will have you starting with the simplest of doughs then tackling much more complex amalgams. Cleaning a squid, making an Italian sponge or pastry, or transforming a custard into a delicious Italian ice-cream will become simplicity itself.

And that actually is the essence of Italian food and cooking: simplicity. With good ingredients, the most basic of cooking techniques and inspired combinations of delicious flavours, you can cook authentic Italian food with ease – and do it well. As my Italian grandmother always said, if you love your family, you must cook properly for them. I sincerely hope that this book helps you to cook properly and well.

pasta and its sauces

making fresh egg pasta

Once pasta would have been made in the home every day but, since the advent of dried pasta, home-made fresh has become less popular. It is now known in Italy as 'Sunday pasta'.

INGREDIENTS

The major ingredient in fresh pasta is flour, and the type used differs across Italy. In the south, we use a mixture of '00' plain flour and a fine durum wheat semolina. This latter makes the pasta stronger (which is ideal for filled pastas) and it comes in several grades of texture – the finest is what you need here. In the north, they use '00' plain flour exclusively. It is also used for cakes, pastries and sauces, and gives deliciously gossamer-light results.

Eggs are used with the flour for fresh pasta, as without them the paste would be far too tough for home rolling out and shaping. (Most dried pasta is made from semolina alone, and this can only be mixed and extruded by machine. There is also an egg and semolina dried pasta.) Italian eggs, with their bright orange yolks, come from chickens fed on a rich corn diet. So buy the freshest free-range and/or organic eggs you can: they add protein and colour to the pasta and enable it to become springy and light.

Salt and oil are the only other ingredients in fresh egg pasta. Use a fine salt, as flakes would cause holes in home-made pasta. Use olive oil rather than extra virgin, as it is lighter and less assertive in flavour. You will also need a good rolling pin, one that is long and straight, without 'handles'.

VARIATIONS

The fresh pasta recipe (right) can be varied by adding 'colourings', although you may need to increase the proportions of flour to eggs to prevent the mixture from becoming too wet. For green pasta, add 85g (3oz) well-drained, puréed cooked spinach; for red pasta, add 1½ tablespoons tomato purée; for black pasta, add 1 teaspoon cuttlefish ink.

You can keep pasta dough in the fridge for several days, or freeze what you don't need (for up to 3 months).

BELOW, FAR LEFT: make a crater in your flour, then crack your eggs into the crater.

LEFT AND ABOVE: slowly break up the eggs while simultaneously drawing in the flour with the other hand. Continue until you have a pasta dough – here spinach has been added to make green pasta.

150g (5½oz) Italian '00' plain flour

150g (5½oz) fine semolina flour

a pinch of fine sea salt

2 large eggs

1 tbsp olive oil

1 Pile the flours on to a work surface, then blend them together with the salt into one large volcano-like pile. Make a crater in the centre.

2 Break the eggs into the crater and add the oil. With a fork in one hand, slowly break up the eggs, at the same time drawing in the flour with the other hand to make a paste.

3 When all the flour is mixed in you should have a ball of dough. If it seems too dry, add a little more oil or water; if it seems too damp, knead in a little more flour. At first the mixture will be soft and sticky, but carry on kneading until it is smooth, silky and, when you press a finger into it, the depression bounces back. Wrap in cling film and allow the dough to rest in the fridge for about 20 minutes before rolling out (see page 14).

SERVES 4-6

rolling out and cutting fresh pasta

ROLLING PASTA BY HAND

Divide your rested dough (see pages 12-13) in half. Keep one half covered and place it back in the fridge. Put the remaining dough on the work surface and start rolling it out with your rolling pin. Keep the dough piece even-sided as you roll, to make it neat. Flour the surface if it is too sticky; this will depend on the ambient temperature (I always try to work in a rather cool kitchen, as pasta likes cold conditions).

Roll the dough backwards and forwards, flipping it over as you go, until the pasta is so thin that you can see the colour of your flesh through it (a little thicker, about 3-4mm/^{1}/$_8$in, if it is for lasagne or cannelloni). You will now have a large piece of pasta, which will start to dry out quickly if it is thin enough. Connoisseurs say that pasta rolled by hand is the ultimate because of the pressure the pasta has been put under, with the constant rolling and the body weight of the person making it.

ROLLING PASTA BY MACHINE

Roll out your rested pasta dough to a long thinnish oval that will just fit into the width of the pasta machine (you may need to divide it into several pieces first). Start with the machine rollers set at their widest setting, and then pass the dough through the machine several times. Change the machine rollers to the next widest setting, and repeat the process. Continue down the settings in this way. By the time you have passed the dough several times through the settings one up from the narrowest (which I never use, as I find it produces pasta so fine that it is too difficult to handle), the pasta should be ready for shaping. It should be as thin as specified above.

CUTTING PASTA

For dishes such as lasagne and cannelloni, you can use these pasta sheets just as they are, trimming them to the required shape. The same applies to making filled pasta shapes: cut plain sheets of rolled-out pasta dough into

strips, then squares, rectangles or circles, as required in the individual recipes. To make pasta noodles by machine, pass the dough through the selected cutter to provide the shape required. To cut by hand, roll the sheet of dough into a wide flat sausage, and cut across the sausage into appropriately sized strips (thick for pappardelle, medium for tagliatelli, or thin for tagliolini or vermicelli). Shake out to separate, and leave to dry in a nest shape for 5-7 minutes. If not dried a little, the pasta will stick to itself during cooking. For filled pasta, see page 25.

Keep any leftover dough, cut it into small pieces and dry these with the rest of the pasta. They can be added to soup as a thickener.

BELOW LEFT: to hand-roll fresh pasta, roll the dough backwards and forwards until you can see the colour of your flesh through it – it should be about 2mm, or a little thicker if it is for cannelloni or lasagne.

ABOVE: to machine-roll fresh pasta, start by rolling it through the widest possible setting, and then gradually narrow down the settings one increment at a time until the pasta is the thickness you require.

cooking and eating pasta

Cook all pasta in rapidly boiling water. (I actually prefer to cook my pasta in bottled water: the purity of the water makes the pasta more flavoursome as pasta actually absorbs a lot of water.) Bring back to the boil as quickly as possible and keep at a rolling boil until *al dente*, or 'to the tooth' (that is, tender with a centre resistant to the bite). Only salt the water when it is boiling: if the salt is put in too early it will disperse around the sides of the pan and the water will not be salty enough. A little olive oil helps prevent fresh lasagne sheets from sticking together.

COOKING FRESH PASTA

This is never as firm as dried pasta when cooked, but it should still have some resistance. Fresh pasta can be cooked in as little as 4-5 minutes, although this will depend on the shape and size. Fresh lasagne, vermicelli and tagliatelle can actually cook in 30 seconds, and often, for lasagne, say, I don't pre-cook it at all (it will be 'cooked' in the sauces during its oven cooking).

Stuffed pasta shapes require more gentle handling or they may burst open and release their filling into the water. Accordingly, add them to the boiling salted water, bring it back to the boil as quickly as possible, then reduce the heat and poach rather than boil the pasta shapes. Keep them at a gentle simmer, stirring carefully during cooking.

COOKING DRIED PASTA

Always cook dried pasta in a large pan in plenty of boiling salted water so that there is plenty of room for it to expand, as it absorbs water as it cooks. The cooking time will be longer: cook following the instructions on the packet, or until *al dente*. Taste after about 6 minutes, and return to the pan to cook further if not done enough.

When cooking spaghetti and other long dried pasta, you need to coil the pasta into the boiling water as it softens so it will fit into the pan. Take a handful at a time and dip it in the boiling water so it touches the bottom of the pan. As the spaghetti starts to soften, coil the strands using a wooden spoon or fork until they are submerged.

No-cook lasagne sheets are available, and these do not need pre-boiling. Simply layer them with the sauces, and bake according to the recipe.

EATING PASTA

Do so in warm plates, with a fork only, using it to lift the pasta and sauce together. Make a small space at the side of your plate and twist only a little around the fork at a time. Add freshly grated Parmesan cheese to most pasta dishes, apart from mushroom or fish and shellfish pasta dishes, for which the flavour of the cheese is too strong.

RIGHT: When cooking spaghetti or other long dried pasta, hold a handful in the pan until the pasta submerged in the boiling water softens, and then coil the strands around a wooden spoon or fork until they are completely submerged.

lasagne con polpettini

lasagne with meatballs

Most lasagnes are made with a Bolognese sauce, but in this one, although I am still using beef (with some pork as well), I have made part of the meat mixture into meatballs, which adds an interesting twist. The recipe is traditional to Campania. Lasagne always involves quite a lot of preparation (as this and the following recipes will show), but it is well worth it, as its is such good family food.

1 recipe fresh pasta dough (see page 12)

or 300g (10¹/₂oz) dried or pre-cooked lasagne sheets (white or green)

1 recipe balsamella sauce (see page 22)

MEATBALLS AND MEAT SAUCE

300g (10¹/₂oz) minced beef

300g (10¹/₂oz) minced pork

1 extra large egg

55g (2oz) fresh white breadcrumbs

5 tbsp freshly grated Parmesan cheese

2 tbsp chopped fresh flat-leaf parsley, plus extra to garnish

2 garlic cloves, peeled and crushed

sea salt and freshly ground black pepper

4 tbsp olive oil

1 onion, peeled and finely chopped

1 carrot, scrubbed and finely chopped

1 celery stalk, finely chopped

2 x 400g cans chopped Italian plum tomatoes

2 tsp finely chopped fresh oregano or basil

1 If using fresh pasta, make, roll out, cut and rest the dough as described on pages 12-14. If using dried lasagne, cook in plenty of rolling, boiling, salted water until *al dente*. Drain and set aside. The fresh or pre-cooked lasagne sheets need not be blanched.

2 To make the meatballs, put 175g (6oz) each of the beef and pork in a large bowl. Add the egg, breadcrumbs, 2 tbsp of the cheese, half of the parsley, half of the garlic, and plenty of salt and pepper. Mix everything together with a wooden spoon, then use your hands to squeeze and knead the mixture so it becomes smooth and sticky.

3 Wash your hands and rinse them under cold water, then pick up small pieces of the mixture and roll them between your palms to make about 30 walnut-sized balls. Place on a tray and chill in the refrigerator, covered, for30 minutes.

4 To make the meat sauce, heat half the oil in a medium saucepan. Add the onion, carrot, celery and the remaining garlic, and stir over a low heat for 5 minutes, or until soft. Add the remaining meat and cook slowly for 10 minutes, stirring frequently and breaking up any lumps. Stir in salt and pepper to taste, then add the tomatoes, the remaining parsley, and the oregano or basil. Stir well, cover, and leave to simmer for 45-60 minutes, stirring occasionally.

5 Meanwhile, heat the remaining oil in a large non-stick frying pan over a medium to high heat. When hot, cook the meatballs in batches for about 5-8 minutes, until brown all over. Shake the pan from time to time so the meatballs roll around. As they cook, transfer them to paper towels to drain.

6 Preheat the oven to 190°C/375°F/gas mark 5.

7 To assemble the dish, spread about one-third of the meat sauce in the bottom of a large, shallow baking dish. Add half of the meatballs, then spread with one-third of the balsamella sauce and cover with half the lasagne sheets. Repeat these layers, then top with the remaining meat sauce and balsamella. Sprinkle the remaining cheese evenly over the surface.

8 Bake for 30-40 minutes, until golden brown and bubbling. Let stand for 10 minutes, then serve. If you like, garnish each serving with parsley.

SERVES 6-8

lasagne con melanzane

lasagne with aubergines

Lasagne has been enjoyed in Italy since Roman times. Baking pasta in layers with vegetables is healthy, tasty and very filling, and this is a perfect dish for sharing with family or friends.

½ recipe fresh pasta dough (see page 12)

or 175g (6oz) dried or pre-cooked lasagne sheets (white or green)

4 tbsp good-quality olive oil

1 large garlic clove, peeled and crushed

1 large white onion, peeled and chopped

1 x 400g can chopped Italian plum tomatoes

3 tbsp red wine

sea salt and freshly ground black pepper

1 large, firm, ripe aubergine

450g (1lb) mozzarella cheese, sliced

a handful of fresh basil leaves

1 If using fresh pasta, make, roll out, cut and rest the dough as described on pages 12-14. If using dried lasagne, cook in plenty of rolling, boiling, salted water until *al dente*. Drain and set aside. The fresh or pre-cooked lasagne sheets need not be blanched.

2 In a large saucepan, heat half the olive oil, then add the garlic and cook gently for a few minutes. Add the onion and sauté until soft. Lower the heat, add the tomatoes, wine, salt and pepper, and simmer for 20 minutes. Set aside.

3 Cut the aubergine into lengthways slices 3mm (⅛in) thick, and place in layers in a colander. Sprinkle salt between the layers and leave for 15 minutes. Rinse to remove the salt, and pat dry. (This prevents the aubergine soaking up too much oil and improves the flavour.)

4 Meanwhile, preheat the oven to 200°C/400°F/gas mark 6.

5 In a frying pan, heat some of the remaining oil, just enough to cover the bottom. Sauté the aubergine slices quickly, about 2 minutes on each side, or until soft. Drain on kitchen paper. Continue in this fashion, using more oil as needed.

6 To assemble the lasagne, spread one-third of the tomato sauce over the base of a lasagne dish (about 25cm/10in square). Add one-half of the lasagne sheets and then a little more sauce, then half the aubergine and mozzarella slices. Season the cheese and sprinkle with some basil leaves. Repeat these layers, finishing with a layer of tomato sauce. Cover with foil.

7 Bake for 25 minutes, until bubbling.

SERVES 4

lasagne de radicchio alla trevigiana
radicchio lasagne

I have a tremendous love for radicchio, having watched it being grown by my father. From planting to harvest is 6 weeks, so it is a good vegetable to grow at home. There are two varieties: the round, which is the most common, and the Treviso, which is long and thin. Do try to get the Treviso – order it from your greengrocer – as it is very much less bitter and much more flavourful.

1 recipe fresh pasta dough (see page 12)

or 300g (10½oz) dried or pre-cooked lasagne sheets (white or green)

3 heads Treviso radicchio

3 tbsp olive oil

FENNEL AND DOLCELATTE SAUCE

1 medium fennel bulb, peeled and quartered

1 onion, peeled and finely chopped

85g (3oz) unsalted butter

55g (2oz) Italian '00' plain flour

1 garlic clove, peeled and crushed

500ml (18fl oz) milk

sea salt and freshly ground black pepper

150g (5½oz) dolcelatte cheese, cut into cubes

1 If using fresh pasta, make, roll out, cut and rest the dough as described on pages 12-14. If using dried lasagne, cook in plenty of rolling, boiling, salted water until *al dente*. Drain and set aside. The fresh or pre-cooked lasagne sheets need not be blanched.

2 Preheat the oven to 200°C/400°F/gas mark 6.

3 Quarter the radicchio, wash well and pat dry. Place on a baking tray and drizzle the olive oil over it. Bake (or put under a preheated grill) for 10 minutes. The radicchio pieces will change colour and become slightly charred; this is correct, as the flavour will be at its best. Set aside.

4 Meanwhile, start the sauce. Steam the fennel pieces over boiling water, for about 12 minutes (it should be slightly *al dente*). Remove and finely chop.

5 Cook the onion in a saucepan in the butter until it is softened and golden. Add the flour, garlic and steamed fennel, and cook for a few minutes to remove the raw taste from the flour. Now add the milk and some salt and pepper. Remove from the heat and stir vigorously with a wooden spoon.

6 Place back on the heat and bring to the boil, stirring continuously, until thickened. Add the cubed dolcelatte, and stir well. Check the seasoning.

7 To assemble the dish, place a layer of sauce in a suitable ovenproof dish followed by a layer of radicchio and a layer of pasta. Continue in this fashion until all the sauce, radicchio and lasagne have been used up. Finish with sauce on top.

8 Bake (still at the same temperature as above) for 20 minutes, until the lasagne is golden and bubbling.

SERVES 4

lasagne tricolore

spinach, fennel and tomato lasagne

Lasagne is eaten a lot in the south of Italy, and this particular recipe, which incorporates the colours of the Italian flag (red, white and green), is the one my family makes.

1 recipe fresh pasta dough
(see page 12)

   or 300g (10½oz) dried or
   pre-cooked lasagne sheets
   (white or green)

8 ripe plum tomatoes

sea salt and freshly ground
black pepper

2 garlic cloves, peeled and
finely chopped

1 tbsp olive oil

2 fennel bulbs

500g (18oz) spinach,
washed, tough stalks removed

finely grated zest of 1
unwaxed lemon

125g (4½oz) Parmesan
cheese, freshly grated

350g (12oz) ricotta cheese

unsalted butter for greasing

175g (6oz) mozzarella
cheese, sliced

a handful of fresh basil leaves

**EVERYDAY BALSAMELLA
SAUCE**

600ml (1 pint) milk

1 onion, peeled and quartered

1 bay leaf

6 black peppercorns

45g (1½oz) unsalted butter

35g (1¼oz) Italian '00' plain
flour

freshly grated nutmeg

1 If using fresh pasta, make, roll out, cut and rest the dough as described on pages 12-14. If using dried lasagne, cook in plenty of rolling, boiling, salted water until *al dente*. Drain and set aside. Fresh pasta does not need blanching.

2 For the sauce, put the milk with the onion, bay and peppercorns in a pan, bring just to the boil, and turn off the heat. Cover and leave to infuse while you prepare the other ingredients.

3 Preheat the oven to 180°C/350°F/gas mark 4. Cut the tomatoes in half and arrange them, cut side up, on a baking tray. Sprinkle with salt, pepper, garlic and olive oil, and bake until softened and wilted, about 35 minutes.

4 Pull off the tough outer layers of the fennel bulbs and cut off the tops where they meet the bulbs. Slice 4mm (⅛in) from the root end, then cut lengthways into thin slices. Drop into plenty of salted simmering water and cook for 5 minutes, until the root ends feel tender but firm when prodded with a fork. Drain.

5 Put the spinach in a pan with 1cm (½in) water. Cover and cook over a high heat until the leaves start to wilt. Stir, replace the lid, and cook until completely wilted (1-2 minutes). Drain in a colander and, when cooled slightly, squeeze dry in your hands. Form the spinach into small marble-sized balls.

6 Beat the lemon zest and about half of the Parmesan into the ricotta, and correct the seasoning.

7 Now finish the sauce. Melt the butter, stir in the flour and cook gently for about 1 minute, stirring all the time, until the mixture is quite smooth and pale yellow. Take the pan off the heat and pour in the milk through a sieve to strain out the flavourings. Whisk briskly until smooth. Put the pan back on the heat and bring back to the boil, whisking all the time, until the sauce thickens. Season with salt, pepper and nutmeg, and simmer gently for a minute or two.

8 To assemble the lasagne, butter a baking dish about 23cm (9in) square. Pour half the sauce into the bottom of the dish and cover with a single layer of pasta. Spread the pasta with half the ricotta mixture, and arrange the tomato halves, sliced mozzarella, basil and fennel slices in that order evenly on top. Follow this with another layer of pasta, spread with the rest of the ricotta, and dot with the spinach balls. Arrange a final layer of pasta on top, pour over the rest of the sauce and sprinkle evenly with the remaining grated Parmesan.

9 Bake until the lasagne is golden and bubbling, about 30 minutes. Serve at once.

SERVES 8

cannelloni con fave e ricotta

cannelloni with broad beans and ricotta

The combination of pasta and beans – a double carbohydrate – is truly delicious and nutritious. The subtle colours and flavours make this a very special dinner party dish – particularly with its very special balsamella – and something to look forward to during the all-too-brief broad bean season. Here the broad beans are cooked with mint: this is a classic combination, as the two are often grown together (because the mint helps keep blackfly away).

1 recipe fresh pasta dough (see page 12)

or 300g (10½oz) dried lasagne sheets (white or green)

sea salt and freshly ground black pepper

semolina for dusting

unsalted butter for greasing

extra grated Pecorino Romano

FILLING

1kg (2¼lb) broad beans in the pod, podded

350g (12oz) ricotta cheese

115g (4oz) Pecorino Romano cheese, freshly grated

1 large garlic clove, peeled and crushed

a large handful of fresh mint leaves, chopped

SPECIAL BALSAMELLA SAUCE

600ml (1 pint) milk

2 slices onion

1 bay leaf

1 blade mace

3 parsley stalks, bruised

5 whole black peppercorns

55g (2oz) unsalted butter

40g (1½oz) '00' plain flour

150ml (5fl oz) white wine

1 If using fresh pasta, make the dough as described on page 12. Roll out the pasta dough wafer thin and cut into 7.5cm (3in) squares. Sprinkle lightly with semolina and let dry on a tray for 10-15 minutes. Once almost dry, cook the pasta squares in boiling salted water. Drain when cooked but still firm to the bite. If using dried lasagne, cook in plenty of rolling, boiling, salted water until *al dente*. Drain and set aside.

2 To make the filling, boil or steam the broad beans until tender, about 10 minutes. Drain and leave to cool. Once cool, put half of the beans in a food processor and pulse, leaving some texture. Add the ricotta, Pecorino, garlic, mint and salt and pepper to taste. Add the remainder of the whole broad beans and mix well with a wooden spoon.

3 Preheat the oven to 200°C/400°F/gas mark 6.

4 To start the *balsamella*, place the milk in a pan with the onion slices, bay leaf, mace, parsley stalks and peppercorns. Heat over a medium to low heat, bring to a simmer, then remove from the heat and leave to infuse for 8-10 minutes.

5 Melt 25g (1oz) of the butter in a saucepan and stir in the flour. Stir over the heat for 1 minute, then remove from the heat. Strain in the infused milk and mix well. Return the saucepan to the heat and stir or whisk continuously until boiling. Add the remaining butter and the wine, and simmer for 3 minutes. Season with salt and pepper to taste.

6 On each pasta square spread 1 tbsp of the broad bean filling, and roll up into a cylinder. In a suitable greased casserole or baking dish, spread half the *balsamella* sauce. Place in the filled cannelloni and layer with the remaining *balsamella*. Sprinkle with extra grated Pecorino and bake for 15 minutes. Serve immediately.

SERVES 6

cannelloni con frutta di mare

seafood cannelloni with saffron sauce

The Trattoria Serra Gambetta in Apulia is run by Signora Perna Lanera and her son Domenico. It is on the coast, and surrounded by olive groves, vineyards, wheat fields and almond trees. They love seafood, and although this recipe – adapted from one of their classics – appears time-consuming, it's very easy.

1 recipe fresh pasta dough
(see page 12)

  or 300g (10¹/₂oz) dried or
  pre-cooked lasagne sheets
  (white or green)

semolina

unsalted butter for greasing

FILLING

25g (1oz) unsalted butter

300g (10¹/₂oz) firm-fleshed
white fish fillets, cut into
bite-sized pieces

8 medium scallops, shelled
and cut into bite-sized pieces

sea salt and freshly ground
black pepper

juice of 1 unwaxed lemon

300g (10¹/₂oz) ricotta
cheese, drained

1 large egg, lightly beaten

1 tsp finely chopped fresh
flat-leaf parsley

2 tsp snipped fresh chives

freshly ground nutmeg

SAFFRON SAUCE

25g (1oz) unsalted butter

2 shallots, peeled and finely
chopped

1 garlic clove, peeled and
crushed

a pinch pure saffron powder

300ml (10fl oz) single cream

1 If using fresh pasta, make the dough as described on page 12. Roll out the pasta dough wafer thin and cut into 7.5cm (3in) squares. Sprinkle lightly with semolina and let dry on a tray for 10-15 minutes. Once almost dry, cook the pasta squares in boiling salted water. Drain when cooked but still firm to the bite. If using dried lasagne, cook in plenty of rolling, boiling, salted water until *al dente*. Drain and set aside.

2 Preheat the oven to 180°C/350°F/gas mark 4.

3 To make the filling, melt the butter in a saucepan and cook the fish and scallops for 2-3 minutes on each side, or until just opaque. Season to taste with pepper and lemon juice. Transfer to a large bowl, using a slotted spoon. Pour off the pan juices and reserve.

4 Add the ricotta, egg, parsley and chives to the bowl with the seafood, and season to taste with nutmeg. Mix together to combine.

5 To make the sauce, melt the butter in a pan and cook the shallots and garlic for 4-5 minutes. Add saffron to taste and cook for 1 more minute, then pour in the cream and reserved seafood juices, and season to taste with salt and pepper. Bring to the boil, reduce the heat and simmer, stirring occasionally, for 5 minutes, or until the sauce thickens slightly. Strain and discard any solids.

6 To make the cannelloni, place about 1 tbsp of the seafood filling down the centre of each pasta square. Roll up to form a thick tube. Arrange the filled cannelloni in a suitable greased ovenproof dish. Pour the sauce over it and cover with foil. Bake for 20 minutes, or until heated through. Serve immediately.

SERVES 4

cappellacci alla Bolognese
cheese cappellacci with Bolognese sauce

Cappellacci are little filled pasta shapes, twisted round the finger to make each look like a bishop's mitre. If you feel uncertain about making these, simply cut the pasta into strips to make ravioli of whatever size you prefer. In Emilia-Romagna it is traditional to serve these *cappellacci* with a rich meat sauce but, if you prefer, you can serve them with a tomato sauce (see page 32) or just melted butter.

1 recipe Bolognese sauce
(see page 30)

1 recipe fresh pasta dough
(see page 12)

Italian '00' plain flour for
dusting

2.8 litres (5 pints) beef broth
(see page 299)

freshly grated Parmesan
cheese

fresh basil leaves

FILLING

250g (9oz) ricotta cheese

85g (3oz) Taleggio cheese,
rind removed, diced very
small

4 tbsp freshly grated
Parmesan cheese

1 medium egg

freshly grated nutmeg

sea salt and freshly ground
black pepper

1 First make the Bolognese sauce as described on page 30.

2 Make the pasta, and leave to rest, wrapped in cling film, for at least 20 minutes while you prepare the filling.

3 Put the ricotta, Taleggio and Parmesan in a bowl and mash together with a fork. Add the egg, a pinch of freshly grated nutmeg, salt and pepper to taste, and stir well to mix.

4 By hand on a floured board or, easier, using a pasta machine, roll out one-quarter of the pasta dough into a 92-100cm (36-40in) strip. Cut the strip with a sharp knife into 2 x 46-50cm (18-20in) pieces. Using a 5-7.5cm (2-3in) square ravioli cutter, cut 6 or 7 squares from one of the pasta strips.

5 Mound 1 tsp of filling in the middle of each square. Brush a little water around the edge of each square, then fold the square diagonally in half over the filling to make a triangle; press to seal the edges. Wrap the triangle around one of your index fingers, bringing two corners together. Pinch the ends together to seal, then press with your fingertips around the top edge of the filling to make an indentation so the 'hat' looks

like a bishop's mitre. Put the *cappellacci* on floured, clean tea-towels, sprinkle with flour, and let dry while you roll, cut and fill the remaining pasta dough. You want to make about 48-56 *cappellacci*.

6 When the sauce is nearing completion, bring the broth to the boil in a large pot over a high heat. Drop the *cappellacci* into it in batches, bring back to the boil, lower the heat and poach for 4-5 minutes. Drain well, and cook the remainder in the same way.

7 Divide the *cappellacci* between 6-8 warmed bowls. Spoon the hot Bolognese sauce over the *cappellacci* and sprinkle with the Parmesan and basil leaves. Serve immediately.

SERVES 6-8

ravioli con cicoria

green chicory ravioli

We Italians love our greens. As a filling for ravioli, the slightly bitter cicoria or endive leaves provide a perfect foil for the sweeter tomato sauce, but you could use spinach, Swiss chard or rocket instead. I first enjoyed this dish in Venice in a little café on a very cold day in February before the Carnival. It was cooked by the grandmother of the family. I went back for dinner and had the same dish again, just so that I could commit the flavour to memory.

1 recipe fresh pasta dough
(see page 12)

FILLING

500g (18oz) green chicory or
endive leaves, trimmed

sea salt and freshly ground
black pepper

250g (9oz) ricotta cheese,
fresh if possible

1 garlic clove, peeled and
crushed

a pinch of dried chilli
(peperoncino) to taste

1 large egg

100g (3½oz) Parmesan
cheese, freshly grated

TO SERVE

55g (2oz) unsalted butter,
melted

freshly grated Parmesan
cheese

tomato sauce (see page 32)

1 Make the pasta as described on page 12. Roll as described on pages 14-15, then cut into 7.5cm (3in) wide strips. Cover while you start the filling.

2 Boil the trimmed chicory leaves in boiling salted water for 7-10 minutes until tender, then drain them well and finely chop.

3 Mix together the ricotta, garlic, chilli, egg, Parmesan, salt and pepper to taste. Make little balls and put them on a pasta strip, about 6cm (2½in) apart. Cover with another pasta strip, seal and cut apart with a ravioli cutter. Continue until all the dough and filling are used up. Dry for a while.

4 Simmer the ravioli in salted water for about 8 minutes, or until they bob to the top of the water. Drain and serve with the melted butter, Parmesan and warmed tomato sauce.

SERVES 4

raviolini al finocchio con salsa di zafferano

fennel ravioli with a roasted vegetable and saffron sauce

This dish looks very cheerful with its white, red and yellow, and brightens up many a dinner table! The saffron sauce is excellent with other vegetable and pasta dishes, so will make a great addition to your repertoire. I've had it just with tagliatelle, which was delicious, but it is particularly good here, with the fennel pasta. In fact, this is a dish for the true fennel lover, with fennel inside the *raviolini* as well as in the sauce.

1 recipe fresh pasta dough
(see page 12)

sea salt and freshly ground
black pepper

fresh basil, flat-leaf parsley
and Parmesan cheese
shavings, to serve

FILLING

1 small fennel bulb, finely
chopped

225g (8oz) ricotta cheese

15g (1/2oz) fresh basil leaves,
shredded

55g (2oz) Parmesan cheese,
grated

**ROASTED VEGETABLE AND
SAFFRON SAUCE**

2 fennel bulbs, trimmed and
sliced

4 small red onions, peeled
and cut in wedges

5 tbsp extra virgin olive oil

1 garlic clove, peeled and
finely chopped

2 shallots, peeled and finely
chopped

a large pinch of saffron
strands

250ml (9fl oz) dry white wine

350g (12oz) mascarpone
cheese

1 Make, roll out, cut and rest the dough as described on pages 12-15.

2 To start the filling, lightly steam the fennel for 5 minutes over a pan of simmering water. Allow to cool slightly, then beat with the ricotta, basil and Parmesan. Season to taste.

3 Use a 7.5cm (3in) fluted cutter to cut out about 54 pasta circles. Spoon a scant tsp of the filling into the centre of each circle of dough. Brush the edges with a little water, fold each circle in half and pinch the edges together to seal.

4 Arrange the finished *raviolini* on a wire rack and leave to dry for at least 15 minutes. While the pasta is drying, preheat the oven to 190°C/375°F/gas mark 5.

5 To make the sauce, place the fennel and onions on a large baking tray and drizzle over 4 tbsp of the oil. Season with salt and pepper and roast for 25 minutes, until just beginning to char.

6 Meanwhile, heat the remaining olive oil in a pan and sweat the garlic and shallots for 5 minutes over a low heat until softened. Stir in the saffron and wine, bring to the boil and simmer until reduced by half.

7 Stir in the mascarpone and beat the mixture until smooth. Cook over a low heat, stirring, for 5 minutes. The more you cook the sauce, the more yellow it will become as the saffron gradually infuses into the mixture.

8 Bring a large pan of slightly salted water to the boil and add the *raviolini*. Return to the boil and cook for 3-4 minutes (frozen pasta will take 5-6 minutes). Drain and toss with the roasted vegetable and saffron sauce, and serve sprinkled with Parmesan shavings, basil leaves and chopped parsley.

SERVES 6

ravioli di patate e herbe

herbed potato ravioli

This is a good example of the northern Italian love for double carbohydrates – potato and pasta in the same dish. The generous soft herbs and the classic Venetian touch of a little cinnamon in the dressing imbue this dish with fresh flavour.

1 recipe fresh pasta dough
(see page 12)

STUFFING

350g (12oz) floury potatoes

4 tbsp olive oil

1 small onion, peeled and finely chopped

sea salt and freshly ground black pepper

1 large egg yolk

1 tbsp each of snipped fresh chives and torn basil leaves

2 tbsp chopped fresh marjoram

1 tsp freshly grated nutmeg

3 tbsp freshly grated Parmesan cheese

TO SERVE

55g (2oz) unsalted butter

1 tsp powdered cinnamon

25g (1oz) Parmesan cheese shavings

1 First make the fresh pasta, then wrap it in cling film and put it aside to rest for at least 20 minutes while you prepare the stuffing.

2 Boil the potatoes in their skins. When cool, peel them and purée them through a food mill or potato ricer into a bowl.

3 Heat the olive oil in a frying pan and sauté the onion for a few minutes to soften. Add to the potato purée with some salt and pepper. Mix in the egg yolk, herbs, nutmeg and Parmesan. Mix well to combine.

4 Unwrap the dough and place on a floured work surface. Divide in half, and roll out one-half to an ideal thickness of about 2mm (1/16in). Work 1 sheet of dough at a time, keeping the rest covered to stop it drying out. Cut the rolled-out sheet into 8cm (3¼in) squares.

5 Place a mound of stuffing the size of a walnut on one square and cover with another square. Seal the dough all around with dampened fingers. Place the little pasta parcels on clean tea-towels. Repeat with the second sheet of dough.

6 When all the ravioli are made, bring a large saucepan of water to the boil. Add salt, then gently slide in half the ravioli, and cook for 4 minutes. When the pasta bobs to the top of the pan, retrieve it with a slotted spoon and transfer it, well drained, to a large heated shallow dish. Cook the second batch and keep warm.

7 Melt the butter and cook until it begins to brown. Pour this over the ravioli and sprinkle with the cinnamon. Arrange the Parmesan shavings on top and serve at once.

SERVES 6

ragu bolognese

bolognese sauce

This is a classic sauce from Bologna in Emilia Romagna. There are many variations, some including chicken livers, but this combination of pork, beef and pancetta is particularly delicious. (You can make the sauce with all beef, however, and it will still be good.) The cream added at the end may seem unusual, but it makes the sauce less acidic, softening it and making it more luxurious. You can use this sauce with spaghetti, in a lasagne, and with the *cappellacci* on page 25. If you made it a little dryer, you could use it as a filling for *crespelle* or cannelloni.

25g (1oz) unsalted butter

1 tbsp olive oil

1 onion, peeled and chopped

2 carrots, finely chopped

2 celery stalks, trimmed and finely chopped

2 garlic cloves, peeled and finely chopped

85g (3oz) pancetta, cut into small cubes

250g (9oz) lean minced pork

250g (9oz) lean minced beef

sea salt and freshly ground black pepper

125ml (4fl oz) dry white wine

2 x 400g cans chopped Italian plum tomatoes

225-350ml (8-12fl oz) beef broth (see page 299)

7 tbsp double cream

1 Heat the butter and oil in a large saucepan until sizzling. Add the vegetables, garlic and *pancetta*, and fry over a medium heat, stirring frequently, for about 10 minutes, or until the vegetables are soft.

2 Add the meats, lower the heat, and cook slowly for 10 minutes, stirring frequently and breaking up the meat with a wooden spoon. Stir in salt and pepper to taste, then add the wine and stir again. Simmer, uncovered, for about 5 minutes, until reduced.

3 Add the tomatoes and 225ml (8fl oz) of the broth, and bring to a boil. Stir well, then lower the heat, half cover the pan, and simmer very slowly for 2 hours. Stir occasionally during this time, adding more broth as it becomes absorbed.

4 Add the cream to the meat sauce. Stir well to mix, then simmer the sauce for about 30 minutes longer, stirring often.

SERVES 4-8

spaghetti alla carbonara

spaghetti with eggs, bacon and cream

'Carbonara' is a famous pasta dish, usually spaghetti, seasoned with a sauce made with beaten egg and *pancetta* or bacon. This version has plenty of *pancetta*, and is not too creamy (I use crème fraîche), but you can vary the amount of the ingredients as you please.

2 tbsp olive oil

1 small onion, peeled and finely chopped

8 rashers pancetta or rindless smoked streaky bacon, cut into 1cm (1/2in) strips

350g (12oz) spaghetti

4 large eggs

4 tbsp crème fraîche

4 tbsp freshly grated Parmesan cheese, plus extra to serve

1 Heat the oil in a large saucepan, add the onion and cook over a low heat, stirring frequently, for about 5 minutes, until softened but not coloured.

2 Add the strips of *pancetta* or bacon to the onion, and cook for about 10 minutes, stirring most of the time.

3 Meanwhile, cook the pasta in a pan of salted boiling water until *al dente*.

4 Put the eggs, crème fraîche and grated Parmesan in a bowl. Grind in plenty of pepper, then beat together well.

5 Drain the pasta, tip it into the pan with the *pancetta* or bacon and toss well to mix. Turn the heat off under the pan. Immediately add the egg mixture and toss vigorously so that the egg cooks lightly and coats the pasta.

SERVES 4

salsa di carbonara di cinque verdure

carbonara sauce with five vegetables

This is my vegetarian version of *carbonara*. It's good served with farfalle (pasta bows).

250g (9oz) broccoli florets

4 tbsp olive oil

2 garlic cloves, peeled and chopped

2 courgettes, trimmed, diced

1 leek, white part only, washed and chopped

2 carrots, peeled and diced

1 red pepper, seeded, diced

a handful of fresh basil leaves, torn

2 large eggs, lightly beaten

100g (3 1/2oz) Parmesan, cheese, freshly grated

1 Blanch the broccoli florets in boiling salted water for 2 minutes. Drain and set aside.

2 In a frying pan, heat the olive oil. Add the garlic and all the vegetables and sauté for 8 minutes. Season and add the basil.

3 In a bowl, combine the eggs with the Parmesan.

4 Cook the pasta as usual until *al dente,* then drain and toss with the vegetables over a high heat for a few seconds.

5 Turn down the heat. Stir in the egg-and-cheese mixture until well combined and 'set', then season again. Serve immediately, with some extra freshly grated Parmesan if you like.

SERVES 4

salsa napoletana

tomato sauce

There are many different recipes for tomato sauce, but this is my grandmother's basic one. Naples is famous for its tomatoes, particularly the San Marzano, which is known as the 'true' Italian plum tomato. It is different from the others in shape and flavour: it has 'shoulders', and a drier but sweeter flesh. This is also the tomato most commonly dried in the hot southern sun.

3 tbsp best-quality olive oil

1 onion, peeled and chopped

750g (1lb 12oz) ripe tomatoes, skinned and roughly chopped

sea salt and freshly ground black pepper

a handful of fresh basil leaves, torn

25g (1oz) unsalted butter, cut into pieces

1 Heat the oil in a heavy pan, add the onion and fry gently for 5 minutes. Add the tomatoes, and some salt and pepper. Cook gently, covered, for 20 minutes.

2 Add the torn basil and the butter, and mix well. Serve immediately with hot cooked pasta.

SERVES 4

salsa di pomodori al forno

oven-roasted tomato sauce

This is a simple but flavoursome recipe, which can be prepared in several ways. In the winter I use oven-roasted tomatoes because they are more savoury, but during summer try using fresh plum tomatoes if you can find them. The finishing touch is some peppery, spicy pecorino, which you shave and toss into the pasta and sauce – you need about 100g (3½oz) peppered pecorino (or regular pecorino plus freshly ground black pepper).

450g (1lb) ripe plum tomatoes, halved

½ tbsp chopped fresh rosemary

3 tbsp chopped fresh thyme

1½ tsp caster sugar

3 garlic cloves, peeled

6 tbsp olive oil

a handful of fresh basil leaves, torn

sea salt and freshly ground black pepper

shavings of Pecorino cheese, to serve

1 Preheat the oven to 150°C/300°F/gas mark 2.

2 To oven-roast the tomatoes, place the plum tomatoes on a baking sheet, cut-sides up. Sprinkle with the rosemary, 1 tbsp of the thyme and the sugar. Chop 2 of the garlic cloves finely and sprinkle over the tomatoes with 4 tbsp of the oil. Roast for 2 hours. Allow the tomatoes to cool.

3 Heat the remaining olive oil in a frying pan. Add the remaining whole garlic clove and sauté until lightly golden, about 1-2 minutes. Remove the garlic from the pan and discard. Add the oven-roasted tomatoes and the basil and cook for 2-3 minutes over a medium heat. Adjust the seasoning with salt and pepper to taste.

4 Mix the cooked pasta with the tomatoes in the frying pan, then add the remaining thyme and the Pecorino shavings. Toss and serve immediately.

SERVES 4

salsa di pomodori e rucola di andrea

andrea's tomato and rocket sauce

Penne is the ideal pasta shape for this sauce, as the sauce clings to the pasta shape, making the dish deliciously substantial. This is one of my sister Andrea's favourite dishes.

16 fresh tomatoes, skinned, seeded and diced

2 garlic cloves, peeled and finely chopped

2-3 tbsp olive oil

a handful of fresh basil leaves, torn

sea salt and black pepper

16 rocket leaves, cut into strips

freshly grated Parmesan cheese, to serve

1 Combine the tomatoes, garlic, oil and basil in a large bowl, then season and allow to rest.

2 Turn the cooked pasta into the bowl with the tomato mixture, and toss well. Sprinkle the top with the rocket and Parmesan. Toss and taste for seasoning. Add a little of the hot pasta water if a thinner sauce is desired. Serve with extra freshly grated Parmesan if you like.

SERVES 4-6

salsa marchigiana

tomato and vegetable sauce

The tremendous advantage of this simple sauce for pasta is that all its ingredients are available in winter. For this dish, local cooks would choose the greenest verdicchio or vino cotto, a syrup made by simmering grape juice over a gentle heat for several hours until it is thick.

2 tbsp olive oil

1 small onion, peeled and finely chopped

1 celery stalk, chopped

1 carrot, peeled and chopped

100g (3½oz) pancetta or streaky bacon, diced

150ml (5fl oz) white wine

2 tbsp tomato purée

450g (1lb) ripe tomatoes, skinned and chopped

chopped plum tomatoes

3 sprigs each fresh thyme and marjoram

sea salt and black pepper

1 Heat the oil in a medium saucepan, then sauté the onion, celery and carrot for a few minutes.

2 Add the *pancetta* and mix. Add the wine and let it reduce until it has almost evaporated.

3 Add the tomato purée, tomatoes, herbs and seasoning, bring to the boil, then turn down the heat and simmer, covered, for 20 minutes.

SERVES 4-6

salsa di pomodori con menta

tomato sauce with mint

I have a passion for mint and tomatoes, as they are such great partners. I first enjoyed this combination in Sicily, one breathtakingly hot lunchtime. The sauce would be good with penne, and it would also be delicious served on bruschetta.

500g (18oz) fresh sun-ripened tomatoes

1 onion, peeled and chopped

2-3 fresh bay leaves

1 dsp capers, rinsed

2 handfuls fresh mint leaves

2 garlic cloves, peeled

1 tsp caster sugar

sea salt and freshly ground black pepper

1 tsp dried chilli (peperoncino)

2 tbsp extra virgin olive oil (estate bottled and fruity)

1 Cut the tomatoes into quarters. Heat the oil in a medium-sized saucepan and cook the tomatoes with the onion and bay leaves for 20 minutes. Remove the bay and press the tomatoes through a sieve or food mill. Return the sauce to the pan and simmer for about 25 minutes to thicken.

2 While the sauce is cooking, blend the capers, mint and garlic together and then set aside.

3 When the sauce is almost ready, add the sugar, salt and pepper and chilli. Taste and adjust the seasoning. Cook on a very low heat for 10 minutes. Turn off the heat and stir in the mint mixture and the oil. The sauce is now ready.

SERVES 6

salsa di mascarpone e spinaci

mascarpone and spinach sauce

In Italy, spinach is available in delicatessens, cooked and prepared, squashed and squeezed into a ball ready to take home and dress simply with oil and lemon. Here I've used it in a simple pasta sauce – good with tagliatelle or bucatini.

20g (3/4oz) unsalted butter

1 garlic clove, peeled and left whole

300g (10½oz) fresh spinach leaves, washed and finely chopped

150ml (5fl oz) double cream

140g (5oz) mascarpone

freshly grated nutmeg

1 Melt the butter, add the whole garlic, and cook gently, allowing the garlic to turn golden brown, but taking care not to burn the butter. Add the finely chopped spinach and cook over a low heat until tender, a few minutes only.

2 In a separate pan, simmer the cream and mascarpone gently for a few minutes.

3 Turn the cooked pasta into a warm serving bowl and add first the cream sauce, and then the spinach, having removed the garlic. Season with salt, pepper and nutmeg and mix well. Serve at once.

SERVES 4

salsa di cipolle

onion sauce

Experiment with the many different types of onion available. Red onions from Tropea, in Calabria, are delicious because the soil is so good. You could use white onions instead, which have a very good flavour, or a combination of the two. Simple, satisfying and surprisingly good, especially with tagliatelle.

100g (3½oz) unsalted butter

450g (1lb) onions, peeled and thinly sliced

150ml (5fl oz) double cream

sea salt and freshly ground black pepper

a large pinch of freshly grated nutmeg

a handful of fresh flat-leaf parsley, finely chopped

1 Melt the butter and cook the onions in a covered pan over a low heat until soft. Do not let the onion turn brown. Cover with a little water, approximately 4 tbsp, and cook with the lid on, simmering for 20 minutes.

2 Purée the cooked onion, then add the cream, salt, pepper, nutmeg and parsley.

3 Warm through, then serve with cooked pasta.

SERVES 4

salsa norcina

truffle or mushroom sauce

Truffles are synonymous with Italy. The white Alba truffle is the principal prize in Piedmont. To sniff them out, dogs are specially trained from puppies using cheese scented with truffles. Black truffles from Norcia, in Umbria, are not so prized, but in my opinion have more flavour. Winter truffles, *d'inverno*, have more flavour than those of the summer, *l'estate*.

1 black truffle or 55g (2oz) dried porcini mushrooms (ceps)

2 tbsp olive oil

1 garlic clove, peeled and crushed

a handful of fresh flat-leaf parsley, chopped

sea salt and freshly ground black pepper

a handful of fresh basil, torn

1 Slice the truffle thinly. If using the dried porcini mushrooms, soak them in cold water for 15 minutes, dry them with kitchen paper and chop them coarsely (keep the soaking water, and strain it to use as stock).

2 Heat the oil in a heavy pan, add the truffle or drained porcini, and cook gently for 5 minutes.

3 Remove from the heat and add the garlic and parsley. Return to the heat and cook gently for a few more minutes. Season to taste with salt and pepper.

4 Pour the sauce over the cooked pasta (spaghetti is good), add the finely torn basil leaves and mix well.

SERVES 3-4

sugo di noci

walnut sauce

My sister has two magnificent walnut trees in her garden in England, and they produce a profusion of nuts. One day I found her on her hands and knees picking up nuts from the ground and wondering in despair what she could do with them. I remembered this recipe – it's a sort of winter pesto – from a recent trip, and we spent the afternoon shelling walnuts and making the sauce. We had enough to keep her going for quite a while – and to give as Christmas presents! The sauce is wonderful with pasta and potato gnocchi (see page 80); use a little of the pasta or gnocchi water to slacken the sauce prior to serving.

175g (6oz) shelled walnuts (for perfection, just out of the shell or vacuum-sealed which tend to be sweeter)

1 garlic clove, peeled

a handful of fresh basil leaves, roughly torn

55g (2oz) Pecorino cheese, freshly grated

55g (2oz) Parmesan cheese, freshly grated

40g (1½oz) unsalted butter

4 tbsp extra virgin olive oil

sea salt and freshly ground black pepper

90ml (3fl oz) double cream

1 Place the walnuts and garlic in a food processor. Process until finely chopped.

2 Add the basil, cheeses, butter and oil, and process just a little bit more.

3 Transfer the mixture to a bowl and season with salt and pepper. Mix in the cream. Refrigerate until needed. It will last 1 week.

SERVES 6

salsa di cozze, pomodori e arancia

mussel, tomato and orange sauce

Although called a sauce, which would be superb with pasta, this could also be served as a fish dish, a **secondo piatto** (second course). One would never imagine mussels and oranges would go together well, but this Sicilian recipe, with its dash of chilli, will surprise you.

1½ tbsp olive oil

1 onion, peeled and chopped

1 garlic clove, peeled and chopped

½ tsp dried chilli (peperoncino)

2 x 400g cans chopped Italian plum tomatoes

200ml (7fl oz) dry white wine

3 tsp finely chopped fresh oregano, or 1 tsp dried

½ tsp caster sugar

3 tbsp orange juice

freshly ground black pepper

16 mussels, cleaned and scrubbed (see page 166/7)

2 tsp finely grated orange zest from an unwaxed orange

a handful of fresh flat-leaf parsley, finely chopped

1 Heat the oil in a large saucepan and cook the onion, garlic and chilli for 5 minutes. Mix in the tomatoes, half the wine, the oregano, sugar and orange juice. Season to taste with pepper. Bring to the boil, then reduce the heat and simmer for 40 minutes, or until the sauce reduces and thickens.

2 Preheat the oven to 200°C/400°F/gas mark 6.

3 Place the mussels in a baking dish and pour in the remaining white wine. Bake for 8 minutes, or until the mussels open. Discard any unopened shells.

4 Combine the orange zest and parsley. Toss the mussels into the sauce, then mix with cooked pasta. Sprinkle with the parsley mixture and serve.

SERVES 4

salsa di bottarga

bottarga sauce

Bottarga, which looks like a grey-brown hard salami, is actually grey mullet roe preserved in salt. The flavour is very unusual, fishy and intense, and I think it is rather addictive. It is becoming increasingly available (see also page 174), and it can be made into a simple Sardinian sauce for pasta, particularly spaghetti.

3 dsp olive oil

12 very thin slices bottarga

juice of ½ unwaxed lemon

freshly ground black pepper

1 garlic clove, peeled and finely crushed

a handful of fresh flat-leaf parsley, roughly chopped

1 Heat the olive oil in a small saucepan and add the bottarga. Add a little hot water (or some of the cooking water from the pasta pot). As soon as the bottarga has dissolved, add the lemon juice.

2 Mix the cooked pasta with the bottarga sauce. Dust with pepper, garlic and parsley, and serve immediately. That's it!

SERVES 4

salsa di aragostine

lobster sauce

The best lobsters are tiny and sweet and are found in Sicily. The richness of their flavour contrasts wonderfully with the simplicity of pasta, especially spaghetti. Twirl the pasta in the usual way, but dive in with your hands as well – something the Italians love to do.

3 small live lobsters or lobster tails, weighing about 400g (14oz) each

3 tbsp olive oil

2 garlic cloves, peeled and chopped

a generous pinch of dried chilli (peperoncino), crumbled

125ml (4fl oz) dry white wine

a handful of fresh flat-leaf parsley, roughly chopped

2 tbsp extra virgin olive oil

1 Bring a pan of salted water to the boil and drop in the lobsters. Simmer for 12 minutes and leave to cool. Halve the lobsters and remove the flesh from the bodies, discarding the stomach sacs. Crack the pincers and remove the meat. Keep to one side.

2 Heat the olive oil in a sauté pan, then add the garlic and chilli. Sauté for a couple of minutes, then add the wine. Bring to the boil, add the cooked lobster meat and the parsley, and simmer for 4 minutes. Season with salt and pepper.

3 Toss the sauce with cooked pasta, drizzle with good extra virgin olive oil (use one from Sicily), and serve at once.

SERVES 4

salsa di casorza

prawn sauce

This is one of the quickest, tastiest and simplest recipes and I first enjoyed it with spaghetti in a little seaside town in Liguria. It's so easy to replicate at home, but you must ensure that you use the very best ingredients. I think this could easily become part of your weekly cooking repertoire!

400g (14oz) raw tiger or king prawns

4 tbsp olive oil

2 garlic cloves, peeled and crushed

a handful of fresh flat-leaf parsley leaves, roughly chopped

1 fresh chilli, finely chopped

5 tbsp dry white wine

300g (10½oz) canned Italian plum tomatoes, chopped

1 Shell and clean the prawns.

2 Heat the oil in a large casserole and add the garlic, parsley and chilli, stirring constantly so as not to burn them. Now add the prawns and cook for 1 minute. Stir in the wine and tomatoes and cook for 2-3 minutes.

3 Add the cooked drained pasta to the pan with the sauce, season to taste and serve immediately.

SERVES 4

salsa di pesce

swordfish and aubergine sauce

Sicilians love swordfish, and aubergine is equally highly prized in their cooking. This recipe combines the two in a pasta sauce, which is delicious with tagliatelle.

1 medium aubergine, cut into 2.5cm (1in) cubes

5 tbsp olive oil

3 garlic cloves, peeled and thinly sliced

1 x 400g can chopped Italian plum tomatoes

500g (18oz) swordfish steak, cut into 1cm (½in) cubes

a small handful each of fresh flat-leaf parsley and marjorum, finely chopped

1 Put the aubergine cubes in a colander, sprinkle them with salt and leave to 'degorge' for 20 minutes. (This stops them from soaking up too much oil, and they taste better too.) Rinse and then dry the aubergines thoroughly.

2 Heat half the olive oil in a pan, add the garlic and cook for 2 minutes, stirring. Add the tomatoes, season to taste with salt and pepper, and then simmer for 10 minutes.

3 Meanwhile, heat the remaining oil and fry the aubergine in batches, adding more oil if necessary. Drain on paper towels and season with salt and pepper.

4 Add the aubergine, swordfish and most of the herbs to the tomato sauce, and simmer slowly for 10 minutes. Mix the cooked pasta into the sauce. Garnish with the remaining herbs and serve.

SERVES 4

salsa di fegatini di pollo e funghi

chicken liver and mushroom sauce

This is a variation on a sauce said to have been created for the great singer, Caruso. Chicken livers are much loved in Italy, where they tend to use everything from an animal – an example of Italian frugality. The sauce is best served with spaghetti or tagliatelle.

1 tbsp olive oil

55g (2oz) unsalted butter

1 onion, peeled and finely diced

2 garlic cloves, peeled and crushed

12 small button mushrooms, halved

1 x 400g can chopped Italian plum tomatoes

1 tsp caster sugar

300ml (10fl oz) chicken broth (see page 299)

salt and freshly ground black pepper

225g (8oz) chicken livers, trimmed and sliced

1 tsp finely chopped fresh thyme

90ml (3fl oz) Marsala wine

1-2 tbsp finely chopped fresh flat-leaf parsley

85g (3oz) Parmesan cheese, freshly grated

1 Heat the oil and half the butter in a saucepan, and cook the onion until soft. Add the garlic and mushrooms and cook for 2-3 minutes longer. Combine the tomatoes and sugar, add to the mushrooms, and cook over a low heat for 10 minutes. Stir in the broth and simmer for 30 minutes, or until the sauce reduces and thickens. Season to taste with some black pepper.

2 To cook the chicken livers, melt the remaining butter in a saucepan, then add the chicken livers and thyme and cook over a medium heat until brown, stirring from time to time. Increase the heat, stir in the Marsala and cook for 1-2 minutes. Stir in the parsley.

3 Arrange half of your cooked spaghetti on a warm serving platter, top with half the chicken liver mixture, then half the tomato sauce and mix. Sprinkle over half the Parmesan, then repeat the layers. Mix together and serve immediately.

SERVES 4

ragu di salsiccia

fresh sausage sauce

Sausages are a passion of the Italians. Don't feel limited to Italian sausages, though; buy any that are tasty. I once used some venison sausages from the local farmers' market.

2 tbsp olive oil

2 x 400g cans chopped Italian plum tomatoes

500g (18oz) your favourite herb sausages, skinned and cut into 2.5cm (1in) lengths

1 celery stalk, diced

1 carrot, peeled and diced

1 small onion, peeled and chopped

$^1/_2$ tsp caster sugar

sea salt and freshly ground black pepper

1 Heat the olive oil and tomatoes together in a large saucepan. Add the sausage, celery, carrot, onion and sugar. Add enough water to just cover the ingredients and combine well.

2 Season to taste and simmer for 45 minutes.

3 Add cooked pasta to the sauce and toss well.

SERVES 4-6

pesto alla genovese
basil pesto

This is the original pesto, made with basil, and it comes from Genoa in Liguria. It is delicious with pasta, traditionally served with **trofie** (hand-made pasta twirls) or **trenette**, but it can also be used in many other ways. It's good with gnocchi, and as the final flourish on a bowl of minestrone (see page 154). I have used it in the dough of a wonderful bread, and it's very tasty on crostini or bruschetta. You can make pesto in a food processor instead of a mortar and pestle, but the flavour is not quite so pungent. It can be made with rocket too, using the same ingredients but adding the finely grated zest of 1 unwaxed lemon.

1 garlic clove, peeled and sliced

2 tsp pine nuts

2 tbsp extra virgin olive oil, and more if needed

1 tbsp freshly grated Parmesan cheese

1 tbsp freshly grated Pecorino cheese

20 basil leaves

1 Using a mortar and pestle, pound the garlic together with the pine nuts until fine textured.

2 Add the oil, cheeses and basil, in that order, pounding until you have a thick pesto sauce.

3 Adjust the olive oil content to achieve the desired consistency. Cover and chill.

SERVES 4

pesto di menta

mint pesto

You don't have to use basil to make a pesto, as these recipes reveal. This one, made with mint, is good with pasta, but it is also very special used with aubergine and mozzarella as a pizza topping.

a large handful of fresh mint, chopped, plus sprigs to garnish

55g (2oz) pine nuts

55g (2oz) Parmesan cheese, freshly grated

1 small garlic clove, peeled

2 tbsp olive oil

1 Put all the ingredients in a mortar and, using the pestle, grind until the mixture is a paste. Alternatively, use a food processor.

SERVES 4

pesto di limone

lemon pesto

This can be served as a pasta sauce, but it is also delicious with vegetables – try it with gently steamed grated courgette and onion.

juice and finely grated zest of 2 unwaxed lemons

a large handful of fresh basil leaves

4 garlic cloves, peeled

75g (2¾oz) pine nuts

4 tbsp extra virgin olive oil

sea salt and freshly ground black pepper

3 tbsp freshly grated Parmesan cheese

1 Put all the ingredients in a mortar and, using the pestle, grind until the mixture is a paste. Alternatively, use a food processor.

SERVES 4

risotto,
polenta, gnocchi
and crespelle

making risotto

Perfect risotto is easy to achieve. The key ingredients are a good suitable pan, a good-quality risotto rice and home-made stock. You'll also need to put in 18-20 minutes of constant stirring while the rice cooks; there are no short-cuts.

EQUIPMENT

As well as the main risotto pan, you need one to heat the stock or broth. The stock pan can be any size, but obviously must be large enough for the amount of stock specified. The risotto pan is a little more specialised: it must be wide-rimmed and of medium height, not shallow and not deep (what I would call a sauté pan). The rice will double in size as it cooks, so the diameter needs to be fairly large. The width of the pan alsoallows the rice to absorb the broth evenly. As well as these two pans, you will need a wooden spoon for stirring the rice and a ladle for spooning the hot broth gradually into the rice.

INGREDIENTS

Risotto is made with short-grain rice, which absorbs a lot of liquid without the grains losing their bite. There are three main varieties of this type of rice: *arborio*, *carnaroli* and *vialone nano*. Each one lends a slightly different texture to the dish. *Arborio*, perhaps the best known, produces a dense risotto that can become too stiff if overcooked. *Carnaroli* is the most expensive, but its tender yet firm grain is ideal for risotto and it is the least likely to overcook. *Vialone nano* is favoured by Venetian cooks and I think it is the best rice of all, giving a creamy, voluptuous texture. Italian delis and an increasing number of supermarkets now sell a good range of risotto rice.

A good home-made broth is almost as important to risotto as the rice. Use vegetable broth for vegetable and vegetarian risottos, a chicken broth for meat and poultry risottos, and a fish broth for fish-based risottos. (*Carnaroli* rice is perfect for a seafood risotto; the grain is slightly larger and less creamy, but will absorb the fish flavours well.)

TECHNIQUE

Good risotto is made in stages. Flavourings are sweated first in unsalted butter (onion, celery etc.), then the rice is added and turned over in the fat. Now the hot, flavourful stock is added to the rice in the pan a ladleful at a time, and you have to stir constantly, until all the liquid has been absorbed and the rice is tender but still firm – *al dente*, or 'to the tooth'. It should never be dry or sticky, but should have a mobile consistency, *all'onda* ('like a wave'). A risotto should stand for 2 minutes, covered, before being served, then be spooned into warmed bowls, not plates, and served with a fork, never a spoon. Grated Parmesan is an optional extra, but there is a golden rule that you should never add cheese to a fish dish.

COOKING THE LEFTOVERS

Any leftover risotto is made into rice croquettes, **_suppli di riso_**. These are firm balls of rice with mozzarella cheese inside, or sometimes Bolognese sauce. They are also called **_arancia_**, meaning 'little orange'. They are shaped into rounds or pyramids, which are floured, egged and coated in breadcrumbs then deep-fried. Served warm, they make great snack food.

BELOW LEFT: one of the three types of risotto rice: _arborio, carnaroli_ and _vialone nano_.

ABOVE: risottos are started by sweating the flavourings in butter and oil, adding the rice, and then turning it over so that it is covered in fat.

risotto alla Parmigiana

Parmesan risotto

This is a good family recipe that children love; at least, my nieces and nephews do. It is rich, creamy and flavoursome without being too overpowering.

100g (3½oz) unsalted butter

1 tbsp olive oil

6 shallots, peeled and finely chopped

sea salt and freshly ground black pepper

350g (12oz) carnaroli risotto rice

1 litre (1¾ pints) hot vegetable broth (see page 299)

3-4 tbsp dry white wine

150g (5½oz) Parmesan cheese, freshly grated

1 Melt the butter and oil in a medium saucepan, add the shallots and some pepper, and fry for 5 minutes, until they have softened.

2 Add the rice and stir well to coat in oil and butter. Now add the hot vegetable broth, ladle by ladle, stirring between each addition, until the rice is tender but firm and the stock is used up. This will take about 18-20 minutes.

3 When the rice is creamy, stir in the wine, some salt and pepper and the Parmesan cheese.

4 Cover and stand for 1 minute to let the rice rest, before serving on hot plates, with extra grated Parmesan if desired.

SERVES 4

risotto alla milanese
classic saffron risotto

Milan is the home of risotto, and although this particular risotto is very simple, it is probably the most enjoyed, most households making it at least once a week. The smell of saffron is haunting and the risotto is very comforting.

150g (5½oz) unsalted butter

1 tbsp olive oil

6 shallots, peeled and finely chopped

sea salt and freshly ground black pepper

7 tbsp dry white wine

1 litre (1¾ pints) hot vegetable broth (see page 299)

350g (12oz) risotto rice (*vialone nano* is the best here)

¼ tsp pure saffron powder

100g (3½oz) Parmesan cheese, freshly grated

4 tbsp single cream

a handful of fresh flat-leaf parsley, finely chopped

1 Melt the butter and oil in a medium saucepan, add the shallot and some pepper, and fry for 5 minutes, until they have softened.

2 Add the wine and 7 tbsp of the stock, and boil until reduced by half.

3 Add the rice to the shallot and reduced liquid, and cook for 5 minutes, stirring constantly on a medium heat. Add the saffron and then the hot stock, a ladleful at a time, stirring well between each addition, until the rice is tender but firm, and the stock is used up. This should take about 18-20 minutes.

4 Remove from the heat and add some salt, the Parmesan, cream and parsley, and mix well.

5 Leave to stand for 1 minute to allow the rice to rest. Serve on hot plates, with extra grated Parmesan if desired.

SERVES 4

risotto alla zucca

pumpkin risotto

Pumpkin is eaten all year round in Italy, not just during its season. Fresh pumpkins are put in straw in cellars to preserve them; the flesh is bottled in olive oil and eaten as an *antipasto*. It is also used in pasta sauces, in *tortelli*, and in vegetable bakes.

2 garlic cloves, peeled

25g (1oz) unsalted butter

2 tsp olive oil

6 shallots, peeled and finely chopped

500g (1lb 2oz) pumpkin, peeled, deseeded and chopped

350g (12oz) *carnaroli* risotto rice

1 litre (1¾ pints) hot vegetable broth (see page 299)

sea salt and freshly ground black pepper

a handful of flat-leaf parsley, chopped

60g (2¼oz) Parmesan cheese, freshly grated

1 Fry the garlic in the butter and oil until coloured. Add the shallot and pumpkin, and cook gently so that the latter softens.

2 Add the rice and stir to coat in the pumpkin mixture. Add a ladleful of hot broth at a time, stirring continuously, until the broth is all used up and the rice is creamy. This should take approximately 18-20 minutes.

3 Stir in some salt and pepper, the parsley and Parmesan.

4 Cover for 1 minute to allow the rice to rest, then serve at once on warmed plates, with extra grated Parmesan if desired.

SERVES 4

risotto con i funghi

wild mushroom risotto

This risotto is very popular in the mushroom season: September and October, and then January and February. You can use a variety of interesting mushrooms which you can find easily in supermarkets and specialist shops. Think of chestnut mushrooms, girolles, oyster mushrooms – and, of course, ceps or penny buns, the famous *porcini* of Italy.

200g (7oz) mixed wild mushrooms

2 garlic cloves, peeled and crushed

6 shallots, peeled and finely chopped

115g (4 oz) unsalted butter

sea salt and freshly ground black pepper

1 sprig fresh rosemary, finely chopped

350g (12oz) *vialone nano* risotto rice

1 litre (1³/4 pints) hot vegetable broth (see page 299)

125ml (4fl oz) white wine, preferably dry

a handful of fresh flat-leaf parsley, chopped

85g (3oz) Parmesan cheese, freshly grated

1 Wipe the mushrooms well to remove any grit, and then slice them.

2 Fry the garlic and shallot in half the butter until slightly coloured, then add the mushrooms, pepper and rosemary.

3 Add the rice and stir to coat in the mixture. Add a ladleful of hot broth and stir well until it has been absorbed by the rice. Keep adding the broth in this way, a ladleful at a time, until the rice is creamy and the broth is used up, stirring all the time. This takes about 18–20 minutes.

4 Add some salt, the wine, parsley, remaining butter and the Parmesan. Adjust the seasoning to taste.

5 Cover for 1 minute to allow the rice to rest. Serve on hot plates, with extra grated Parmesan if desired.

SERVES 4

risotto al porri con noci e vin santo

leek risotto with nuts and vin santo

This is my variation on a classic Tuscan risotto. Risotto is a great two-pan meal – one for the broth, one for the cooking – and you know it will be ready in about 18-20 minutes. It's good to get the family involved in the constant stirring a risotto requires – perhaps 10 minutes per child or friend!

85g (3oz) unsalted butter

3 shallots, peeled and thinly sliced

4 young tender leeks, cleaned and finely chopped

1 tsp green peppercorns, crushed in a pestle and mortar

115g (4oz) shelled fresh walnuts, coarsely minced

350g (12oz) *carnaroli* risotto rice

125ml (4fl oz) Vin Santo

1 litre (1³/4 pints) hot vegetable broth (see page 299)

100g (3¹/2oz) Parmesan cheese, freshly grated

sea salt and freshly ground black pepper

a handful of fresh flat-leaf parsley leaves, chopped

1 Melt 55g (2oz) of the butter in a large saucepan and sauté the shallots and leek until translucent. Add the green peppercorns and walnuts and fry for 1 minute.

2 Add the rice and fry until it becomes golden. Then pour about three-quarters of the Vin Santo over the rice and simmer until it is absorbed. Add the hot stock, ladle by ladle, stirring all the time; this will take about 15-18 minutes, never adding more until the last ladle has been absorbed. Then add the remaining Vin Santo and cook until the rice is *al dente*.

3 Turn off the heat and stir in the Parmesan and remaining butter. Season to taste. Let the mixture stand for 1 minute for the rice to rest. Serve at once sprinkled with the chopped parsley.

SERVES 4

risotto con fontina e noci

walnut and fontina risotto

This is a northern recipe that uses the Aosta Valley's fontina cheese, whose wonderfully nutty flavour blends beautifully with the walnuts. This is a good store-cupboard risotto. Keep shelled walnuts in the fridge as they soon become rancid; buy them in the shell when fresh (in the autumn) and use quickly.

55g (2oz) unsalted butter

1 tbsp olive oil

8 shallots, peeled and finely chopped

1 garlic clove, peeled and crushed

350g (12oz) risotto rice of choice

75ml (2¹/₂fl oz) white wine

1 litre (1³/₄ pints) hot vegetable broth (see page 299)

100g (3¹/₂oz) fontina cheese, cut into cubes

100g (3¹/₂oz) Parmesan cheese, freshly grated

55g (2oz) shelled walnuts, coarsely chopped

a handful of fresh flat-leaf parsley, coarsely chopped

sea salt and freshly ground black pepper

TO SERVE (OPTIONAL)

shelled walnuts, coarsely chopped

freshly grated Parmesan cheese

1 Heat the butter and olive oil in a sauté pan or heavy-based casserole over a medium heat. Add the shallot and cook for 1-2 minutes, until softened but not browned. Add the garlic and mix well.

2 Add the rice and stir, using a wooden spoon, until the grains are well coated and glistening (about 1 minute). Pour in the wine and stir until it is absorbed.

3 Add a ladleful of hot broth and simmer, stirring, until it has been absorbed. Keep adding the broth in this way, a ladleful at a time, until the broth – all but 1 ladleful – is used up, stirring continuously. This takes about 18-20 minutes. Reserve the last ladleful.

4 Add the reserved broth, fontina, Parmesan, walnuts, parsley and some salt and pepper. Stir well. Remove from the heat, cover and allow to rest for 1 minute.

5 Spoon into warmed bowls, sprinkle with walnuts and grated Parmesan if using, and serve immediately.

SERVES 6

risi e bisi

risotto with peas

This recipe has become a speciality of Venice because of the wonderful soil of the Veneto, where peas grow in abundance. In the pea season, there is often such a glut that the vendors don't bother to weigh them out but just pour the pods freely into your bag, so as to ensure that you can enjoy them at their very finest and sweetest.

1kg (2¼lb) sweet fresh pea pods, young and tender

6 shallots, peeled and finely sliced

2 garlic cloves, peeled and finely chopped

55g (2oz) unsalted butter

2 tbsp olive oil

a handful of fresh flat-leaf parsley, chopped

1 litre (1¾ pints) hot vegetable broth (see page 299)

350g (12oz) *vialone nano* risotto rice

125ml (4fl oz) dry white wine

sea salt and freshly ground black pepper

a handful of fresh mint, chopped

55g (2oz) Parmesan cheese, freshly grated

1 Shell and rinse the peas. Fry the shallot and garlic in the butter and oil until lightly coloured, then stir in the parsley, peas and just enough hot broth to barely cover the ingredients. Simmer gently for 2 minutes.

2 Add the rice, wine and some pepper, and stir to coat the rice with this mixture, using a wooden spoon. Now add the hot broth ladleful by ladleful, stirring well between each addition, until all the broth has been absorbed and the rice is creamy. This should take 18-20 minutes.

3 Stir in some salt, then the mint and Parmesan.

4 Cover for 1 minute to allow the rice to rest, then serve on warmed plates, with extra grated Parmesan if desired.

SERVES 4

risotto con zucchini e fiori

risotto with courgettes and their flowers

This is a slightly indulgent recipe, as courgette flowers are not readily available unless you grow them yourself. I have seen them in shops – at a price – but they always look rather tired, although they can be revived in iced water. Give them a shake before use to dislodge any insects that might be lurking inside. Whenever I see **fiori di zucchini**, it means the onset of summer for me.

5 tbsp olive oil

8 young, tender and thin courgettes, sliced, whole flowers detached

6 shallots, peeled and sliced

350g (12oz) *carnaroli* risotto rice

sea salt and freshly ground black pepper

1 litre (1³⁄₄ pints) hot vegetable broth (see page 299)

a handful of fresh mint, finely chopped

a handful of fresh flat-leaf parsley, finely chopped

25g (1oz) unsalted butter

55g (2oz) Parmesan cheese, freshly grated

1 In a deep frying pan heat the oil, and fry the sliced courgettes for 2 minutes until tender.

2 Add the shallots and the rice, and stir until coated in oil, then season with black pepper. Begin to add the hot broth, a ladleful at a time, stirring continuously. Wait for the rice to absorb this before adding any more. Continue until all the broth has been used up and the rice is creamy. This should take approximately 18-20 minutes.

3 Stir in the whole courgette flowers, and season with some salt, the mint, parsley, butter and Parmesan.

4 Cover for 1 minute to allow the rice to rest, then serve on warm plates and eat at once. Extra Parmesan may be sprinkled on top.

SERVES 4

risotto con asparagi selvatici

risotto with asparagus

The flavour of asparagus blends particularly well with rice. If wild asparagus is not available, use sprue or tender young spears, rather than the fat white ones, which can be a bit woody.

500g (18oz) asparagus, trimmed and well washed

1 tbsp olive oil

150g (5½oz) unsalted butter

6 shallots, peeled and chopped

350g (12oz) vialone nano risotto rice

1 litre (1¾ pints) hot vegetable broth (see page 299)

7 tbsp white wine

100g (3½oz) Parmesan cheese, freshly grated

a handful of fresh basil leaves

sea salt and freshly ground black pepper

1 Cut the tips off the asparagus and keep to one side. Cut the spears into 3 pieces.

2 Heat the oil and butter together in a deep-sided sauté pan. Sauté the shallot over a low heat for 5 minutes, stirring frequently. Add the chopped asparagus spears and cook over a low heat for about 4 minutes, then add the rice. Mix so that all the grains are glistening.

3 Add 3 tbsp of hot broth and stir until absorbed. Add the wine and continue stirring until you need more liquid. Add the hot broth a ladleful at a time, stirring well between each addition, and not adding more until the last ladleful has been absorbed. Continue until all the stock has been absorbed and the rice is creamy. This should take 18-20 minutes. Add the asparagus tips about 5 minutes before the end of cooking.

4 Stir in the cheese, salt, pepper and basil, place the lid on the pan and leave to rest for 1 minute.

SERVES 4

risotto di spinaci

spinach risotto

This is dedicated to real spinach lovers like me. In Italy spinach appears on the menu at all times of the year, as Italians believe that, eaten daily, it is the essence of good health. We have many ways of enjoying it, as a result, and this recipe is one.

1kg (2¼lb) spinach, washed

85g (3oz) unsalted butter

6 shallots, peeled and finely chopped

350g (12oz) *arborio* risotto rice

125ml (4fl oz) white wine

sea salt and freshly ground black pepper

1litre (1¾ pints) hot vegetable broth (see page 299)

freshly grated nutmeg

85g (3oz) Parmesan cheese, freshly grated

1 Steam the spinach for a few minutes until soft. Drain very thoroughly, squeeze dry and chop finely.

2 Melt half the butter and fry the shallot until softened. Add the rice and stir together for a few minutes, then add the spinach, wine and some black pepper and mix well.

3 Add a ladleful of hot broth, and stir until this has been absorbed by the rice. Continue to add broth, ladleful by ladleful, stirring continuously, until it has all been used up and the rice is creamy. This should take about 18-20 minutes.

4 Remove the pan from the heat and stir in the nutmeg, the rest of the butter, some salt and the Parmesan.

5 Cover for 1 minute to allow the rice to rest. Serve at once on hot plates, and add extra Parmesan at the table if desired.

SERVES 4

risotto al salto

crisp risotto cake

When Milanese cooks have some risotto left over, they sauté it in a very thin layer until it is golden and crisp. You could serve this by itself as an **antipasto**, cut into wedges, or as a crunchy lid for a piping hot, creamy risotto.

300g (10½oz) saffron risotto (see page 53)

55g (2oz) unsalted butter

6 tbsp freshly grated Parmesan cheese

1 If you make the risotto from scratch, spread it out on a board and let it stand until cooled.

2 Melt half the butter in a frying pan. Cover the bottom with a layer of cooked rice 5mm (¼in) thick, pressing down lightly. Brown over a low heat for 20 minutes.

3 Invert the rice cake on to a flat saucepan lid or a plate for a moment. Add the remaining butter to the frying pan. Slide the rice back into the pan and brown the other side, shaking the pan to prevent sticking.

4 Place the rice cake on a serving plate and sprinkle with Parmesan.

SERVES 6

supplí di riso

deep-fried risotto with shallots, orange zest and mozzarella

This recipe is not for a risotto, but risotto rice is cooked in almost exactly the same way, before being flavoured, then formed into little balls and fried. In the south of Italy, we call them **arancini**, or 'little oranges'. We always seem to eat them when travelling on the boat to Sicily.

55g (2oz) unsalted butter

280g (10oz) *arborio* risotto rice

800ml (29fl oz) hot vegetable broth (see page 299)

175g (6oz) mozzarella cheese, grated or diced

6 shallots, peeled and finely chopped

a handful of mixed fresh herbs, chopped

finely grated zest of 1 large unwaxed orange

6 tbsp freshly grated Parmesan cheese

sea salt and freshly ground black pepper

1 egg

55g (2oz) fresh breadcrumbs

6 tbsp olive oil

1 Melt the butter in a large saucepan, add the rice and brown for a few minutes. Stir in a ladleful of hot stock and cook until the liquid has been absorbed. Continue doing this until the rice is cooked and all the stock has evaporated, stirring continuously. This should take about 18-20 minutes.

2 Now add the mozzarella, shallots, herbs, orange zest, Parmesan, salt and pepper. Mix in and leave to cool.

3 Form the flavoured rice into balls the size of a plum. Beat the egg and dip the rice balls first into the egg and then into the breadcrumbs.

4 Heat the oil in a frying pan and fry the rice balls until golden on all sides. Drain well on kitchen paper and serve hot or cold.

SERVES 4

making polenta

In Roman times, 'polenta' was a porridge made from indigenous grains such as barley, and, indeed, a polenta made from chestnut flour was eaten in northern Italy until fairly recently. But when maize was introduced from the New World in the 16th century, it was used to make polenta, and this is still a staple of the northern Italian diet today. Maize flour is known in Italy as *farina gialla* or *granturco*, and it is available in a variety of forms: very coarse, medium or fine. The coarser the flour, the more yellow its colour; a white polenta is used in the Veneto. Quick-cook polentas are useful, but not so tasty.

INGREDIENTS AND TECHNIQUE

Whatever the type of flour used, polenta is always made in a special large copper pan. The flour is gradually added to a pan of hot water and the mixture is stirred constantly throughout the long cooking time with a long wooden stick, a *mestolo* (it must be long to prevent your hands being scalded). The polenta is ready when it is like a thick porridge, and it can then be served 'wet' or 'set'. To serve it 'wet', it is traditionally spread on to a wooden board and eaten hot. Because plain boiled polenta is rather bland, it is often accompanied by a strongly flavoured sauce or with grated cheese. Or you can add some flavourings to taste while it is still hot (see ingredients list below).

If the polenta is to be served 'set', the boiled and/or flavoured polenta is left to cool and set, after which it can be sliced and fried or grilled, and served with a sauce or topped with cheese and vegetables. Cold polenta is eaten as an alternative to bread in some parts of northern Italy (particularly during bad weather, when visits to the bakery are not possible). Set cold polenta can also be eaten as a dessert: deep-fry, then drench in sugar and lemon juice and serve with mascarpone cheese.

1 litre (1¾ pints) vegetable broth (home-made is best, see page 299) or water

1 tsp sea salt

200g (7oz) coarse polenta

ADDITIONS (OPTIONAL)

coarse black pepper

unsalted butter

chopped fresh herbs

crushed garlic

freshly grated Parmesan cheese

olive oil for frying

1 In a large heavy-based saucepan, bring the broth or water and the salt to the boil. Return to a simmer, then gradually add the polenta, letting it run through your fingers in a thin stream, stirring constantly to prevent lumps forming.

2 Simmer for 30-40 minutes, until the mixture is thick and comes away from the sides of the pan, stirring frequently. Add some flavourings of your choice and serve hot.

3 Alternatively, while the plain or flavoured polenta mixture is still hot, spread it on a dampened baking sheet or wooden board into a cake shape about 5cm (2in) thick. Leave for 1 hour, until set.

4 When cold cut out into sections and then into slices of whatever size you like. Fry in olive oil – or grill – for about 3 minutes on each side until crisp. Serve hot.

SERVES 4-6

polenta con due salse

polenta with two sauces

It is considered a show of true friendship for Italians to eat their polenta together from the same board. These two sauces, spelled out separately from the main recipe, would also be very good with pasta.

1 recipe polenta (see page 68)

2 garlic cloves, peeled and crushed

115g (4oz) unsalted butter

115g (4oz) Parmesan cheese, freshly grated

TO SERVE

mushroom sauce (see below)

tomato and celery sauce (see page 72)

1 Cook the polenta according to the instructions on page 68. When it starts to pull away from the sides of the pan, add the garlic, butter, Parmesan and seasoning, and continue stirring until smooth and glossy. The whole process should take 40 minutes.

2 Meanwhile, make and warm the sauces. Pour your chosen sauce on the polenta – or try a little of both! Serve.

SERVES 6

salsa di fungh

mushroom sauce

This is a classic sauce, made by every Italian cook. It's good with polenta, pasta, in a risotto or as a layer in a lasagne.

675g (1½lb) mixed mushrooms (porcini or ceps and field)

1 tbsp olive oil

55g (2oz) unsalted butter

1 small hot red chilli pepper, seeded and chopped

sea salt and freshly ground black pepper

a handful of fresh flat-leaf parsley leaves, chopped

1 Clean the mushrooms by trimming away any dry ends, brushing away any soil or grit, and wiping with a damp cloth.

2 Coarsely chop the mushrooms and combine with the oil, butter and chilli in a large saucepan. Season to taste, cover and cook gently for 10-12 minutes. Mix in the parsley, then pour on to the polenta and serve.

SERVES 4

salsa di pomodoro i sedano

tomato and celery sauce

The balance of flavours here – of the onion, garlic and celery – is particularly interesting; the celery creates an interesting texture as well, which complements the softness of the polenta.

1 small onion, peeled and minced

2 tbsp olive oil

1 garlic clove, peeled and crushed

1 celery stalk, minced

a handful of fresh flat-leaf parsley leaves, finely chopped

16 ripe plum tomatoes, diced

sea salt and freshly ground black pepper

a handful of fresh basil leaves, torn

1 Cook the onion in the olive oil until translucent. Add the garlic, celery and parsley, mix well and cook until tender over a low heat, about 20 minutes.

2 Add the tomatoes and season generously with salt and pepper. Place the lid on the pan and simmer until thick, for 20 or so minutes. Adjust the seasoning and add the basil.

SERVES 4

funghi porcini in umido con polenta

braised porcini mushrooms with polenta

My mother had the answer to the slow cooking of polenta – up to 40 minutes – when we were children. As we were four girls, we all took a turn at stirring, so it wasn't really a chore, either for her or us!

1 recipe polenta (see page 68)

extra virgin olive oil

BRAISED MUSHROOMS

250g (9oz) fresh porcini mushrooms (ceps)

1 tbsp olive oil

1 garlic clove, peeled and crushed

a handful of mint leaves, torn

1 x 115g can chopped Italian plum tomatoes, liquid reserved

1 Brush and wipe the mushrooms, and peel them if necessary. Remove the stalks, and keep – but look carefully, as they can harbour grubs (which are easy to remove and won't do you any harm anyway). Slice the mushrooms.

2 Heat the oil in a large frying pan, add the garlic, and sauté for a minute. Stir in the mushrooms and mint and cook for 5 minutes over a low heat.

3 Add the tomatoes along with 2 tbsp of the reserved tomato liquid, plus salt and pepper, and continue to cook for 10 minutes, stirring continually.

4 When the polenta is coming away from the side of the pan, remove from the heat and distribute between bowls.

5 Top with the mushrooms and a generous amount of extra virgin olive oil. Serve immediately.

SERVES 4-6

impastoiata

polenta and cannellini beans

Impastone means to knead, and **impastoiata** is a mixture similar to a dough. This double carbohydrate dish, so typical of the north of Italy, is made to celebrate the arrival of the new beans in the autumn. It's a humble dish, but the flavours are stunning. This recipe uses fresh cannellini beans, but you can use dried (to cook, see page 148).

300g (10½oz) fresh cannellini beans

2 tbsp olive oil

1 small onion, peeled and finely chopped

1 garlic clove, peeled and finely chopped

4 fresh sage leaves, chopped

2 sprigs fresh rosemary, chopped

sea salt and freshly ground black pepper

400g tin chopped Italian tomatoes

1.5 litres (2¾ pints) vegetable broth (see page 299)

225g (8oz) coarse polenta

freshly grated Parmesan cheese

extra virgin olive oil

1 Stir the beans into a large pot filled with cold water to cover. Bring to the boil, lower the flame and simmer until the beans are tender (about 40 minutes). Drain well.

2 Meanwhile, make the sauce. Put the oil, onion, garlic, sage, rosemary, 1 tsp salt and plenty of pepper in a saucepan and cook for 10 minutes over a low heat. Add the tomatoes and cook until the sauce has thickened (20-25 minutes).

3 While the sauce is cooking, make the polenta. Heat the vegetable broth. When it begins to bubble at the side, add the polenta in a thin stream while beating hard with a wooden spoon. Cook, stirring, for 40 minutes. When the polenta has cooked and is coming away from the sides of the pan, mix in the beans and season.

4 Serve the sauce with the polenta, sprinkling Parmesan and extra virgin olive oil on top.

SERVES 6

spiedini di polenta

polenta and roasted vegetable skewers

The maize for polenta may be grown on the plains of Italy, but polenta is also popular in the mountains because it can sustain you during hard winters. Polenta has had a bad press because by itself it can be bland, but it has a magical ability to absorb flavours.

1 recipe polenta (see page 68)

55g (2oz) unsalted butter

85g (3oz) Parmesan cheese, freshly grated

1 garlic clove, peeled and crushed

freshly ground black pepper

225g (8oz) cherry tomatoes

2 tbsp olive oil

450g (1lb) flat mushrooms

2 sprigs fresh rosemary

115g (4oz) dolcelatte cheese

freshly grated Parmesan cheese for sprinkling

1 Make the polenta as described on page 68. When it is hot and coming away from the sides of the pan, add the butter, Parmesan, garlic and some black pepper.

2 Spread the hot mixture on to a dampened baking sheet to a 5mm (¼in) thickness. Leave for about 1 hour, until set.

3 Meanwhile, preheat the oven to 200ºC/400°F/gas mark 6.

4 Cut the tomatoes in half and place on a baking sheet. Drizzle with a little of the olive oil. Thickly slice the mushrooms and place on the same or another baking sheet. Sprinkle with the remaining olive oil and place some rosemary on top. Bake the tomatoes and mushrooms in the oven for 20 minutes.

5 Using a 2.5cm (1in) round cutter, cut the cold polenta into rounds. Cut the dolcelatte into cubes.

6 Thread the halved tomatoes, mushrooms, polenta rounds and cheese on to cocktail sticks or kebab sticks. Sprinkle with Parmesan cheese.

7 To serve, grill for about 7 minutes, until golden.

SERVES 6 AS AN ANTIPASTO

polenta pasticciata
baked stuffed polenta

This is a special dinner-party polenta dish, which can be made a day ahead, leaving you more time to concentrate on other courses on the day itself. Never economize when you are buying polenta. Get the real thing, the kind that needs long cooking.

1.5 litres (2¾ pints) water

sea salt and freshly ground black pepper

225g (8oz) coarse polenta

90g (3¼oz) unsalted butter

a handful of fresh oregano sprigs, chopped

1 small aubergine

1 red pepper

1 courgette

450g (1lb) flat field mushrooms

3 tbsp olive oil, plus extra for drizzling

25g (1oz) Italian '00' plain flour

300ml (10fl oz) milk

55g (2oz) blue cheese, eg Gorgonzola

a handful of fresh flat-leaf parsley, finely chopped

115g (4oz) Parmesan cheese, freshly grated

1 Dampen a 1kg (2¼lb) loaf tin. In a large heavy saucepan bring the water to simmering point. Add 1½ tsp salt, pour in the polenta, then cook as described on page 68.

2 Now add 55g (2oz) of the butter and stir in well. Add some salt and pepper and the chopped oregano. Stir until the butter has melted. Pour into the loaf tin and leave to set for 20-30 minutes.

3 Preheat the oven to 200°C/400°F/gas mark 6.

4 Slice the aubergine lengthways, sprinkle with salt, place in a colander, cover and weigh down for 20 minutes.

5 Meanwhile put the red pepper in a baking tray and roast for 20 minutes, until deflated, turning once during cooking. Leave to cool.

6 Trim the ends of the courgette, then slice it lengthways. Slice the mushrooms. Heat the olive oil in a frying pan and fry the courgette, then drain and reserve. Now fry the mushroom until tender, season with salt and pepper and reserve. Rinse the aubergine slices, pat dry and fry until golden. Drain and reserve. When the pepper is cool, peel off the skin and chop the flesh, discarding the core and seeds.

7 Now make the sauce. In a saucepan, melt the remaining butter. Add the flour and cook the roux for 3 minutes, stirring. Remove the pan from the heat and gradually beat in the milk. Return to the heat and slowly bring to the boil, beating all the time until thickened. Stir in the Gorgonzola, mushrooms and some salt and pepper.

8 Turn the set polenta out of the tin on to a board and cut into 5 slices lengthways. Put one slice back in the tin, and layer the polenta with all the fillings, sauce and the Parmesan. Drizzle on some olive oil and bake at the same temperature as above for 20 minutes.

SERVES 4

panini con polenta, mozzarella e prosciutto

polenta, mozzarella and Parma ham

The Trattoria Sorelle Carboni in Recco, near Genoa, serves simple, honest food. This recipe is one of its specialities in the polenta season, from January to April. These small polenta 'sandwiches' are ideal as an antipasto, or they could be served as an appetizer with drinks. Polenta is incredibly versatile, and this is one of the many ways — rather unusual — in which it can be used.

750ml (26fl oz) water

350ml (12fl oz) milk

sea salt and freshly ground black pepper

250g (9oz) coarse polenta

85g (3oz) unsalted butter

85g (3oz) Parmesan cheese, freshly grated, plus extra to serve

1 tbsp any mustard (optional)

350g (12oz) buffalo mozzarella cheese, sliced

200g (7oz) Parma ham, thinly sliced

115g (4oz) Italian '00' plain flour

2 large eggs, beaten

115g (4oz) fresh breadcrumbs

vegetable oil for deep-frying

1 Bring the water, milk and a pinch of salt to the boil. Slowly whisk in the polenta, and then cook as described on page 68.

2 Remove from the heat, add the butter, Parmesan and some black pepper, then mix well.

3 Pour a thin layer of about half the polenta into a lightly oiled tray and spread evenly. Allow to cool. Keep the rest of the polenta warm.

4 When this first layer has cooled, spread a thin layer of mustard over it, if using, and arrange the mozzarella to cover the area. Lay the Parma ham over the mozzarella. Pour over the remaining warm polenta and spread it thinly to cover the filling. Cool in the tray for at least 1 hour.

5 When cold, turn the entire tray out in one piece and cut into small neat triangles. Heat the oil for deep-frying. Coat each piece in flour, then the beaten egg, and finally coat with breadcrumbs. Deep-fry until crisp and golden brown.

SERVES 6

making gnocchi

TYPES OF GNOCCHI

The word 'gnocchi' in Italian means 'little lumps' and refers to a host of different types of *gnocchi* that are eaten the length and breadth of Italy. Potato-based *gnocchi* are the most common, and are enjoyed with many different sauces, usually tomato. In Tuscany, in autumn, potato *gnocchi* are eaten with a walnut pesto or *salsa di noce*, which is delicious, my husband's favourite (see page 38).

However, *gnocchi* are also made of ricotta, the Italian curd cheese, which is mixed with flour or semolina, and then flavoured with cheeses or spinach (which also colours it). Then there are semolina *gnocchi*. The semolina is cooked in milk, enriched with egg yolks, butter and cheese, and is left to set before being stamped into rounds; these are then baked, overlapping each other (a wonderful Roman speciality). And finally, there are even *gnocchi* made with stale bread, for in Italy a good cook never wastes anything!

INGREDIENTS

To make potato *gnocchi,* it is essential that you use old potatoes of an even size. I recommend Pentland Crown, King Edward, Desirée and Maris Piper. Old potatoes are used because the starch content is fully developed, and this allows the *gnoccho* to cohere and stay together in a 'little lump'.

TECHNIQUE

Once the potato has been boiled in its skin and is tender, you need to cool it down, then peel and process either through a *mouli de légumes* or a potato ricer. Hold the machine up high so that the potato will fall from a height (this makes it lighter). Then mix in the other recipe ingredients.

Potato and other *gnocchi* are made in the same way from now on. Knead the paste or dough lightly and form into sausage shapes. These shapes now need to be rolled with floured hands into 2.5cm (1in) thick rolls – or roughly the diameter of your little finger – then cut into pieces about 2-2.5cm (^{3}/$_4$-1in) long. You can leave the *gnocchi* plain, or you could press a finger into each piece to flatten it, then draw your finger towards you to curl the sides. You could also roll each *gnoccho* against the tines of a fork to pattern it. See recipes for further details.

BELOW LEFT AND LEFT: to make potato gnocchi, begin by sifting Italian '00' plain flour into a bowl. Make a well in the centre and crack your eggs into It. Push the cooked potatoes through a sieve or ricer, holding it high above the bowl to get air into it. Add salt and butter, mix, then knead until soft.

ABOVE: to cut the gnocchi, with floured hands roll the dough on a floured surface into a 2.5cm (1 inch) sausage shape, then cut it into pieces about 2cm (¾in) long. Press a finger into each piece to flatten it.

COOKING

To cook *gnocchi*, bring a large pan of salted water to the boil and drop in about 20 gnocchi. Lower the heat and cook gently for 2-3 minutes, allowing the gnocchi to pop to the top of the pan, then counting for 30 seconds. Remove the *gnocchi* with a slotted spoon and keep warm. Repeat with the remaining *gnocchi*. Warm up your chosen sauce. When the *gnocchi* are cooked, toss in the sauce and serve sprinkled with Parmesan cheese. Alternatively, *gnocchi* can be baked.

STORING

Potato *gnocchi* can be frozen very successfully or stored in the fridge for 2 days. Coat them well with flour and cover, or else the humidity of the fridge will make them very squashy. Semolina *gnocchi* will keep for 3-4 days in the fridge, and I think really improve with keeping. The flavour is retained, and the texture is better too. Ricotta *gnocchi* will keep in the fridge for 3-4 days, acquiring a fuller flavour too, but don't freeze, as the cheese will split. Don't keep bread *gnocchi*; eat them straightaway.

gnocchi di patate

potato gnocchi

There are so many poor **gnocchi** imitations ready-prepared for us to buy, that I urge you to spend some time making them yourself. The results are infinitely superior, and it's certainly not difficult (in fact, it's fun!). The tomato sauce here, made with broth and tomato purée, is slightly different from the others in the book, but it can be replaced by the others – or by the walnut sauce on page 38.

900g (2lb) even-sized old potatoes (see page 78)

225-280g (8-10oz) Italian '00' plain flour

2 small eggs

sea salt

55g (2oz) unsalted butter, softened and cubed

freshly grated Parmesan cheese to serve

TOMATO SAUCE

1 tbsp olive oil

1 small onion, peeled and finely chopped

450g (1lb) ripe tomatoes or 1 x 400g can chopped Italian plum tomatoes

1 garlic clove, peeled and crushed

150ml (5fl oz) vegetable broth (see page 299) or water

1 tbsp tomato purée

a pinch of caster sugar

a handful of fresh basil leaves (optional), torn

sea salt and freshly ground black pepper

1 tbsp dry white wine

1 Make the sauce first. If using fresh tomatoes, put them in a bowl, cover with boiling water for 30 seconds, then plunge into cold water. Using a sharp knife, peel off the skins, cut in half, discard the seeds, then roughly chop the flesh.

2 Heat the oil in a saucepan, add the onion and cook gently for 5 minutes until softened. Add the tomatoes and garlic, cover and cook over a gentle heat for 10 minutes, stirring occasionally.

3 Add the broth or water, tomato purée, sugar, basil (if using) and salt and pepper to taste. Half cover the pan and simmer for 20 minutes, stirring occasionally.

4 Sieve the tomato mixture into a clean pan. Bring to the boil, add the wine and keep to one side, off the heat.

5 Meanwhile, for the gnocchi, cook the potatoes in their skins in boiling water for 20 minutes until tender (or longer, depending on size). Drain well and, when cool enough to handle, peel off the skins.

6 Sift the flour into a bowl or on to the work surface, and make a well in the centre. Crack the eggs into the well.

7 Push the still-warm potatoes through a sieve on to the flour and eggs from a height, to enable the potato to lighten with air as it falls. Add plenty of salt and the butter. Mix thoroughly and then knead until soft, adding more flour if it is necessary.

8 With floured hands, roll the dough into 2.5cm (1in) thick rolls, then cut into pieces about 2cm (³/4in) long. Press a finger into each piece to flatten then draw your finger towards you to curl the sides.

9 Bring a large pan of salted water to the boil and drop in about 20 gnocchi. Lower the heat and cook gently for 2-3 minutes, allowing the gnocchi to pop to the top of the pan, then counting for 30 seconds. Remove the gnocchi with a slotted spoon and keep warm. Repeat with the remaining gnocchi.

10 Warm up the tomato sauce. When all the gnocchi are cooked, toss in the sauce and serve sprinkled with some Parmesan cheese.

SERVES 4

gnocchi di ricotta e salsa di gorgonzola

ricotta and nutmeg dumplings with gorgonzola sauce

At first glance you might think these dumplings would be heavy and artery-clogging, but in reality they are light, fluffy and delicious. The Gorgonzola really enhances the taste of the ricotta. They are simple to prepare and can be made ahead of time. Serve with a green salad.

400g (14oz) ricotta cheese

2 tbsp freshly grated Parmesan cheese

3 large egg yolks

5 tbsp fine semolina

a good pinch of freshly grated nutmeg

sea salt and freshly ground black pepper

1 tbsp chopped fresh flat-leaf parsley, to serve

GORGONZOLA SAUCE

15g (1/2oz) unsalted butter

2 tbsp double cream

115g (4oz) Gorgonzola cheese, crumbled

1 Preheat the oven to 180°C/350°F/gas mark 4.

2 In a bowl, mash the ricotta with 2 tbsp Parmesan, the egg yolks, semolina, nutmeg and some salt and pepper to taste. Mix well together to form a paste.

3 On a lightly oiled surface, roll the paste into thin sausages about 1cm (1/2in) in diameter, then cut with a sharp knife into balls or pieces 2cm (3/4in) long.

4 For the sauce, melt the butter with the cream in a saucepan. Add the Gorgonzola and cook over a very low heat, crushing and stirring the cheese until you have a well-blended sauce.

5 Bring a large pan of water to the boil and lower the dumplings in, one at a time, on a slotted spoon. Let them simmer for about 2 minutes, or until they rise to the surface, count for 30 seconds, then remove with the slotted spoon and drain thoroughly.

6 Put the dumplings in an oven-proof dish, pour the sauce over the top, sprinkle on the chopped parsley and the last tbsp grated Parmesan. Bake for 15-20 minutes.

SERVES 6

tondore

ricotta gnocchi

This recipe is from my village in Italy, and has many variations and stories attached to it. It is served in virtually every **trattoria** along the Amalfi coast. My father loves this dish, and always laughs that everyone ends up with tomato sauce plastered on their clothes. He says it's a sign that you've eaten well.

300g (10½oz) ricotta cheese

85g (3oz) Italian '00' plain flour, plus extra for dusting

1 garlic clove, peeled and crushed

2 large egg yolks

sea salt and freshly ground black pepper

a little freshly grated nutmeg

TO COOK AND SERVE

200g (7oz) tasty cherry tomatoes, halved

2 tsp dried chilli (peperoncino)

2 tbsp olive oil

a handful of fresh basil leaves, torn

grated Parmesan cheese, to taste

1 Mix all the gnocchi ingredients together in a bowl. Knead lightly on a floured surface. Roll into a sausage-shaped log the thickness of your little finger. Cut at an angle to create shapes the length of the first joint of your index finger.

2 Boil the gnocchi in batches in a large pan of boiling salted water. When they rise to the top of the pan, after about 2 minutes, count for 30 seconds, then skim out into a frying pan.

3 Add the tomatoes, chilli and olive oil to the frying pan, and sauté until the gnocchi are stained with tomato. Serve with torn basil and grated Parmesan.

SERVES 4

gnocchi di pane

bread gnocchi

In Italy, a good cook never wastes anything. As bread stales so quickly, many recipes have been created to utilise it. These bread **gnocchi** are very light and full of herby flavour, and are delicious with a tomato sauce as here, or any of the others on pages 32-5, or a pesto (see pages 46-7).

250g (9oz) stale bread, crusts discarded, finely chopped

a handful of fresh mint leaves, torn

1 tsp each of finely chopped fresh marjoram, thyme and rosemary leaves

1 tsp minced rosemary

140g (5oz) Parmesan cheese, freshly grated

2 large eggs, beaten

2-3 tbsp milk

a generous pinch of freshly grated nutmeg

sea salt and freshly ground black pepper

Italian '00' plain flour

TO SERVE

250g (9oz) tomato sauce with mint (see page 36)

a handful of rocket leaves, cut into strips

shavings of Parmesan cheese (optional)

1 To make the **gnocchi**, combine the bread, herbs, cheese, eggs, milk, nutmeg, salt and pepper. Knead until the mixture holds together. Add some more milk if the mixture is too dry or some of the flour if it is too wet.

2 Turn the mixture out on to a floured work surface and cut into 4 pieces. Shape each piece into a 2.5cm (1in) thick log, and cut each log into 1cm (1/2in) pieces.

3 Cook the gnocchi in a large pan of boiling salted water until they float to the surface. Count 30 seconds, then remove with a slotted spoon to a heated bowl.

4 Fold in the warmed tomato sauce and top with the rocket. You may like to serve them with extra shavings of Parmesan. I often add a fine drizzle of exceptional extra virgin olive oil.

SERVES 6

making crespelle (pancakes)

Crespelle are pancakes, and Italian pancakes differ from French *crêpes* in that they have melted butter in the batter. The texture is completely different, slightly thicker than conventional pancakes, but just as melt-in-the-mouth. The home of the *crespella* is Piacenza in Emilia-Romagna, the gastronomic capital of Italy, where so many wonderful dishes have originated (also the homeland of Parmesan cheese).

Crespelle are very easy to make and can be made ahead of time and kept covered in the fridge for up to 3 days. They can also be frozen very successfully too. The fillings vary considerably from region to region and season to season. In fact, you can use anything you like: there are a few choices here. I once enjoyed them filled with courgette flowers and pecorino cheese in Apulia. They were totally memorable, and I've since tried to reproduce the recipe (with little success).

EQUIPMENT

It is very important to use the correct type of pan and the correct size of pan. A heavy-based pan is vital, as even and steady heat conduction will allow an even browning of the pancake. And the size of the pan will of course define the size of the pancake. For the 'cannelloni' recipe on page 91, I would use a 15-20cm (6-8in) pan (to make 8 pancakes): for the other *crespella* dishes here, I would use a 30cm (12in) pan (to make 4-6 pancakes)

SERVING

Pancakes can be filled, then presented in a cylinder or parcel shape. There are no particular rules, although the first side cooked must always be the presentation side (it just looks better). Traditionally in Italy, *crespelle* are eaten in a savoury context, but during the summer, at beach-side cafés, French-style sweet *crêpes* with their various sauces are enjoyed.

225g (8oz) Italian '00' plain flour

sea salt and freshly ground black pepper

1 1/2 tsp freshly grated nutmeg (optional)

2 large eggs, beaten

1 large egg yolk, beaten

350ml (12fl oz) milk

1 tbsp unsalted butter, melted, plus extra for greasing

1 Sift the flour, 1/2 tsp salt and nutmeg (if using) into a bowl. Add the beaten eggs, milk and melted butter, and whisk until smooth. If it seems too thin, add a little more flour; if too thick, a little more milk. Pass the batter through a sieve.

2 To cook, brush a round heavy-based frying pan with melted butter and set over a moderate heat. Pour a small ladleful of the batter into the pan and swirl the pan to make sure it is evenly coated with a thin layer of batter. Cook for 2 minutes or until lightly browned on the underside. Flip the *crespella* over and cook the other side until lightly browned.

3 Remove the *crespella* to a piece of kitchen paper and repeat the process. Lightly grease the pan every so often to prevent the batter from sticking.

MAKES 6-8 CRESPELLE

LEFT: crespelle cooking; they are thicker than traditional French crêpes.

crespelle con funghi

mushroom pancakes

These pancakes could be served as the equivalent of the pasta course, but are wonderful as a light lunch. As with foods such as fish baked in baking paper, there is an element of surprise when a filling is encased in a pancake. This mushroom filling is classically Italian, but you can vary the ingredients as you like.

I recipe crespelle (see page 86)

freshly grated Parmesan cheese

FILLING

55g (2oz) unsalted butter

2 shallots, peeled and finely chopped

1 garlic clove, peeled and crushed

375g (13oz) field mushrooms, wiped and sliced

125g (4¹/₂oz) mixed wild mushrooms, cleaned and sliced

225g (8oz) mozzarella cheese, diced

85g (3oz) Parmesan cheese, grated

225g (8oz) ricotta cheese

a handful of fresh basil leaves, torn

sea salt and freshly ground black pepper

1 Make 6-8 pancakes according to the recipe on page 86. Stack on a plate and cover while you make the filling.

2 Preheat the oven to 180°C/350°F/gas mark 4.

3 To make the filling, melt two-thirds of the butter in a large frying pan, add the shallot, garlic and both kinds of mushrooms, and sauté until golden, stirring constantly. In a medium mixing bowl, combine the mushroom mixture with the remaining filling ingredients, season to taste and set aside.

4 Put a spoonful of the filling in the centre of each pancake and fold over 2 edges to meet in the centre, then fold over the other 2 edges, making a parcel. Place on a greased, high-sided baking tray, joins down. Brush with the remaining melted butter and sprinkle with Parmesan to taste.

5 Bake for 10-15 minutes. Serve immediately.

SERVES 6-8

crespelle con spinaci e mozzarella

pancakes stuffed with spinach and mozzarella

These pancakes come from Piacenza in Emilia, and no matter how many times I make them, they are always welcomed by my friends and guests. In fact, it's a very useful dish altogether. One of its main merits is that it can be cooked in advance and reheated when needed – a great boon when we are all so busy.

I recipe *crespelle* (see page 86)

freshly grated Parmesan cheese

FILLING

55g (2oz) unsalted butter

85g (3oz) Italian '00' plain flour

200ml (7fl oz) milk

300g (10½oz) cooked spinach, chopped

sea salt and freshly ground black pepper

a pinch of freshly grated nutmeg

225g (8oz) mozzarella cheese, diced

55g (2oz) Parmesan cheese, freshly grated

1 Make 6-8 pancakes according to the recipe on page 86. Stack on a plate and cover while you make the filling.

2 To make the filling, melt two-thirds of the butter in a saucepan, add the flour and cook for 1 minute to make a roux. Slowly add the milk, stirring all the time, and cook over a moderate heat, stirring constantly, until the sauce has thickened. Add the spinach with a pinch of salt and cook for a further minute. Fold in the remaining ingredients and leave to cool.

3 Preheat the oven to 180°C/350°F/gas mark 4.

4 Put a spoonful of the filling in the centre of each pancake and fold over 2 edges to meet in the centre, then fold over the other 2 edges, making a parcel.

5 Place on a greased, high-sided baking tray, joins down. Brush with the remaining melted butter and sprinkle with Parmesan to taste. Bake for 10-15 minutes. Serve immediately.

SERVES 6-8

cannelloni con verdure e formaggio

pancakes with vegetables and cheese

I have a great affinity with cannelloni, and in Italy we have many varieties. Many cannelloni dishes are made with pasta, but this one, again traditional to Piacenza, is constructed from *crespelle*, and is particularly light. It can be made into a wonderful *antipasto* dish.

I recipe *crespelle* batter (see page 86)

3 tbsp freshly grated Parmesan cheese

sea salt and freshly ground black pepper

FILLING

350g (12oz) ricotta cheese, well drained

1 large egg

175g (6oz) lightly cooked broccoli, chopped

3 tbsp freshly grated Parmesan cheese

5 ripe tomatoes, skinned, seeded and chopped

a handful of fresh flat-leaf parsley, chopped

1 tsp finely grated zest of unwaxed lemon

TO COOK AND SERVE

3 tbsp melted unsalted butter

freshly grated Parmesan cheese to taste

1 Preheat the oven to 180°C/350°F/gas mark 4.

2 Make the *crespella* batter as described on page 86, and then finally beat in the Parmesan and some pepper. Cook the *crespelle* as described on page 86.

3 For the filling, in a large bowl combine the ricotta and egg. Add the remaining filling ingredients and mix.

4 Spread about an eighth of the filling over each crespella and roll up into a cylinder. Place them in a single layer, seam-side down, in a suitably sized, buttered ovenproof dish. Drizzle the melted butter over them and sprinkle with Parmesan.

5 Bake for 10-15 minutes, until piping hot and golden. Serve immediately.

SERVES 6-8

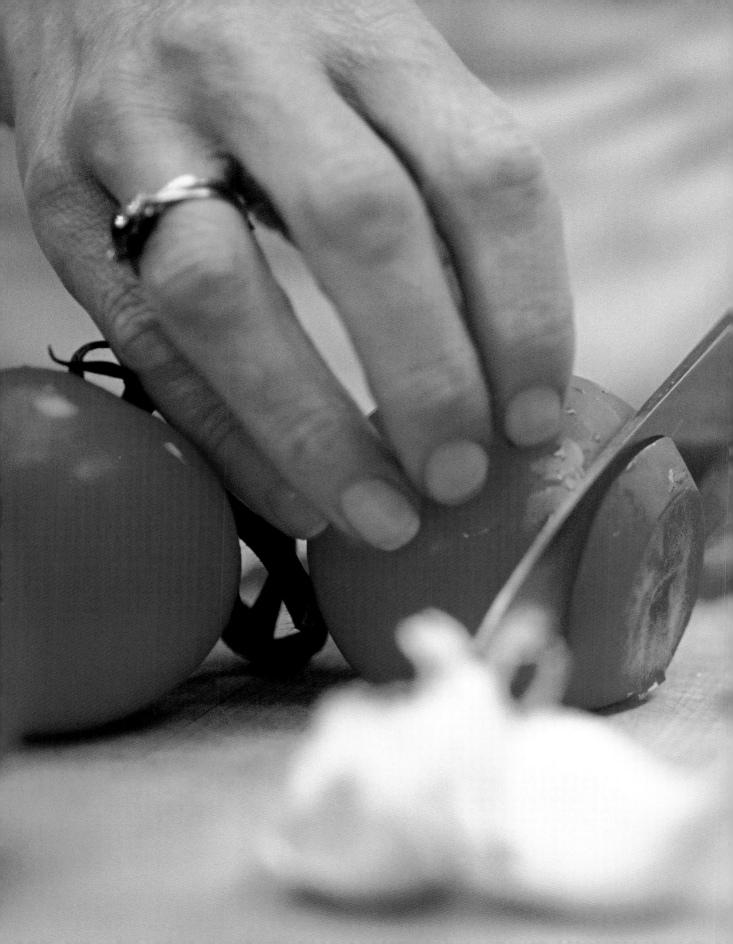

vegetables

making frittate

La frittata is Italy's answer to the French omelette, but it is easier and quicker to make since you don't have to flip or fill it: the filling is blended into the beaten eggs, or vice versa (quite similar to a Spanish *tortilla*). Although the main ingredient is eggs, *frittate* are used as a major vehicle for vegetables, which is why they appear in the vegetables chapter!

INGREDIENTS

The best *frittate* are composed of a simple blend of eggs, seasonings and the vegetable flavour or flavours of the season. For the best possible result, it is essential that you use the best possible ingredients. Italian-style eggs really make an enormous difference, and throughout the book I have referred to them constantly. Italian chickens are fed on a diet of corn, which turns the yolks almost orangey-red in colour, and also enriches the flavour of the eggs.

I know that it may prove impossible for many of you to find eggs such as these, so try and source the freshest, free-range, possibly organic eggs that are produced as locally to you as possible. I am delighted that eggs do seem to be improving these days. Over the many years that I have been teaching cooking, I have seen an ever-expanding range of eggs becoming available – among them quail's, duck's and some from unusual chicken breeds.

If eggs are key to the success of *frittate*, so too are the other simple ingredients which go to make up the best ones. A good olive oil should be used, but not extra virgin, which has too strong a flavour. Oil is needed to pre-cook the vegetable or other ingredients, such as pancetta or courgettes, for example. All of these need to be cooked beforehand, because once the eggs are in the pan, the *frittata* takes no time at all to cook. Cheese is another basic of the best *frittate*, and the type used varies from region to region. Pecorino is used greatly in the south, particularly Pecorino Romano, while in the north they use Parmigiano Reggiano. Herbs too are a great *frittata* flavour enhancer: I tend to use flat-leaf parsley and mint.

The frying pan for *frittate* is as important as that for French omelettes. It should be good quality, to conduct heat effectively, enabling the egg and vegetable mixture to set and become evenly golden. It should have a lid, so that the *frittata* can set on top as well as on the base. I recommend you use a pan of about 25cm (10in) in diameter.

SERVING

Served hot, warm or cold, a *frittata* should be light and tasty. When I'm teaching I always recommend a *frittata* for picnics; a large wedge with salad is a deliciously simple alfresco food. My baby loves *frittate* and I will cook her one regularly in summer with tomatoes, in spring with peas. In fact there are no boundaries when it comes to a *frittata*, and you can allow your imagination free rein.

ABOVE: A *frittata* does not need flipping; simply cook it in a frying pan for 5-7 minutes until firm but moist.

frittata con piselli e pancetta

frittata with fresh peas and pancetta

This is the sort of **frittata** I make for my baby, Antonia, in spring, when the first new peas appear. She has a couple of slivers, I eat most of the rest, and then there is always a little left over to be eaten cold when my husband Richard comes home.

8 large eggs

60g (2¼oz) freshly grated Parmesan cheese

fine sea salt and freshly ground black pepper

a handful of chopped fresh flat-leaf parsley

1 tbsp olive oil

115g (4oz) pancetta, cubed

200g (7oz) podded fresh peas

1 Beat the eggs in a medium mixing bowl and blend in the Parmesan cheese with a pinch of salt, plenty of pepper and the parsley.

2 Heat the oil in a 25cm (10in) frying pan over a medium heat, add the pancetta and cook until golden brown. Add the peas and mix well together while still on the heat.

3 Pour in the egg, cheese and parsley mixture and, over a medium heat, cook, covered, until the **frittata** is firm but moist, about 5-7 minutes (it all depends on the heat and the pan).

4 Cut into wedges and serve immediately.

SERVES 4

frittata con la zucchine

courgette omelette with fresh mint and cheese

In Rome, favourite **frittata** ingredients range from leftover pasta to onions, pancetta and fresh vegetables – especially courgettes, sweet peppers and artichokes. (The first recorded frittata, in the writing of Apicius, dating from some 20 centuries ago, calls for fresh peas.)

8 large eggs

4 tbsp freshly grated Pecorino Romano cheese

fine sea salt and freshly ground black pepper

4 small courgettes

3-4 tbsp olive oil

4 tbsp minced fresh mint

1 Beat the eggs in a medium mixing bowl and blend in the Pecorino Romano with a pinch of salt and plenty of pepper.

2 Rinse the courgettes, pat them dry and slice them into thin rounds.

3 Heat the oil in a 25cm (10in) frying pan over a medium heat. Add the courgette and sauté, stirring, flipping and tossing for 5-6 minutes. Lower the heat to minimum, cover the frying pan, and simmer until tender, about 3-4 minutes.

4 Add the mint and a tiny pinch of salt and pepper to the courgette, then pour in the beaten egg. Lift and tilt the pan to distribute the contents. Cook, covered, until the **frittata** is firm but moist, about 5-7 minutes (it all depends on the heat and the pan).

5 Cut into wedges and serve immediately.

SERVES 4

fave con cipolla rossa e formaggio

broad beans sautéed with red onion and goat's cheese

In the restaurant of a smart hotel outside Rome, I asked if they had broad beans on the menu. Moments later arrived a beautiful platter covered with chunks of ice on which were arranged sheaves of fresh young broad beans in the pod. This is how most Italians enjoy broad beans: young and raw. However, cooking them is also delicious.

1kg (2¼lb) broad beans in the pod, podded and skinned

1 medium red onion, peeled and chopped

2 tbsp olive oil

sea salt and freshly ground black pepper

1 x 200g packet goat's cheese

paprika

1 Boil or steam the podded and skinned broad beans until tender, this should take about 10 minutes.

2 Sauté the onion in the olive oil for about 5 minutes, then add the hot drained beans, and season to taste. Mix together well.

3 Serve in a dish, with thinly sliced goat's cheese in a stripe across the top. Sprinkle with paprika.

SERVES 4

fave al vino

broad beans with a wine sauce

On every street corner in the spring you can see groups of little old men passing the time eating young broad beans straight from the pod. This recipe is a way to use broad beans when they are not so young and tender, and cannot be eaten raw.

1kg (2¼lb) broad beans in the pod

25g (1oz) unsalted butter

½ onion, peeled and finely chopped

25g (1oz) plain flour

1 sprig fresh marjoram, chopped

1 tsp caster sugar

300ml (10fl oz) white wine

150ml (5fl oz) vegetable broth (see page 299)

sea salt and black pepper

1 Shell the broad beans.

2 Melt the butter in a pan and cook the finely chopped onion for 4 minutes until it is golden. Stir in the flour, and cook until you have a thick roux, about 1 minute.

3 Add the podded beans and the marjoram, salt and pepper, sugar and white wine, and mix all together.

4 Add the broth, mix and simmer gently for 20-25 minutes, until the beans are tender.

SERVES 4

frittata di asparagi

asparagus omelette

I often cook *frittata* when I've just come back from holiday and there's nothing else in the fridge. I either pick the vegetable from the garden or stop off and buy it on the way home. It's good eaten hot or at room temperature.

400g (14oz) asparagus, trimmed and well washed

8 large eggs

2 garlic cloves, peeled and crushed

a good pinch of dried chilli (peperoncino)

4 tbsp whole milk

2 tbsp freshly grated Parmesan cheese

sea salt and freshly ground black pepper

3-4 tbsp olive oil

1 Preheat the oven to 200°C/400°F/ gas mark 6. Roast the asparagus for 6 minutes, turning once, then cut each spear in 3.

2 Beat the eggs lightly and mix in the asparagus and all the remaining ingredients, apart from the oil.

3 Heat the olive oil in a 25cm (8in) frying pan and, when hot, pour in the egg mixture. Over a medium heat, cook, covered, until the *frittata* is firm but moist, about 5-7 minutes (it all depends on the heat and the pan).

4 Cut into wedges and serve immediately.

SERVES 4

torta di asparagi

asparagus flan

Wrapped up in a clean napkin or in paper, this flan is easy to transport in a basket or hamper for a spring (or summer) picnic. It looks good, tastes good, and is wonderful with fruit, salad and wine. It's a real boon for the cook as it can be made ahead of time. (And the pastry is really simple to make – a real confidence booster!)

PASTRY

150g (5½oz) Italian '00' plain flour

55g (2oz) unsalted butter

1 large egg, lightly beaten

3 tbsp whole milk

FILLING

sea salt and freshly ground black pepper

375g (13oz) asparagus, trimmed and well washed

25g (1oz) unsalted butter

2 tbsp Italian '00' plain flour

4 large eggs, lightly beaten

250g (9oz) ricotta cheese, fresh if possible

2 garlic cloves, peeled and crushed

¼ tsp freshly grated nutmeg

55g (2oz) Parmesan cheese, freshly grated

1 To make the pastry, combine the ingredients in a food processor. Gently knead on a work surface then wrap in greaseproof paper or cling film and chill for 30 minutes.

2 Heat the oven to 200°C/400°F/gas mark 6.

3 To make the filling, bring a pot of water to a rapid boil. Add salt. Lower the asparagus into the water and cook until just tender, about 3-6 minutes. Transfer the asparagus to a bowl of cold water.

4 Make a roux by melting the butter in a small heavy saucepan over a medium heat. Add the flour and stir until dissolved and foaming. Remove from the heat and let the roux cool.

5 Drain the asparagus, then cut off the tips and set to one side. Cut the stems into 2cm (¾in) pieces, and combine these in a bowl with the eggs, ricotta, garlic, nutmeg, Parmesan, some salt and pepper and the roux.

6 On a lightly floured board, roll out two-thirds of the pastry into a 28cm (11in) round, 3mm (⅛in) thick. Line a 23cm (9in) greased tart tin with the pastry. Trim off excess dough and prick the bottom of the tart with a fork.

7 Spread the filling evenly over the pastry and top with the asparagus tips. Roll out the remaining pastry into a smaller round also 3mm (⅛in) thick. Cut the pastry into 2cm (¾in) wide strips, using a fluted pastry wheel. Arrange the strips over the filling in a lattice pattern.

8 Bake the flan for 30 minutes until golden. Cool on a wire rack.

SERVES 6

bianchetti di zucchini e patate novelle con erbe

new potatoes with courgettes and herbs

This delicious recipe is very characteristic of the south, where courgettes grow prolifically. The best potatoes to use are Elvira and Spunta. In Italy they come to the markets covered in the dark, southern volcanic soil, which gives them a fantastically earthy flavour. The flesh is bright yellow. All the potatoes should be the same size.

500g (18oz) new Italian potatoes, peeled

300ml (10fl oz) double cream

150ml (5fl oz) water

4 shallots, peeled and finely chopped

sea salt and freshly ground black pepper

250g (9oz) courgettes, sliced into rounds

juice of 1 lemon

a handful each of fresh flat-leaf parsley and mint, roughly chopped

1 In a large saucepan, combine the potatoes, cream, water, shallots and some salt, and bring to the boil over a medium to high heat. Cover and continue to cook for 10 minutes.

2 Add the courgettes to the potatoes and cook for another 10 minutes.

3 Add the lemon juice, some pepper and the herbs. The potatoes should be tender and creamy. Season as required and serve.

SERVES 6

fiori di zucca ripieni

courgette flowers stuffed with mozzarella and anchovies

My love of courgette flowers developed when, as a child, I was learning about cookery from my grandmother in the south of Italy. They can be eaten in a variety of ways.

16 large courgette flowers

8 salted anchovies, rinsed and filleted, or 16 marinated anchovies in oil, drained

85g (3oz) mozzarella cheese, cut into 16 cubes

3 large eggs, beaten

100g (3½oz) dried breadcrumbs

olive oil

sea salt and black pepper

1 Remove the stems and stamens from the flowers. Rinse them under cold water and pat dry with paper towels.

2 Stuff each flower with an anchovy fillet and a cube of mozzarella. Twist the top of the flower to seal it. Dip in the beaten egg then coat with breadcrumbs.

3 Heat 2.5cm (1in) oil in a large frying pan. When the oil is hot add the flowers, a few at a time. Fry until they are golden, turning once. Remove with a slotted spoon and drain on kitchen paper.

4 Sprinkle with salt and pepper and eat.

SERVES 6

preparing carciofi (globe artichokes)

The globe artichoke is one of Italy's favourite vegetables, flourishing in the warm south, and it is increasingly available in the UK. Its preparation daunts many people, but once you have learned the basic techniques, you can enjoy eating artichokes – boiled, steamed, baked, stuffed or marinated – as often as you like!

Globe artichokes are giant thistles related to the cardoon. The part that we eat is the immature flower bud, which can vary in colour from purple to green, and in size from tiny to large and globular (thus their English name!). There are two main varieties: those with a pointed head and prickly leaves, *spinosa sarda*, and those with a rounded head and no prickles, *spinosa romanesco*. In Italy during the short artichoke season, they are truly celebrated in the markets. The vendors will prepare them for you, dipping them into lemon juice as they go, so you can buy them, rush home, cook them quickly and enjoy.

PREPARING AND COOKING A WHOLE ARTICHOKE

The preparation of an artichoke depends to a great extent on what you intend to do with it. As the flesh discolours very easily, begin by soaking it for 20 minutes in a large bowl of water acidulated with the juice of half a lemon. Use the other half of the lemon to rub the artichoke as the inner flesh is exposed. If you want to eat it in the 'British' fashion – boiled whole – you need only trim off the tough tops of the leaves and a little bit of the stem. When the artichoke has boiled to tender, you eat it leaf by leaf, dipping them into melted butter, vinaigrette or hollandaise, and scraping off the tasty flesh with your teeth. When you reach the heart, you will have to scrape out the fuzzy choke, and discard it. Then you can enjoy the tender flesh of the heart.

STUFFED ARTICHOKES

If you want to stuff a large artichoke, raw or cooked, you must trim it as above, then open out the leaves and reach in with a spoon to scrape out the choke. You could also cut artichokes in halves or quarters, and scrape out the chokes that way, before braising, say.

ARTICHOKE HEARTS

If you want to use the heart and tender inner leaves only, you must trim the raw artichoke of all its tough, inedible parts. Begin at the base and snap off the dark green leaves. As the leaves become lighter in colour, remove only the green portion, leaving the tender yellow part closest to the base. Stop when the leaves are completely yellow. Cut off and discard 2.5cm (1in) from the top of the artichoke. Open it carefully to remove the prickly inner leaves and scrape out the fuzzy choke with a teaspoon. Rinse the artichoke under cold water then dip it into the acidulated water again.

ARTICHOKE STEMS

Most of the stem is edible. Trim off the dry end and remove the outer green casing, leaving only the tender white core. Trim away any additional dark green that remains on the artichoke and return it to the lemon water.

carciofi con spinaci

artichoke hearts with spinach

In Italy, artichokes are sold along the roadside from lorries during the artichoke season, which is April, May and October. This recipe comes from the Marche region, famous for delicious artichokes, as well as spinach.

6 tbsp olive oil

1 small onion, peeled and finely chopped

1 garlic clove, peeled and crushed

1kg (2¼lb) spinach, washed, drained and finely chopped

25g (1oz) plain flour

sea salt and freshly ground black pepper

8 young globe artichokes

55g (2oz) dried breadcrumbs

55g (2oz) Parmesan cheese, freshly grated

a handful of fresh mint leaves, finely chopped

a handful of fresh flat-leaf parsley leaves, chopped

1 Heat half the oil in a large heavy pan, add the onion and garlic, and fry gently for 5 minutes. Add the spinach and cook for 2 minutes.

2 Stir in the flour and salt and pepper to taste, cover and cook gently for 5 minutes.

3 Preheat the oven to 200°C/400°F/gas mark 6.

4 Clean the artichokes, discarding the hard outer leaves, spikes and chokes (see page 104). Stand them close together in an oiled ovenproof dish, then cover with the spinach.

5 Scatter with the remaining oil, the breadcrumbs, Parmesan, pepper and mint. Bake for 20 minutes, then sprinkle with parsley and serve.

SERVES 4

carciofi ripieni
stuffed artichokes

I first tasted this recipe in Milan. If the cheeses specified here aren't available, please experiment. So long as the cheeses are strong, the recipe will work.

55g (2oz) Parmesan cheese, freshly grated

40g (1½oz) Fontina cheese, shredded

25g (1oz) Taleggio cheese, finely diced

1½ garlic cloves, peeled and crushed

a handful of fresh basil leaves, torn

5 tbsp olive oil

4 large globe artichokes

1 lemon, halved

a handful of fresh flat-leaf parsley leaves, finely chopped

165ml (5½fl oz) vegetable broth (see page 299)

1 Preheat the oven to 180°C/350°F/gas mark 4.

2 To make the stuffing, combine the 3 cheeses, a third of the garlic, the basil and 2 tbsp olive oil in a bowl. Set aside.

3 Prepare the artichokes for stuffing as described on page 104, using the lemon halves as you go. Remove the stems from the trimmed artichokes, coarsely chop them and set aside. Spoon the stuffing into the cavity of each artichoke, dividing the mixture evenly.

4 Heat the remaining olive oil in a medium-sized casserole over a low heat and add the remaining garlic. Add the parsley, broth and chopped artichoke stems, and simmer for 15 minutes. Arrange the stuffed artichokes in the casserole and cover the dish.

5 Bake for 50 minutes, or until the artichokes are tender. When tender, a small paring knife should slip in and out easily when inserted into the thickest part of the artichoke bottom. Serve immediately.

SERVES 4

carciofi alle mandorle
artichoke hearts with almond sauce

This Calabrian dish is sweet-sour and uses almonds, exhibiting the influence of North Africa.

½ red onion, grated

4 tbsp olive oil

1 garlic clove, crushed

115g (4oz) ground almonds

300ml (10fl oz) vegetable broth (see page 299)

1 tbsp white wine vinegar

1 tbsp caster sugar

juice of 1 lemon

6 fresh cooked artichoke hearts

2 tbsp capers and 2 small pickled gherkins, chopped

1 For the sauce, fry the onion until golden in 1 tbsp of the oil, then add the garlic and allow to colour lightly. Add the almonds and the broth, then simmer for approximately 15 minutes, until thick and creamy.

2 Beat in the remaining oil, the vinegar, sugar, lemon juice and a little salt and pepper, adjusting the quantities to taste. Leave to cool.

3 Arrange the artichoke hearts on individual plates, pour the sauce over them, and garnish, if liked, with capers and pickled gherkins. Serve cold.

SERVES 4

misticanza

sautéed mixed greens

This dish illustrates the importance of greens, which form a fundamental part of Italian eating served as **contorne** (vegetables) throughout the summer season. Tossing the greens in the pan with chilli and garlic (**saltata in padella**) makes them more interesting. And you could then add some fresh lemon juice at the end.

675g (1½lb) mixed greens (spinach, Swiss chard, purple sprouting broccoli, endive)

sea salt and freshly ground black pepper

2 tbsp olive oil

2 garlic cloves, peeled and crushed

1-2 small hot chillies, seeded and finely chopped

extra virgin olive oil

1 Trim and thoroughly wash the leaves and vegetables.

2 Fill a large pan with 3 litres (5¼ pints) water and bring it to the boil. Add salt to taste. Stir in the greens and boil for 3-5 minutes, or until just tender. Drain and refresh under cold water and drain again. Squeeze to eliminate all of the water, then coarsely chop.

3 Heat the olive oil in a large sauté pan over a medium heat. Add the garlic and chillies and cook lightly to soften. Add the greens, and sauté until heated through. Season with salt and pepper.

4 To serve, sprinkle with good extra virgin olive oil.

SERVES 4

peperonata alla campagnola

country style peppers

This is a classic pepper dish from the south of Italy, where peppers grow in profusion. I should think that every household has its own 'blend'. Some *peperonata* in a jar with good olive oil to cover makes a wonderful present to give to friends – the essence of summer!

6 tbsp olive oil

1 red onion, peeled and sliced

2 garlic cloves, peeled and sliced

2 large red and 2 large yellow peppers, seeded and cut into strips

sea salt and freshly ground black pepper

350g (12oz) plum tomatoes, skinned and chopped

350g (12oz) new potatoes (such as Nicola), peeled and cubed

1 fresh red chilli, seeded and finely chopped

a handful of fresh flat-leaf parsley leaves, finely chopped

a handful of fresh oregano leaves, finely chopped

1 Heat the oil in a heavy pan, add the onion and garlic and cook gently for 5 minutes.

2 Add the peppers and some salt and pepper. Cook for a further 5 minutes, stirring occasionally.

3 Add the tomatoes, potatoes, chilli, parsley and oregano to the peppers. Adjust the seasoning to taste, cover and simmer for 20-30 minutes, stirring frequently until thickened.

4 Serve hot or cold as an *antipasto*.

SERVES 4

peperoni e porcini

sweet peppers and porcini

My naughty friend Claudio gave me this recipe. He has a restaurant called **La Taverna** in Perugia. This dish is always on his menu, and it is always cooked to perfection.

85g (3oz) dried porcini mushrooms (ceps)

2 tbsp olive oil

2 garlic cloves, peeled and finely chopped

2 red peppers, seeded and thinly sliced

1 yellow pepper, seeded and thinly sliced

1 medium fennel bulb, thinly sliced

sea salt and freshly ground black pepper

1 Cover the *porcini* with cold water in a bowl, and leave for 10 minutes.

2 Pick the *porcini* out of the water rather than strain them through a sieve, as this ensures you leave any grit in the bowl. Strain the soaking water through a sieve, and retain 2 tbsp (keep the rest for stock). Dice the *porcini*.

3 In a heavy-based medium saucepan, heat the olive oil and sauté the garlic until soft but not too coloured.

4 Add the sliced peppers and fennel and sauté for 5 minutes, then add the *porcini* and their reserved soaking water.

5 Cover the saucepan, and simmer for 5 minutes. Season with salt and pepper, and serve at once.

SERVES 4

fagioli in padella

'ratatouille' of French beans

This is a speciality of Domodossola, an area in Lombardy in the north of Italy. It is a really tasty bean recipe, and even better made the day before as all the flavours will have mingled together. I like it as a simple meal served with crusty bread and a salad to follow.

900g (2lb) French beans

2 tbsp olive oil

1 small onion, peeled and chopped

2 garlic cloves, peeled and crushed

2 tbsp finely chopped fresh flat-leaf parsley

1 tsp torn fresh basil leaves

50ml (2fl oz) dry red wine

225g (8oz) canned tomatoes and their juices, chopped

1 Top and tail the beans, and cut them into 5cm (2in) lengths.

2 Heat the olive oil in a large frying pan and cook the onion, garlic, parsley and basil for 3 minutes.

3 Add the red wine and then cook over a moderate heat until the wine has almost evaporated.

4 Add the beans and tomatoes, season to taste with salt and pepper, and cook gently for 12 minutes, or until the beans are tender and the sauce has thickened. Serve hot..

SERVES 4

fagiolini di sant'anna

green beans in garlic sauce

When I'm writing and running short of recipes, my friend Anna from Perugia helps me out, and this is one of her recipes – simple, straightforward and delicious. You could ring the changes with a handful of toasted pine kernels scattered on at the end, or alternatively you could include cooked new potatoes. Some fresh oregano added towards the end of the cooking would be good as well.

3 tbsp olive oil

2 garlic cloves, peeled and crushed

1 large ripe tomato, skinned and chopped

550g (1¼lb) green beans, topped, tailed and cut in half

100g (3½oz) cooked new potatoes (Nicola or Spunta), halved (optional)

sea salt and freshly ground black pepper

1 Heat the oil in a medium saucepan, add the garlic and fry gently until coloured. Stir in the tomato, then add the beans and potatoes (if using).

2 Add enough water to barely cover the beans, then season to taste and bring to the boil. Lower the heat, cover and simmer for 10 minutes, until the beans are tender.

3 Remove the lid and increase the heat towards the end of the cooking time to reduce the juices. Serve hot or cold.

SERVES 4

torta di melanzana
aubergine cake

One of my all-time favourites: aubergine fried in a coating of egg and Parmesan until golden and crispy, then layered with mozzarella cheese and a fresh tomato sauce. Ideal for entertaining, it can be made in advance and reheated at the last minute. If you have any of the coating egg and cheese mixture left, it makes a delicious tiny *frittata*!

1 medium aubergine, thinly sliced

sea salt and freshly ground black pepper

900g (2lb) fresh ripe tomatoes

6 tbsp olive oil

1 garlic clove, peeled and crushed

1 onion, peeled and finely chopped

1 tsp caster sugar

a handful of fresh basil leaves, torn

2 tbsp strong white unbleached flour

4 large eggs

7 tbsp freshly grated Parmesan cheese

350g (12oz) mozzarella cheese, sliced

1 Sprinkle the aubergine slices with salt, place in a colander, cover and weight down. Leave for 30 minutes. This prevents them from soaking up too much oil, and improves the flavour.

2 Put the tomatoes in a bowl, cover with boiling water for about a minute, then plunge into cold water. Peel off the skins, then chop the tomatoes.

3 In a large saucepan, heat 2 tbsp of the olive oil, add the garlic and cook until coloured, then add the onion and cook gently until softened. Add the tomatoes and sugar, bring to the boil, then simmer for 40 minutes, uncovered, to allow the sauce to reduce. Season and add a few of the basil leaves. The sauce should be thick and concentrated.

4 Preheat the oven to 190°C/375°F/gas mark 5.

5 Rinse the aubergine and pat dry. Dip the slices in flour and set aside. Whisk the eggs in a bowl and add 5 tbsp of the grated Parmesan.

6 In a frying pan, heat the remaining olive oil. Dip the aubergine in the egg mixture and fry until golden on both sides. Drain on absorbent kitchen paper and set aside.

7 Assemble the dish in a 20cm (8in) spring-release cake tin. Place a layer of the aubergines in the bottom, add a third of the mozzarella cheese, tomato sauce and basil leaves. Then add further layers, finishing with a layer of aubergine slices.

8 Sprinkle over the remaining Parmesan cheese and bake for 20-25 minutes, until golden.

SERVES 4

cipolle farcite

baked stuffed onions

These stuffed onions make an ideal **contorno**, a course by themselves. Be inventive with the filling: this one I recommend, but spinach would be good too, and looks wonderful.

4 medium onions, peeled

100g (3½oz) Parmesan cheese, freshly grated

85g (3oz) unsalted butter

3 large eggs

sea salt and freshly ground black pepper

3 tbsp brandy

1 Cook the onions in boiling water for 15 minutes. Drain and cut in half horizontally, then scoop out two-thirds of the cores with a spoon.

2 Chop the onion cores and place in a bowl with the cheese, half of the butter, the eggs, and salt and pepper to taste. Mix thoroughly, then spoon into the onion shells.

3 Preheat the oven to 200°C/400°F/gas mark 6.

4 Melt the remaining butter in a flameproof casserole, put the onions in and then sprinkle with the brandy.

5 Bake for 25 minutes, until golden. Serve right away.

SERVES 4

finocchi al formaggio

baked fennel and cheese

Making this dish once for a group of students, everyone was a little alarmed at my method, as everything seemed to go into the oven very quickly and with very little fuss. The results were good, though, and I think I have made a few converts!

6 fennel bulbs, 3 male, 3 female

sea salt and freshly ground black pepper

55g (2oz) unsalted butter

115g (4oz) Fontina cheese, freshly grated

freshly grated nutmeg

50ml (2fl oz) milk

1 Preheat the oven to 220°C/425°F/gas mark 7.

2 Trim the fennel bulbs and discard the tough outer layers.

3 Cut the bulbs into small wedges and cook in a little boiling salted water until crisp-tender. Drain and place in a greased baking dish with a little of the butter.

4 Season the fennel with salt and pepper. Cover with the grated Fontina, sprinkle with nutmeg and then pour on the milk.

5 Dot with the remaining butter, then bake for 10 minutes. Serve hot.

SERVES 6

zucca fritta con salvia e Parmigiano
pumpkin fritters with sage and parmesan

The pungency of the sage is a great flavour enhancer for the fairly bland pumpkin here. Choosing the right pumpkin is vital. It should not be too large, nor too small; tap it, and it should feel as tight as a drum, heavy for its size. If it's light, the chances are it's old. You'll need at least 1kg (2¼lb) pumpkin to get this amount of flesh after peeling and seeding. Keep the seeds as a cook's treat: wash, dry and bake with sea salt.

750g (1lb 10oz) pumpkin flesh

sea salt and freshly ground black pepper

200g (7oz) Italian '00' plain flour

a handful of fresh sage leaves, finely chopped, plus extra to garnish

115g (4oz) Parmesan cheese, freshly grated

2 garlic cloves, peeled and finely chopped

4 tbsp olive oil

1 Chop the pumpkin flesh into even cubes.

2 Put the pumpkin into boiling salted water and cook for about 8 minutes, until tender. Drain and mash in a bowl. Add the flour, sage, half of the Parmesan, some salt and pepper and the garlic, and knead until smooth.

3 Form into a long sausage and chop into 12 even pieces. Flatten each piece to form a fritter.

4 Heat the oil in a frying pan and fry the fritters for 3-4 minutes on both sides, until golden. Drain well.

5 Serve sprinkled with the remaining Parmesan and extra torn sage leaves.

SERVES 4

funghi al cartoccio

baked mushrooms

Mushrooms, parsley and mint make a classic Umbrian combination. If you have been out on a wild mushroom foray, you could bake a selection of mushrooms all in one go. Instead of wrapping the ingredients in paper, you could encase them in foil and cook them on the barbecue. Both versions preserve the juices – '*in umido*' – and therefore the flavour.

500g (18oz) field mushrooms (or wild), cleaned

15g (1/2oz) unsalted butter, melted

4 garlic cloves, peeled and finely chopped

a handful each of fresh flat-leaf parsley and mint, finely chopped

sea salt and freshly ground black pepper

4 tbsp olive oil

1 Preheat the oven to 200°C/400°F/gas mark 6.

2 Wipe the mushrooms with a clean damp cloth and roughly chop.

3 Brush 4 squares of parchment paper liberally with the butter. Place some of the mushrooms in each square of paper. Sprinkle with garlic, herbs, salt and pepper and olive oil.

4 Bring the corners of each square up to meet in the centre and fold over to seal the contents perfectly.

5 Bake for 10-15 minutes. Serve wrapped in the paper – slash open and let the smell hit your nose.

SERVES 4

cavolfiori di amalfi

Parmesan-fried cauliflower

This is a family recipe, which can be made with broccoli as well. Do try it, as it will change the face and flavour of cauliflower for you. Cauliflower cheese will never be the same again!

1 medium cauliflower

2 tbsp plain flour

2 large eggs

4 tbsp freshly grated Parmesan cheese

sea salt and freshly ground black pepper

a good handful of fresh flat-leaf parsley leaves

6 tbsp olive oil

1 Break the cauliflower into florets, then steam for 6 minutes until tender. Leave to cool completely.

2 Coat the cauliflower florets in flour, one at a time.

3 Beat the eggs, then add the Parmesan, salt and pepper. Finely chop most of the parsley and add it as well. Dip the florets in the egg mixture.

4 Heat the oil in a frying pan and, when hot, shallow-fry the cauliflower florets until golden brown on all sides.

5 Drain and serve hot, cold or warm, scattered with the remaining parsley.

SERVES 4

patate al forno

roast potatoes with garlic, rosemary and lemon

These are healthy 'roast' potatoes, made crispy and flavourful by the lemon juice: the juice caramelizes slightly on the surface starch of the potatoes, and turns them golden. The dish is best made with Italian new potatoes, but you can use other varieties, old or new. I used to make these at my cookery school in Umbria to accompany fish caught in the lake – a wonderful combination.

1kg (2¼lb) Italian new potatoes

125ml (4fl oz) olive oil

1 sprig fresh rosemary, leaves finely chopped

juice of 2 lemons

finely grated zest of 1 unwaxed lemon

3 garlic cloves, peeled and finely chopped

sea salt and freshly ground black pepper

1 Preheat the oven to 200°C/400°F/gas mark 6.

2 Scrub the potatoes and cut into 2.5cm (1in) cubes. Parboil for 10 minutes and drain into a bowl.

3 In a separate bowl, prepare the dressing, using the olive oil, rosemary, lemon juice and zest and the garlic.

4 Pour this dressing over the hot potatoes and mix, then place in a roasting dish. Stirring periodically, bake for 25 minutes, until golden.

5 Season with salt and pepper – salting them before makes the potatoes go a little soggy – and serve warm or cold.

SERVES 4

patate e zucchini al forno con aglio

roast potatoes with courgettes, garlic and herbs

Spunta potatoes, which my father grows, are rich and yellow fleshed, with lots of moisture. Even the soil in which they travel – in hand-sewn sacks – smells good!

6 large Italian new potatoes (Spunta), scrubbed

2 medium courgettes

6 tbsp olive oil

3 garlic cloves, peeled and crushed

2 sprigs fresh rosemary, leaves chopped

sea salt and freshly ground black pepper

1 Preheat the oven to 200°C/400°F/gas mark 6.

2 Cut the potatoes and courgettes into 2.5cm (1in) chunks. Put the courgettes in a bowl and set aside.

3 In a 35 x 23cm (14 x 9in) baking dish, mix the olive oil and the garlic paste. Add the potatoes and coat well with the mixture. Bake for 30-45 minutes and baste frequently.

4 Add the courgettes and rosemary to the baking dish, and toss well, then bake for a further 10 minutes. Sprinkle with salt and pepper and serve at once.

SERVES 4

patate con funghi porcini

potatoes with mushrooms

Along the side of Italian roads in autumn, you will encounter a host of vendors offering fresh porcini mushrooms or ceps, all of them invitingly laid out in boxes, and wrapped with fresh forest leaves. I always find it hard to resist. Hence this recipe, which is a great example of how to enjoy these particular mushrooms.

500g (18oz) Italian potatoes (Elvira or Spunta are best)

400g (14oz) fresh porcini mushrooms (ceps) or a combination of wild mushrooms

5 tbsp olive oil

4-5 garlic cloves, peeled and crushed

a handful of fresh flat-leaf parsley leaves, chopped

sea salt and freshly ground black pepper

1 Preheat the oven to 180°C/350°F/gas mark 4.

2 Scrub the potatoes, and slice them to 3mm ($^1/_8$in) thick. Brush the mushrooms to get rid of any clinging dirt (check the stems too), and slice them to 3mm ($^1/_8$in) thick.

3 Lightly oil a large roasting pan and place a single layer of potatoes in the pan. Top with some mushrooms and sprinkle with some of the garlic, parsley, salt and pepper.

4 Continue layering the ingredients until you finish them. Drizzle with olive oil, then pour into the side of the pan 150ml (5fl oz) of water.

5 Bake for an hour, or until the potatoes are tender and the top is golden brown. If the mixture seems dry, add a little more water. Serve hot.

SERVES 6

salads and soups

insalata della nonna

Grandmother's special salad

This hearty salad is full of goodness. The combination of beans and potatoes also make it a filling snack.

450g (1lb) new potatoes, boiled

sea salt and freshly ground black pepper

450g (1lb) French beans, cut into bite-sized pieces

2 tbsp freshly squeezed lemon juice

4 tbsp extra virgin olive oil

a handful of chopped fresh oregano

1 garlic clove, peeled and finely crushed

6 tomatoes (preferably vine-ripened), roughly chopped

1 Cook the potatoes in boiling salted water for 10-15 minutes, or until tender, depending on their size.

2 Steam the French beans for approximately 7 minutes, or until tender.

3 While the beans and potatoes are cooking, mix the lemon juice and oil together with salt, pepper, the oregano and garlic.

4 Add the tomatoes to the dressing and mix well with the potatoes and beans while still warm. Serve warm or cool.

SERVES 4

patate insalata di Sicilia
Sicilian potato salad

This salad is a real feast for the eyes and palate. It's full of crunch and flavour, and keeps very well (useful for our busy lives). I first enjoyed it on a trip with family friends to Syracuse, a beautiful fishing village. All these flavours are very characteristic of Sicilian cooking.

6 Italian new potatoes
(Spunta, Elvira or Nicola),
scrubbed

a handful of salted capers,
rinsed

8 *pomodorini* cherry tomatoes
on the vine (when they are
sweeter)

4 marinated anchovies,
roughly chopped

8 marinated black olives,
stoned

1 small red onion, peeled and
roughly sliced

sea salt and freshly ground
black pepper

3 tbsp fruity extra virgin olive
oil

a sprinkling of fresh oregano
leaves

1 Peel the potatoes, cut them into 2.5cm (1in) chunks and boil them for about 6-8 minutes, until tender. Drain and leave to cool.

2 Add the capers to the cooled potatoes, plus the tomatoes, anchovies, olives and onion.

3 Season with salt and pepper, add the oil and oregano and mix well. Serve at room temperature.

SERVES 4

insalata di spinaci e patate

spinach and potato salad

The combination of these two ingredients is delicious, creating a salad that is warming and satisfying, with a meaty texture. As these two vegetables are commonly cooked together in the Indian sub-continent, perhaps Marco Polo had a hand in bringing the idea to Europe.

1kg (2¼lb) spinach

55g (2oz) unsalted butter

sea salt and freshly ground black pepper

3 tbsp extra virgin olive oil

1 dsp balsamic vinegar

4 medium Italian new potatoes, scrubbed and thinly sliced

1 Wash the spinach well and remove any tough stems. Cook in a large pan, with only the water clinging to the leaves, until wilted, about 8-10 minutes.

2 Add the butter to the spinach along with some salt and pepper and the oil and vinegar. Mix very well to season all the spinach leaves.

3 Boil the potato slices until tender, about 4-5 minutes, and mix into the spinach. Serve warm.

SERVES 4

broccoli in insalata

broccoli salad

The Italian love of vegetables is amply illustrated by the fact that they even eat broccoli in a salad. A crispness comes from the raw carrot, a softer texture from the cooked broccoli. The lemon juice recognisably enhances the flavour of the broccoli, just as it does many other cooked green vegetables (particularly spring greens, one of my favourite vegetables).

450g (1lb) broccoli florets

sea salt and freshly ground black pepper

4 small carrots

juice of 4 unwaxed lemons

½ tsp dried chilli (*peperoncino*)

2 tbsp fruity olive oil

1 Cook the broccoli florets in rolling, boiling, salted water for 7 minutes. Drain and refresh under cold water to prevent further cooking. Drain again and leave to cool.

2 Scrape the carrots and shred them into thin strips.

3 Mix the carrots and cold broccoli together, and dress with lemon juice, chilli, salt, pepper and oil.

SERVES 4

insalata mezzogiorno

prawn, artichoke and roasted tomato salad

In Italy, '*mezzogiorno*' has two meanings: 'noon' and 'the southern regions of Italy, which are the sunniest'. This salad celebrates the south, using capers from the islands and prawns from the rich seas all around. You can find many prawns in the shops these days, but do try to buy them raw. They will be much better if cooked at home and then mixed with their aromatics while still warm.

6 plum tomatoes

7 tbsp extra virgin olive oil

sea salt and freshly ground black pepper

4 tbsp salted capers

12 baby artichokes

36 raw prawns in the shell

2 bay leaves

1 garlic clove, peeled and crushed

a handful of fresh flat-leaf parsley, chopped

1 unwaxed lemon, sliced

1 tsp white wine vinegar

1 Preheat the oven to 200°C/400°F/gas mark 6.

2 Halve the tomatoes from stem to stamen and place on a baking sheet. Drizzle with 1 tbsp of the oil, and season with salt and pepper. Roast until deflated and slightly brown, about 10-15 minutes, depending on the size of the tomatoes. Cool.

3 Meanwhile, soak the capers in lukewarm water for 20 minutes, changing the water 2-3 times. Drain them well.

4 Remove the tough outer leaves of the artichokes and trim off the leaf tips. Cut the artichokes in half and scrape out the choke (see also page 104). Bring abundant salted water to the boil. Drop in the artichokes and cook for about 10 minutes, until they are tender. Drain and allow to cool.

5 Cook the prawns with the bay leaves in lots of boiling water for a few minutes. Drain, shell (when cool enough) and place in a large bowl. While still warm, season with 2 tbsp of the olive oil, the garlic, parsley and capers.

6 Place the prawns in the centre of a platter and surround them with the artichokes, lemon slices and roasted tomatoes. Sprinkle with vinegar, the remaining olive oil, salt and pepper, and serve.

SERVES 6

insalata di petti di pollo di estate

summer chicken salad

This salad uses many of the ingredients that are so readily found in Italy in the summer. Try to buy the best rocket you can, nothing sold in a packet.

1 whole chicken breast (both sides), about 650g (1lb 7oz), poached (see page 138)

1 red pepper, seeded and thinly sliced into julienne strips

1 large avocado, peeled, stoned and roughly diced

4 medium plum tomatoes, seeded and finely chopped

sea salt and freshly ground black pepper

juice of 1 unwaxed lemon

90ml (3fl oz) extra virgin olive oil

350g (12oz) rocket, trimmed well, washed, dried and shredded

1 When cool enough to handle, skin and bone the poached chicken, and cut the flesh into 5mm (^{1}/4in) julienne strips. Put them in a bowl and add the red pepper, avocado and tomato. Season with salt and pepper, and some of the lemon juice and olive oil.

2 Place the rocket in a large bowl. Pour the remaining olive oil and lemon juice over the rocket. Season with salt and pepper, and toss.

3 Arrange the rocket salad on 6 individual salad plates. Top with the chicken salad and serve.

SERVES 6

insalata con erbe

green salad with wild herbs

This recipe comes from the deeply religious south of Italy, where every facet of life seems to be analysed or dissected in terms of superstition or religion. Here we use seven herbs because seven represents the number of the cardinal virtues.

1 crisp fresh cos lettuce

1/2 Treviso radicchio

a handful of rocket leaves

a large handful in total of 7 wild herbs from the garden (ie basil, parsley, thyme, marjoram, chives, sage and mint)

1 fennel bulb

DRESSING

3 tbsp best extra virgin olive oil

1 tbsp freshly squeezed lemon juice

sea salt and freshly ground black pepper

1 Separate, wash and pat dry all the salad leaves. Wash, dry and finely chop the herbs. Trim the fennel, then finely slice it.

2 Mix the leaves and herbs together, and then toss in the fennel slices.

3 Mix all the dressing ingredients together, seasoning to taste with salt and pepper.

4 To preserve the crispness of the leaves, dress the salad immediately before serving.

SERVES 4

insalata di rucola con fave

rocket salad with broad beans

Try to seek out different varieties of rocket to find which you like best. I'm not too keen on the rocket leaves you find in plastic bags, and would much rather go to my local market and buy bunches tied up with rubber bands, as they do in Italy. The very thin leaves tend to be the wild ones; fatter leaves are what my father calls '***domestica***' or cultivated. The wild in my mind is superior because of its fierce peppery flavour, and it goes very well with young – they must be young – broad beans.

300g (10¹/₂oz) rocket, selvatica or wild variety

300g (10¹/₂oz) oakleaf lettuce

125g (4¹/₂oz) young Pecorino Toscano cheese, thinly sliced

675g (1¹/₂lb) young shelled broad beans

sea salt and freshly ground black pepper

4 tbsp fruity extra virgin olive oil

1 Combine the rocket and lettuce in a large shallow bowl.

2 Place the cheese on top, then scatter with the beans.

3 Add some salt and pepper and the oil, and toss. Serve immediately.

SERVES 6

dressing salads

Italians are passionate about salads, and serve them daily, often after a main course, as they believe they are digestive, helping to settle the stomach. Usually the salads are very simple, and consist of a selection of leaves with the most basic dressing you could imagine, some good olive oil, a sprinkling of lemon juice or balsamic vinegar, and some salt and pepper.

Most of the new salad leaves we see in the shops today emanate from Italy. Think of the wonderful peppery rocket, the lollos (biondo and rosso), cicoria or frisée/endive, and the two radicchios (the round from Chioggia and the long from Treviso). The shape, texture and flavour of the leaves used usually dictates the type of dressing. Fresh and tender lettuces and herbs require a basic, thinnish dressing, like the Italian one below; sturdier leaves with a stronger flavour, such as radicchio or cicoria, can take a thicker and more characterful dressing (perhaps the lemon and Parmesan one below, or something with anchovy in it).

Before preparing and dressing a salad, pick through the leaves. (Always try and buy whole lettuces, not the leaves in bags; the former are usually fresher and are much cheaper.) Discard any wilted outer leaves, and wash them carefully, drying them on a clean tea-towel or in a salad-spinner. The Italians would then put the leaves in a bowl and sprinkle over the dressing ingredients by hand. If you're not this confident, mix up the dressing in a screw-top jar, and toss with the leaves just before serving.

But of course many other ingredients can be and are used in an Italian salad. Salads of cooked vegetables and stronger textures and flavours are often served as an antipasto. These can contain artichokes, aubergines, fennel, tomatoes and other fruits such as orange, as well as the intense flavourings so redolent of Italy, such as olives, anchovies, capers, pine nuts and sun-dried tomatoes. Simplicity is still the key, though, and often there is nothing else in a dressing but virgin olive oil. Italian salads always taste so good because the Italians insist on the best-quality ingredients. But these don't

have to be expensive: an essential frugality was the driving force behind one of Italy's best salads, made with stale bread (see page 136).

BASIC ITALIAN DRESSING
Put 4 tbsp extra virgin olive oil, 2 tbsp freshly squeezed lemon juice and some sea salt and freshly ground black pepper in a bowl and whisk together until well blended. This dressing is good for ordinary lettuces such as round, cos, romaine or little gem.

You could use balsamic vinegar instead of the lemon juice, and this dressing could then be used to dress meat salads and cooked vegetable salads.

SERVES 4

LEMON AND PARMESAN DRESSING
Put the juice of 1 unwaxed lemon, 4 tbsp fruity extra virgin olive oil, 2 tbsp freshly grated Parmesan and some sea salt and freshly ground black pepper in a bowl and then whisk together until well blended and thick. I would use this dressing to enhance bitter leaves such as frisée and rocket.

You could add the finely grated lemon zest as well, with perhaps a crushed half garlic clove, and whiz the whole thing in a blender for ultimate smoothness. This is good with vegetables.

SERVES 4-6

insalata di sicilia

tomato, mint and red onion salad

I have very fond memories of this salad and of eating it in Syracuse, Sicily, with my father. Some friends there grow lettuces, and this salad is what we ate – part of a wonderful meal – after a long dusty drive to their farm. It was the first time I had seen tomatoes, onion and mint together – and it is a stunning combination.

4 firm, bright red tomatoes

½ small red onion, peeled and finely chopped

a handful of fresh mint leaves, finely chopped

3 tbsp extra virgin olive oil

juice and finely grated zest of 1 unwaxed lemon

sea salt and freshly ground black pepper

1 Slice the tomatoes and arrange on a large plain plate.

2 Sprinkle the onion and mint over the tomatoes, and then drizzle with oil and lemon juice. Sprinkle over the finely chopped zest of the lemon, and season with salt and pepper.

3 Allow all the ingredients to come together for 20 minutes, and then serve.

SERVES 4

panzanella alla minori

bread, onion and tomato salad

There are many variations of this salad, which originates in Tuscany. It is a bread salad created, like so many Tuscan dishes, to utilize leftover stale bread. Here, bread mops up all the vegetable juices, and really is a bonus – especially if you have a lot of mouths to feed.

200g (7oz) coarse white bread, crusts removed

5 tomatoes, finely chopped

1 red onion, finely chopped

½ cucumber, finely chopped

2 celery stalks, finely chopped

6 black olives, stoned, chopped

a handful each of fresh basil and mint leaves, torn

90ml (3fl oz) extra virgin olive oil

25ml (1fl oz) white wine vinegar

1 Cut the bread into chunky pieces and put into a salad bowl. Sprinkle with 1 tbsp water.

2 Add all the other vegetable and herb ingredients, and toss.

3 Dress with the oil and vinegar, and season with salt and pepper. Stir well and leave for half an hour before serving.

SERVES 4

insalata di petti di pollo con noci
chicken salad with walnuts

This famous old recipe from Mantua once stipulated breast of capon rather than chicken, because it is more tender. In many regions of Italy capons are bred solely for Christmas dinner, and are served boiled with green sauce or **mostarda di Cremona**, a fruit relish.

POACHED CHICKEN

2 carrots, scrubbed and chopped

2 green celery stalks, trimmed and chopped

a handful of flat-leaf parsley

1 bay leaf

1 whole chicken breast (both sides), about 650g (1lb 7oz)

SALAD

2 tbsp raisins

2 inner white celery stalks

2 tbsp fresh lemon juice

4 tbsp extra virgin olive oil

1 small lettuce, split into leaves

12 walnuts, shelled, chopped

1 Combine the carrot, green celery, parsley, bay leaf and 600ml (1 pint) water in a saucepan. Add sea salt to taste. Bring to the boil and simmer, partially covered, for about 30 minutes.

2 Add the chicken breast and poach, covered, just until firm and cooked through, about 25 minutes. Drain (keeping the liquid as stock), cool, then skin and cut into julienne strips.

3 Meanwhile, soak the raisins in lukewarm water for 30 minutes, then drain them.

4 Cut the white celery stalks into thin julienne and then mix with the cooked chicken and drained raisins in a bowl.

5 Whisk the lemon juice, oil and a pinch of salt to make the dressing.

6 Arrange the lettuce leaves in 6 small bowls or on a serving plate. Spoon the chicken salad into each lettuce leaf. Drizzle with the oil and lemon dressing. Garnish with the walnuts, and serve.

SERVES 6

caponata di napoli
bread and mozzarella salad

This recipe may be simple, but it's delicious so long as you use the best ingredients.

450g (1lb) slightly dry, firm-textured, country-style bread

450g (1lb) mozzarella

4 tomatoes, seeded and diced

a handful of fresh basil, torn

1 tsp dried oregano

125ml (4fl oz) bold, fruity extra virgin olive oil

1 Tear the bread into small chunks and tear the mozzarella into 1cm (½in) chunks. Combine with the tomatoes, basil, oregano and salt and pepper to taste.

2 Drizzle generously with olive oil. Mix well and serve.

SERVES 4

insalata di rucola e fichi

rocket and fig salad

Rocket is a member of the same family as mustard and cress, which is obvious when you bite into it and encounter its bitter, sharp and peppery flavour. It was once cultivated in Britain, but went out of fashion for centuries until very recently, when Italian imports caused a happy renaissance. Now rocket has become the leaf of the moment, appearing in many of the most fashionable salads; it can also be used to make an extremely pungent pesto (see page 46).

225g (8oz) rocket leaves

125g (4½oz) fresh figs, quartered

1 tbsp freshly squeezed lemon juice

2–3 tbsp fruity extra virgin olive oil

sea salt and freshly ground black pepper

1 Wash the rocket well, tear into rough pieces, and dry it thoroughly.

2 Mix the quartered figs with the leaves, and add the lemon juice, oil and seasoning. Serve at once.

SERVES 4

insalata di granchi

crab salad

Serve this with toasted bread rubbed with garlic, and a glass of prosecco.

1 bunch rocket

1 head radicchio

500g (18oz) cooked crabmeat, picked over

2 avocados, stoned, peeled and sliced

2 tomatoes, cut into wedges

6 tbsp extra virgin olive oil

juice of 2 lemons

sea salt and freshly ground black pepper

1 Wash and dry the rocket well and divide between 4 plates. Core the radicchio and shred. Add to the rocket.

2 Place some rocket and radicchio on each plate, then mound a quarter of the crabmeat on top. Surround with some of the avocado and tomato.

3 In a small bowl, whisk together the olive oil, lemon juice and some salt and pepper. Drizzle over the salads and serve.

SERVES 4

insalata di finocchio e arancia

fennel and orange salad

This Sicilian salad is colourful and unusual, and packed with Vitamin C. A traditional story tells that when there is nothing to eat in Sicily there are always blood oranges.

6 medium blood oranges (or navel oranges)

1 medium fennel bulb, trimmed, cut into thin strips

2 tbsp finely minced fennel leaves

1 red onion, finely sliced

3 tbsp finely chopped fresh walnuts

2 tbsp extra virgin olive oil

sea salt and freshly ground black pepper

8 cos lettuce leaves

1 Peel the oranges and remove as much of the pith as possible. Slice the oranges into thin rounds and place them in a shallow dish, slightly overlapping.

2 Sprinkle over the fennel strips, fennel leaves, red onion and walnuts. Drizzle the olive oil over and sprinkle with salt and pepper.

3 Cover and let stand at room temperature for several hours. Every so often, tilt and turn the salad so that the oil and juices that have collected flow over and around the oranges.

4 To serve, arrange the salad on a bed of cos lettuce leaves, and pour the juices over.

SERVES 4

insalata toscana

beef, potato, red onion and parsley salad

The peasants of Tuscany have created many memorable dishes from leftovers, among them this delicious and hearty salad, which has become a staple at many a *trattoria*.

1 x 450g (1lb) beef brisket

1 litre (1³/₄ pints) beef broth (see page 299)

150ml (5fl oz) red wine

1/2 onion, finely chopped

1 carrot, scrubbed and sliced

1 celery stalk, trimmed

1 bay leaf and 3 sage leaves

6 medium potatoes

4 tbsp extra virgin olive oil

1 tbsp red wine vinegar

1/2 tsp dried chilli

1 red onion, coarsely chopped

2 plum tomatoes, finely diced

a handful of flat-leaf parsley

1 Place the meat in a large saucepan with the beef broth, wine, onion, carrot, celery and bay leaf. Bring to the boil over a high heat, then reduce the heat to medium, cover the pan, and simmer for 2 hours.

2 Drain the meat (the broth could be used in a soup; don't throw it away). When cool enough to handle, cut the meat into 1cm (½in) cubes and set aside.

3 Peel and dice the potatoes. Put in a pan with plenty of water and the sage. Bring to a boil and simmer for 8-10 minutes, until tender. Drain and set aside.

4 In a small bowl, mix the extra virgin olive oil, vinegar, salt, pepper and chilli. Finely chop the parsley.

5 In a large bowl, combine the meat, potatoes, red onion, tomato and parsley. Add the dressing, toss and serve the salad warm or cool.

SERVES 6

insalata di melanzane e cipolle

aubergine, potato and onion salad

This recipe came from a family friend in Calabria, Salvatore Veltri. I spent 10 days, one hot summer, learning how to cook delicious red onions, which he grows for export. The Tropea onion is picked in early spring and late summer, and its bulbs are intense violet, round, oval or long. They are sweet and fleshy, and eminently suitable for salads and raw dishes.

1 firm aubergine, weighing about 200g (7oz)

200g (7oz) Italian new potatoes

2 red onions, peeled

a handful of fresh mint leaves

a handful of fresh oregano leaves

1-2 tbsp white wine vinegar

3 tbsp extra virgin olive oil

sea salt and freshly ground black pepper

1 Peel, wash and boil the entire aubergine for 10 minutes in plenty of boiling water. Drain and cool. Cut it into strips and place it on a plate.

2 Peel, slice and boil the potatoes until tender, about 8-10 minutes. Drain and add to the aubergine.

3 Chop the onions finely, and add to the aubergine and potato, along with the herbs, vinegar and oil. Season with salt and pepper, and mix well. Serve at room temperature.

SERVES 4

insalata di pecorino e noci

cheese and walnut salad

This simple salad illustrates how something wonderful can be produced when you use a few ingredients at their peak of perfection: the fennel, walnuts and oil. A good, aged Pecorino is worth seeking out from your local cheese shop – there really isn't a substitute.

400g (14oz) mature Pecorino Toscano cheese

2 fennel bulbs, trimmed

a handful of fresh rocket leaves, washed and dried

12 whole walnuts, freshly shelled

3 tbsp Tuscan extra virgin olive oil

sea salt and freshly ground black pepper

1 Cut the cheese and fennel bulbs into thin slices.

2 Arrange the rocket leaves around the edge of the serving dish. Put the cheese and fennel in the centre and the walnuts on top.

3 Sprinkle with oil, salt and pepper and serve.

SERVES 4

insalata chiantigiana

frisée, caciotta cheese, pancetta and poached egg salad

During harvest time in the Chianti region, peasants used to spend long hours in the vineyards. To lighten their day, the women prepared this appealing and simple cold salad, which features caciotta, a mild sheep's milk cheese. A similar tradition exists in France in the Beaujolais region. I have added the poached egg to enhance the flavours and give it a sunny touch.

2 thick slices open-textured bread, crusts cut off

olive oil

300g (10¹/₂oz) pancetta, cut into strips

2-3 tbsp extra virgin olive oil

1 tbsp balsamic vinegar

sea salt and freshly ground black pepper

1 frisée lettuce, washed, dried and separated into leaves

4 large eggs

300g (10¹/₂oz) caciotta cheese, grated into shavings

1 Make the croûtons first. Preheat the oven to 200°C/400°F/gas mark 6. Cut the bread into even 1cm (½in) cubes, and put on a baking sheet. Drizzle with olive oil and bake for about 8 minutes, or until golden. Drain on paper towels and leave to cool.

2 In a frying pan, cook the pancetta slowly over a medium heat until it is crisp. Drain on paper towels.

3 In a large bowl, whisk together the oil, vinegar and some salt and pepper to taste. Add the frisée and toss well.

4 Bring a shallow pan of water to a simmer. Crack the eggs, carefully slide them into the water, and poach them for 3 minutes.

5 While the eggs poach, arrange the dressed frisée on 4 serving plates. Place a poached egg in the centre of each and surround it with some cheese, pancetta and croûtons.

SERVES 4

jota

bean and cabbage soup

This northern dish is eaten for *pranzo* (lunch), with a hunk of bread during the winter months. It's almost mandatory for all Italians to eat lots of beans during the winter, as they believe them to be synonymous with health, warmth and energy. Make this soup the day before you plan to eat it to allow all the flavours to amalgamate.

350g (12oz) dried cannellini beans, soaked overnight, drained and rinsed

1 medium fennel bulb

1 onion, peeled

2 garlic cloves, peeled

1 green cabbage, shredded

4 tbsp tomato purée

2 tbsp olive oil

a handful of fresh flat-leaf parsley leaves, finely chopped

1 Put the drained beans in a large pan with plenty of cold water, bring to the boil and boil vigorously for 10 minutes. Reduce to a slow simmer and continue cooking for 25 minutes.

2 Meanwhile, chop the fennel and onion and crush the garlic. Stir them, along with the cabbage, tomato purée, salt and pepper, into the beans, and simmer for 30 minutes, or until the beans are tender.

3 Add the olive oil and parsley, adjust the seasoning, and serve.

SERVES 4

pappa con pomodoro e porri

leek and tomato soup

As I've mentioned, we Italians love to make use of every morsel in our kitchens. We always have leftover bread as it goes stale so quickly, and here is a fine example of a straightforward soup, thickened by day-old bread. The use of a sublime oil to finish is essential.

6 baby leeks, sliced

50ml (2fl oz) olive oil

675g (1 1/2lb) ripe tomatoes

1/2 tsp dried chilli

450g (1lb) crusty day-old bread

750ml (25fl oz) vegetable broth (see page 299)

6 fresh basil leaves

extra virgin olive oil (estate-bottled)

1 Wash the leeks well under cold running water. Drain, then chop finely.

2 Heat the olive oil in a large pan, add the leeks and fry gently for 10 minutes.

3 Meanwhile, purée the tomatoes in a blender or food processor. Add to the leeks, with salt, pepper and chilli to taste, then simmer for 30 minutes.

4 Cut the bread into small pieces and add to the pan. Mix well and lightly simmer for 5 minutes. Add the broth, mix well, and simmer for a further 10 minutes.

5 Serve the hot soup in individual bowls. Add a basil leaf and some extra virgin olive oil to each serving.

SERVES 6

cooking pulses

Dried peas, beans and pulses are known collectively as pulses. In Italy we have a vast array of them: borlotti and cannellini beans, *lenticchie* (lentils), *fave* (broad beans), *ceci* (chickpeas) and *piselli* (peas), to name but a few. We eat them mostly in soups.

There are some golden rules you must follow in the cooking of pulses, but otherwise they are blissfully straightforward, quick and easy to prepare. First of all, buy your supplies from a shop with a fast turnover, so that you can be sure they are not too old. All pulses (apart from lentils) must be soaked in lots of cold water, at least overnight, in order to rehydrate them. They should then be covered with fresh cold water, brought to the boil and boiled for 10 minutes; this is in order to inactivate potentially toxic substances many pulses contain. Thereafter, continue cooking the pulses – perhaps with some added flavouring (see the individual recipes) – for another 40 minutes, at a slow simmer, or

until they are tender. Lentils do not require soaking, and they will only need simmering for about 40 minutes. Salt pulses only after cooking: doing so before will toughen the skins.

A handy rule of thumb is that pulses, when cooked, roughly double in volume and weight: so 250g (9oz) dried beans will become roughly 500g (18oz) after cooking. And don't be ashamed to use canned pulses if you haven't got time. Heat them through for a few minutes before using in a recipe.

farro con fagioli

farro and bean soup

Barley-like and light brown, farro has recently been rediscovered and is now valued both for its taste and nutritional value. Farro is cultivated almost exclusively in the Garfagnana, the mountainous region of Tuscany, and its use has brought a fresh recognition to Tuscan cooking. This soup is typical of the Garfagnana.

250g (9oz) dried borlotti beans, soaked overnight, drained and rinsed

2 medium white onions, peeled

5 sage leaves

3 garlic cloves, peeled

4 tbsp olive oil

1 medium red onion, peeled

2 carrots, scraped and diced

2-4 celery stalks, trimmed and diced

a handful of fresh flat-leaf parsley leaves

275g (9½oz) canned Italian plum tomatoes and their liquid

6 tbsp extra virgin olive oil (estate bottled)

200g (7oz) farro, soaked overnight, drained and rinsed

sea salt and freshly ground black pepper

1 Place the beans in a large saucepan with 1 onion, half the sage, 1 of the garlic cloves, and enough water to cover by at least 5cm (2in). Cover and boil vigorously for 10 minutes. Reduce the heat and simmer for a further 50 minutes, or until tender.

2 When the beans are cooked, pass all the contents of the pan either through a food processor or a *mouli di légumes*.

3 Heat the oil in a large saucepan. Add the red onion and the remaining white onion, both of which have been finely chopped. Add the carrots, celery, most of the parsley, remaining garlic and sage leaves, the tomatoes and 1.2 litres (2 pints) hot water, and continue to cook for 10 more minutes.

4 Add the farro and simmer on a low heat for 30 minutes, until tender. Add salt and pepper and the bean mixture. Stir and warm through until hot. Add more water if the soup is too thick for your taste. Adjust the seasoning and serve with drizzlings of olive oil and the remaining parsley.

SERVES 8

minestra di ceci e castagne

chestnut soup with chickpeas

My father really loves this recipe, as he grows chestnuts in Avellino, in Campania. In Minori, my village, we have a torchlight festival at the end of October to celebrate the chestnut harvest. This soup is one of many ways in which we use chestnuts locally.

450g (1lb) fresh chestnuts

200g (7oz) dried chickpeas, soaked overnight

3 celery stalks

4 bay leaves

7 tbsp olive oil

4 garlic cloves, peeled

sea salt and freshly ground black pepper

4 slices country-style bread

1 Preheat the oven to 200°C/400°F/gas mark 6.

2 Score the chestnut skins on the outside – cutting into the skin slightly – and put on a baking tray. Bake for 40 minutes. Leave to cool slightly and peel off the thick outer skin, then the inner skin.

3 Meanwhile, drain the soaked chickpeas. Rinse them and put them in a large saucepan with 2.5 litres (4½ pints) water. Add the celery, bay leaves and 2 tbsp of the oil. Bring to the boil, boil vigorously for 10 minutes, then reduce the heat and simmer for 40 minutes, until tender.

4 Heat the remaining oil in a frying pan and fry the peeled chestnuts and garlic until golden.

5 Remove the bay leaves and celery from the chickpea soup and stir in the chestnuts, garlic and oil. Season with salt and pepper.

6 Toast the bread slices. Put them in the bottom of a soup tureen and pour over the soup. Leave for 2-3 minutes before serving.

SERVES 4

minestra di ceci e peperoni

chickpea and pepper soup

This is a family soup which is often served in our village, as we produce so many peppers and chickpeas. It's colourful, full of flavour and very satisfying.

150g (5½oz) dried chickpeas, soaked overnight, drained and rinsed

2 red onions, peeled and chopped

2 tbsp fruity olive oil

2 medium potatoes, peeled and diced

3 red peppers, seeded and cut into strips

1 carrot, peeled and finely chopped

3 ripe tomatoes, cut into chunks

2 garlic cloves, peeled

sea salt and freshly ground black pepper

a handful of fresh flat-leaf parsley, finely chopped

extra virgin olive oil

grated Parmesan cheese, to serve (optional)

1 Put the chickpeas in a large saucepan with 2 litres (3½ pints) water. Bring to the boil, boil vigorously for 10 minutes, reduce the heat and simmer for 40 minutes, or until tender.

2 Meanwhile, fry the onion in the olive oil for a few minutes, then add the potato, peppers, carrot, tomato, garlic and 4 tbsp of water. Bring to the boil and cook for 15 minutes over a moderate heat, stirring constantly to stop any of the vegetables from sticking (add a little more water if necessary). Season well.

3 The moment the chickpeas are cooked, pour the prepared sauce into them, stirring gently.

4 Serve the soup in bowls sprinkled with parsley and extra virgin olive oil. You may like to offer some grated Parmesan to sprinkle on top.

SERVES 4

zuppa di pollo con peperoni arrostiti

chicken and roasted pepper soup

This recipe is based on a dish from the Ristorante Solferino in Tuscany, and it uses '*duchese*' olive oil. This is made from olives grown on the restaurant's own land and pressed locally. It is named after a family member. Use the best extra virgin oil you can get for the garnish.

12 red peppers

10 chicken thighs

sea salt and freshly ground black pepper

2 tbsp olive oil

1 onion, peeled and chopped

2 garlic cloves, peeled and crushed

1.5 litres (2¾ pints) chicken broth (see page 299), warm

a handful of fresh basil leaves, torn

a handful of fresh mint leaves, roughly chopped

2 tsp fresh marjoram leaves

Duchese oil or the best-quality extra virgin olive oil

1 Preheat the oven to 200°C/400°F/gas mark 6. Roast the peppers for 25 minutes, then leave to cool. Scrape out the seeds and slice the peppers thinly.

2 At the same time, cook the chicken thighs. Season them with salt and pepper and roast alongside the peppers for 20 minutes, or until cooked through. Cool. Discard the chicken skin and bones and shred the meat finely.

3 Heat the oil in a large saucepan, add the onion and sauté until golden. Add the strips of pepper and the garlic.

4 Add the broth to the peppers along with the chicken shreds and herbs. Adjust the seasoning and simmer the soup for 5 minutes.

5 Ladle into warmed soup bowls and serve with some good oil on top. .

SERVES 6

zuppa di pesce con pasta

fish soup with macaroni

Every *trattoria* on the coast of Italy will serve a fish soup like this – plain, pure and simple.

250g (9oz) monkfish steaks

250g (9oz) boneless cod steaks

250g (9oz) sea bass fillets

a handful of fresh flat-leaf
parsley leaves, finely chopped

2 tbsp olive oil

1 onion, peeled and chopped

2 garlic cloves, chopped

400g can chopped tomatoes

200g (7oz) macaroni

1 Cut the fish into fork-friendly chunks. Bring 2.25 litres (4 pints) cold water to the boil. Reduce the heat, add the fish and a third of the parsley and simmer for 10 minutes, until cooked. Transfer the fish to a plate using a slotted spoon, and strain and reserve the cooking liquid.

2 Combine the olive oil, onion, garlic, tomatoes and half the remaining parsley in a clean saucepan. Season and simmer gently for 10 minutes.

3 Add the fish broth and macaroni and cook gently until the pasta is done, about 10 minutes. Add the fish and heat through briefly. Sprinkle with the remaining parsley and serve hot.

SERVES 4

minestrone alla genovese

genoese vegetable soup with pesto

In Genoa, cooks often make **minestrone** like this, with some of their local **pesto** stirred into the soup towards the end of the cooking. I like pesto as a garnish, though. *Maltagliati*, literally meaning 'badly cut', are pasta shapes from Emilia-Romagna, made by cutting sheets of pasta into irregular shapes; small pieces are often used in soup.

3 tbsp olive oil

1 onion, peeled and finely chopped

2 celery stalks, trimmed and finely chopped

2 carrots, scrubbed and finely chopped

115g (4oz) thin green beans cut into 5cm (2in) pieces

1 medium courgette, trimmed and thinly sliced

1 medium potato, peeled and cut into 1cm (½in) cubes

¼ head Savoy cabbage, shredded

115g (4oz) cooked cannellini beans (see page 146) or rinsed canned

2 Italian plum tomatoes, chopped

1.4 litres (2½ pints) vegetable broth (see page 299)

sea salt and freshly ground black pepper

100g (3½oz) dried vermicelli or *maltagliati* (see above)

TO SERVE

½ recipe basil pesto (see page 46)

1 Heat the oil in a large pot over a a low heat. Add the chopped onion, celery and carrot, and fry, stirring frequently, for 5-7 minutes.

2 Stir in the green beans, courgette, potato and cabbage, and stir-fry over medium heat for about 3 minutes. Add the cannellini beans and tomatoes, and stir-fry for 2-3 minutes longer.

3 Pour in the broth and add some salt and pepper to taste. Bring to the boil, stir well, cover, and simmer, stirring occasionally, until all the vegetables are tender, about 20-30 minutes.

4 Break the pasta into small pieces and add it to the soup. Simmer, stirring frequently, for 5 minutes, or until the pasta is *al dente*, or tender but still firm to the bite.

5 Taste and adjust the seasoning, if necessary. Serve the minestrone in warm bowls. You can dress the soup with any of the other versions of pesto in the book such as the rocket, mint or lemon pestos on pages 46-7.

SERVES 4-6

minestrone con riso e fagioli

vegetable soup with rice and beans

In Italy there is a multitude of vegetable soups or '*minestrone*': roughly translated, the word means a 'mixture'. There are countless ways of mixing good wholesome ingredients in a soup – one for every day of the year – and this is a particular favourite of my family.

2 garlic cloves, peeled

1 celery stalk, finely chopped

1 red onion, peeled, sliced

2 tbsp olive oil

8 fresh red tomatoes, skinned

500g (18oz) cooked borlotti beans (see page 148)

200g (7oz) arborio rice

1/2 tsp dried chilli

a handful each of flat-leaf parsley and mint, chopped

extra virgin olive oil

1 Finely chop and then sauté the garlic with the celery and onion in the olive oil until softened. Add the tomato and simmer for 10 minutes.

2 Pour this sauce over the cooked beans, then add the rice and 450ml (16fl oz) water, stirring well. Add the chilli, parsley and mint, and cook for 20 minutes until the rice is tender. You will need to add more water if the soup looks too thick.

3 Season with salt and pepper, and serve with a drizzle of extra virgin olive oil.

SERVES 4

minestra di lenticchie e pancetta

lentil and pancetta soup

The Bible tells of Esau selling his inheritance to Jacob for a dish of lentils. This dish illustrates why they were considered so valuable!

150g (5¹/₂oz) Italian lentils

4 tbsp olive oil

2 sprigs fresh rosemary

2 garlic cloves, peeled

3 bay leaves

1 carrot, finely chopped

1/2 onion, peeled and chopped

2 celery stalks, chopped

115g (4oz) diced pancetta

1 tbsp tomato purée

150ml (5fl oz) dry white wine

extra virgin olive oil to serve

1 Put the lentils in a large pot with cold salted water to cover, half the olive oil, 1 rosemary sprig, the whole garlic cloves and the bay leaves. Cover, and simmer for an hour over a medium heat, until the lentils are tender. Remove the herbs.

2 Meanwhile, in a large heavy pan, heat the remaining olive oil. Add the carrot, onion, celery, remaining rosemary and pancetta. Cook for 10 minutes over a medium heat. Add the tomato purée and wine, and cook until the wine evaporates.

3 Drain a little more than half of the lentils and add to the pan of veg. Place the remaining lentils with the cooking liquid in a food processor and whizz until smooth. Add to the veg pan and cook for 30 minutes over a low heat, stirring often.

4 Season with salt and pepper, ladle the soup into bowls, and drizzle with good extra virgin olive oil.

SERVES 6

fish

marinating fish

Italy has 1,500 miles of coastline, so it is not surprising that the Italians love to eat fish. Every region has its special fish dishes, which are sometimes similar in essence, but betray their origin in the use of one simple differing ingredient. For instance, basic soup-stews of fish are served all over the country, but the ***brodetto*** of Romagna is flavoured with vinegar (balsamic vinegar is made in this region), while that of the Marche uses the local saffron, and further south, in the Abruzzi, chilli reigns and tends to be the predominant flavouring.

The Italians cook food simply, and their fish dishes are no exception, whether grilled, baked, roasted, fried, poached or steamed. Fish, of course, cooks very quickly, so it occasionally needs a little protection, which is where marinades come in. This is particularly useful when you are going to griddle, grill, barbecue or roast whole fish, steaks and fillets. An olive oil-based marinade is the norm, the oil helping to prevent tender white fish from becoming too dry during cooking. But white wines, vinegars and citrus juices can be used in marinades too, adding moisture to fish that might become too dry (swordfish is a prime example), and also adding flavour; often this acidic bath can 'cook' the fish a little too (think of the South American ceviche). And many marinades can, of course, be reserved to use first as a basting medium, then in an accompanying sauce for the fish.

Sometimes, though, an even simpler 'marination' can help: sprinkling a fresh fish with salt before cooking it helps improve its texture when cooked. Salt draws excess moisture out (think of 'de-gorging' aubergines). It is not something you should do to a steak, but with fish, half an hour's salt marination can work wonders.

Olive oil (or extra-virgin if you want, and can afford it!) and vinegar, white wine or citrus juice form the basic backbone of a fish marinade, but there are many different flavourings that can be added to suit the particular fish: think of ingredients such as garlic, chilli, shallots or onion, or a fresh herb. Nothing must be overdone, though, as the essential delicacy of fish can so easily be overwhelmed by strong flavours.

As a guideline, to marinate fish for 4 people, use 6 tbsp olive oil to half that of wine, vinegar or citrus juice (or a mixture). Add 2 chopped shallots, 1 tbsp capers and 4 chopped anchovies to an oil-and-white wine marinade for swordfish steaks to be grilled or barbecued. Add 2 chopped garlic cloves, a chopped and seeded fresh chilli and 2 tbsp chopped fresh parsley to an oil-and-lemon juice marinade for whole gutted sardines to be grilled or barbecued. The same marinade would be good for cubes of monkfish to be grilled on skewers, but substitute rosemary for the parsley. And this marinade would be good too for sea bass fillets to be baked: substitute the finely grated zest of an unwaxed lemon for the herb and marinate for an hour before cooking.

salmoriglio

fish marinade/dressing

This oil, lemon and garlic mixture is a classic fish marinade. It can be used as a dressing too.

4 tbsp water

150ml (5fl oz) olive oil

juice and finely grated zest of 1 unwaxed lemon

2 garlic cloves, peeled and sliced

a handful of fresh flat-leaf parsley, finely chopped

1 tsp fresh oregano leaves

1 Scald the water in a pan but do not boil it.

2 Put the olive oil into a bowl and beat in the water, lemon juice and zest, garlic, parsley and oregano. Beat well until amalgamated.

3 Place in a bain-marie (a roasting tray full of hot water), and cook for 5 minutes, stirring all the time.

MAKES ABOUT 150ML (5FL OZ)

taglia di spada

marinated swordfish

When the fish is truly fresh, this is awesomely good. Swordfish is mainly caught in the channel that separates Sicily and Africa. The fish is often cooked on the brace, or barbecue/grill, and served with lemon and capers.

6 swordfish steaks, about 175g (6oz) each

sea salt and freshly ground black pepper

250ml (9fl oz) dry white wine

1 sprig fresh rosemary, leaves finely chopped

4 garlic cloves, peeled and finely chopped

a handful of fresh mint leaves, chopped

4 tbsp olive oil

100g (3½oz) fine dried breadcrumbs

3 tbsp salted capers, rinsed and chopped

juice of 1 unwaxed lemon

1 Place the swordfish steaks in a bowl and season with salt and pepper. Add the wine, rosemary, garlic and mint. Coat the steaks and marinate for at least an hour.

2 Drain the fish, reserving the marinade. Brush a large frying pan with a little oil and heat it. Sprinkle the steaks with a mixture of the breadcrumbs and capers. Add the steaks, 2-3 at a time, to the pan and cook on both sides until nearly cooked through, basting with the marinade. This should take about 8 minutes.

3 Whisk the rest of the oil with the lemon juice in a small bowl. Pour over the fish and cook for a few minutes more; this keeps it tender. Serve immediately.

SERVES 6

spigola al sale

sea bass with salt

Once eaten, this simple recipe is never forgotten, and it became a staple part of the repertoire of many of my students in Italy. John Dory could be prepared in the same way.

1 x 1kg (2¼lb) sea bass, gutted

1kg (2¼lb) large-grain salt

TO SERVE

extra virgin olive oil (optional)

1 lemon (optional)

1 Preheat the oven to 200°C/400°F/gas mark 6.

2 Wash and clean the fish without removing the scales. Distribute a 1cm (½in) thick layer of salt over a baking tray. Place the fish on the salt and cover it with the remaining salt. The fish should be completely hidden by the salt. Put the fish in the oven for 25 minutes.

3 Before serving, remove the salt carefully, extracting the fish, which should be served as it is with no seasoning. However, if desired, a thin drizzle of extra virgin olive oil can be served with the fish, as can lemon juice.

SERVES 4-6

pesce alla griglia con salsa di menta

grilled fish with mint sauce

Mint's fresh flavour blends beautifully with the subtle fish here. The recipe comes from Amalfi, where the cooking is very simple. You could cook the fish on a barbecue.

2 garlic cloves, peeled

2 handfuls of fresh mint

a handful of flat-leaf parsley

190ml (6½fl oz) extra virgin olive oil, plus extra to oil

25ml (1fl oz) white wine vinegar

40ml (1½fl oz) lemon juice

sea salt

1 whole sea bass, 1.2-1.4kg (2¾-3½lb), scaled, gutted

2-3 tsp Italian '00' plain flour

some very good extra virgin olive oil, to serve

1 Chop the garlic and herbs. Make the mint sauce an hour before serving. Combine 175ml (6fl oz) olive oil, half the garlic, the vinegar, lemon and some salt to taste in a medium bowl. Blend well with a whisk and stir in half the mint. Preheat the grill at least 15 minutes before serving. Oil the grill-pan.

2 Rinse the fish in cold water and dry it with kitchen paper. Season the cavity with salt. Combine the remaining garlic and mint with the parsley. Push the mixture into the cavity and drizzle this cavity with 1 tsp of olive oil. Season the surface of the fish with salt, dust with

1 tsp of the flour through a small sieve, and drizzle with more oil.

3 Grill the fish for 8-10 minutes, or until the top is cooked through. To test for doneness, insert a small paring knife into the fleshiest part of the fish; it should be flaky and opaque. Turn the fish using a large metal spatula, sprinkle with salt, flour and oil, and grill the other side for 8-10 minutes, or until cooked.

4 Transfer to a large serving platter, drizzle with extra virgin olive oil, and serve with the mint sauce.

SERVES 4-6

tonno in padella

tuna with dried cep and anchovy sauce

The people of Liguria eat very little fish. However, this recipe is one of the few that have become associated with the region. The sauce is simple, and the meatiness of the anchovies and dried mushrooms complements the fish well. It's a quick recipe, ideal for today's busy lifestyles — and it's healthy and delicious too!

4 fresh tuna steaks, about 600g (1lb 5oz) in total

3 tbsp olive oil

juice of 1 unwaxed lemon

SAUCE

25g (1oz) dried porcini mushrooms (ceps)

2 garlic cloves, peeled and crushed

a handful of fresh flat-leaf parsley leaves, chopped

a few sprigs of fresh marjoram

6 marinated anchovies, drained

1 tbsp salted capers, rinsed

3 tbsp olive oil

1 tbsp Italian '00' plain flour

150ml (5fl oz) dry white wine

sea salt and freshly ground black pepper

1 Soak the porcini in cold water for 15 minutes. Drain and dry on paper towels.

2 Put the porcini on a board with the garlic, parsley, marjoram, anchovies and capers and chop the whole lot together. The garlic absorbs the oils of the herbs, becoming less pungent in the process.

3 Heat the olive oil in a large sauté or frying pan and add the porcini mixture. Sauté for 2 minutes, stirring frequently. Blend in the flour, cook for about 1 minute, and add the wine. Boil for 3-4 minutes then add some salt and pepper. If the sauce seems thick, add 4-5 tbsp boiling water.

4 Remove the skin from the tuna steaks if it is still on. Rinse and dry the steaks with kitchen paper. Heat the olive oil in a frying pan, and cook the steaks for 2-3 minutes on each side, depending on their thickness.

5 Spoon the sauce over the steaks, drizzle with lemon juice and serve immediately.

SERVES 4

tonno fresco al pomodori

fresh tuna with tomatoes

Tuna can be found all along the coastlines of Italy, but it is most common in the warm waters of the south. This Naples recipe has a good dinner-party feel, and the anchovies do great favours to the tuna, giving it a tangy freshness. In Livorno (Leghorn) a little further up the coast, peas are added to this tomato sauce.

1 x 600g (1lb 5oz) piece fresh tuna

sea salt and freshly ground black pepper

Italian '00' plain flour

2 tbsp olive oil

55g (2oz) black olives, stoned

a handful of fresh flat-leaf parsley leaves, chopped

SAUCE

1 tbsp olive oil

1 small onion, peeled and chopped

2 garlic cloves, peeled and chopped

3 marinated anchovy fillets, mashed

5 tbsp white wine

500g (18oz) ripe tomatoes, skinned and roughly chopped

1 bay leaf

1 For the sauce, heat the olive oil in a saucepan, fry the onion well and then add the garlic, mashed anchovy fillets and wine. Bubble briskly until the wine has almost evaporated.

2 Add the tomato to the pan with the bay leaf and some pepper to taste. Simmer until reduced to a sauce consistency.

3 Meanwhile, season the piece of tuna fish and dust with flour.

4 Heat the olive oil in a casserole and fry the fish slowly until it is golden on both sides.

5 Pour the tomato sauce over, cover with the lid, and simmer gently for 20-30 minutes. Add the olives and parsley, then serve.

SERVES 4

pesce al cartoccio

red mullet baked in paper

I love being served something wrapped in paper – there's such a sense of excitement and anticipation! The delicate flavour of the mullet here is enhanced by the fragrance of the herb butter. To make the envelopes for the fish you will need some baking paper.

4 red mullet, about 200g (7oz) each, scaled

4 sprigs fresh fennel fronds

a handful each of fresh basil and rosemary leaves

2 tbsp olive oil

sea salt and freshly ground black pepper

HERB BUTTER

125g (4¹/₂oz) unsalted butter

a handful each of fresh torn basil and chopped rosemary leaves

1 Preheat the oven to 220°C/425°F/gas mark 7.

2 To make the herb butter, soften the butter and mash in the torn and chopped herbs. Chill until ready to use.

3 Wash and gut the fish, leaving the livers in (your fishmonger will always do this for you). Dry the fish well, and put some of the fennel fronds and herbs in each cavity.

4 Cut the parchment paper into rectangles large enough to enclose each fish. Oil each fish and place in the centre of the paper. Add another sprinkling of fennel and some salt and pepper, and close the paper parcels firmly.

5 Place the parcels on a baking tray and bake for 12 minutes.

6 Serve the fish in their fragrant parcels, to be opened at the table, with the herb butter.

SERVES 4

frittelle di sardine con burro

sardine fritters with minted chilli butter

Sardines are abundant in Italian waters, and the idea for the minted chilli butter came from an old friend, Claudio Brugalossi, who runs La Taverna in Perugia. He spent 10 years in America and fulfilled a lifetime ambition to return to Italy with his wife and family to run his own trattoria. We used to teach together in Umbria; I did the vegetables and salads and he did the fish and meat. This recipe can be prepared several hours before cooking. Serve as an *antipasto*. Use the butter in tandem with many other small fish.

12 fresh sardines, scaled

4 tbsp Italian '00' plain flour

1 large egg, blended with 2 tbsp milk

125g (4¹/₂oz) dried breadcrumbs

about 2 tbsp sunflower oil

MINTED CHILLI BUTTER

125g (4¹/₂oz) unsalted butter, softened

3 tbsp finely chopped fresh mint

2 spring onions or peeled shallots, finely chopped

1 garlic clove, peeled and crushed

1 small fresh red chilli, seeded and finely chopped

freshly ground black pepper

1 Cut the heads from the sardines and, using scissors, cut along the underside of the fish. Clean, gut and open out flat. Cut the backbone at the tail end and remove. Separate the two fillets on each, so that you have 24 small pieces of fish. Wash the pieces and dry on paper towel.

2 Coat the sardine pieces in flour, dip in the egg mixture, then coat with breadcrumbs. Cover and chill.

3 To make the minted chilli butter, put the butter, mint, spring onions or shallots, garlic, chilli and some pepper in a bowl and mix well. Place the butter on a piece of cling film and roll into a log shape. Refrigerate.

4 Heat the oil and one-third of the minted chilli butter in a large frying pan and cook the sardine fillets for 2 minutes on each side, or until golden.

5 Serve the sardines topped with a slice of the remaining minted chilli butter.

SERVES 4

preparing squid, scallops and mussels

SQUID

Wash the squid under the cold tap. Separate the tentacles from the body sac by pulling; this will also remove the intestines. Discard the latter (you may want to keep the ink sac, which is small and silvery dark, to use in a black fish risotto or an ink sauce). The head is attached to the tentacles, and this is where you cut; discard the head. There's a little bony piece called the beak (it's the fish's mouth) attached to the top of the tentacles; squeeze the tentacles to remove this. Pull the plastic-like quill from the sac. Cut the flaps from the body sac and set aside. Scrape the semi-transparent membrane from the outside of the sac. Wash all the pieces well. You can either use the body sac whole, by itself or stuffed, or you can cut it into rings about as wide as your index finger. Leave the tentacles and other bits as they are.

Clean cuttlefish in much the same way, removing the cuttle in the middle rather than the quill (and saving it for your budgie). Save the ink sacs as above.

SCALLOPS

Scottish diver-caught scallops are the ultimate in this country, fat, juicy and delicious; Venetian scallops are also wonderful, brought in fresh every day from the Adriatic. Try to buy scallops fresh in-shell rather than off-shell and/or frozen. Some off-shell scallops may appear particularly plump and white, but they may have been soaked in water to make them so; they won't cook nearly so well as fresh.

With the scallop flat-side up, run a long sharp knife through the inside of the rounded part of the shell; this will cut the meat from the shell, breaking the scallop's 'hinges'. Open the two shells. On the rounded side you will see the white central muscle plus the orange roe or coral (the edible parts), plus a frill of innards, including the eyes, which you throw away. (I don't eat the roe or coral of scallops, although many people, including my husband, do – and apparently dogs like them as well!) Rinse the scallop briefly and dry well before cooking.

Clams, although very much smaller, can be opened in much the same way – or simply put them whole into a hot oven for a minute or two, which will open the shells.

MUSSELS

Most mussels we can buy these days come already fully or partially cleaned. I always like to make sure, though. Put the mussels in a sink of cold water. Scrub off any sand or mud, and you may have to scrape off some barnacles. Tug off the beard (the hairy bit that attached the mussel to rock or rope). Discard any mussels that are cracked, and if any mussels remain open after cleaning, discard them too as they are certainly dead and may be toxic (mussels are filter feeders, and can be easily contaminated). Discard any mussels that appear oddly heavy, as they may be full of sand. Wash again before cooking (see individual recipes).

LEFT AND ABOVE: preparing squid may look fiddly, but don't be put off; it's really very straightforward. The ink sack can be kept for use in a sauce or a risotto.

calamari in teglia
baked squid with potatoes

Squid are cephalopods, as are cuttlefish and octopus. They are torpedo-shaped with 8 arms and 2 tentacles, and vary in size from a few centimetres long to science-fiction giants, which are amongst the most formidable of deep-sea predators. Those caught in the Mediterranean – by lure and lights, at night – are small to medium in size, and are very popular in Italy.

12 medium squid, 10-13cm (4-5in) long, with tentacles, cleaned (see page 164), body left whole

1 medium onion, peeled and sliced 5mm (¼in) thick

2 garlic cloves, peeled and crushed

2 large plum tomatoes, skinned, seeded and chopped

a handful of fresh flat-leaf parsley leaves, finely chopped

450g (1lb) Italian potatoes, such as Spunta, peeled and sliced 1cm (½in) thick

1 dried chilli (peperoncino), coarsely chopped

4 tbsp olive oil

STUFFING

150g (5½oz) dry country-style bread, crusts discarded, torn into very small pieces

2 large eggs, beaten

1 garlic clove, peeled and crushed

a handful of fresh flat-leaf parsley leaves, peeled and chopped

sea salt and freshly ground black pepper

1 To make the stuffing, soak the bread in a small bowl of warm water for 5 minutes. Drain and squeeze dry. Mix the bread with the eggs, garlic and parsley, then season with salt and pepper.

2 Stuff the squid with the stuffing mixture, filling them halfway only, as the stuffing will expand when cooked. Seal the open end of the squid with some wooden toothpicks.

3 Arrange the onion, garlic, tomatoes and parsley in a 3 litre (5¼ pint) round flameproof terracotta casserole, at least 22cm (8½in) in diameter, or a cast-iron pot. Season with salt and pepper. Pour 3 tbsp of water into the casserole, cover with the potato slices slightly overlapping, and sprinkle with the chilli.

4 Arrange the squid and the tentacles on top. Drizzle with olive oil. Cover and simmer slowly over a low heat for an hour, or until the squid is cooked and tender. Check the casserole to be sure it remains on a slow simmer.

SERVES 4

capasante con limone, alloro e olio di rosarino
scallops with lemon, bay and rosemary oil

This recipe is so simple that it hardly needs a method. It's from the Naples area, where many of the best fish and shellfish recipes are to be found. The rosemary used here as a skewer grows in profusion all over Italy and it enhances fish dishes wonderfully.

12 fat fresh scallops, corals removed (freeze and keep for stock)

4 tough rosemary stalks, leaves removed and retained

pared zest (cut into 12 pieces) and juice of 2 unwaxed lemons

12 fresh bay leaves

1½ tbsp olive oil

sea salt and freshly ground black pepper

1 Thread 3 scallops on to each rosemary stalk, alternating with 3 pieces of lemon zest and 3 bay leaves. Put the skewers in a roasting tin.

2 Pound the rosemary leaves and oil together until fine and pour over the scallops. Sprinkle with the lemon juice and leave to marinate for 20 minutes.

3 Preheat the oven to 200°C/400°F/gas mark 6.

4 Season the rosemary skewers and put the roasting tin in the oven to bake for 8 minutes only.

SERVES 4

tiella di patate, riso e cozze

potato, rice and mussel casserole

Mussels abound on the east coast of Italy, and the best are said to come from Puglia, a region ruled for years by the Normans, Angevins and Spanish. This casserole is a reflection of its chequered history. *'Tiella'*, the name of the cooking pot as well as the dish, is closely related to *'paella'* (and indeed to the *'tian'* of southern France, where the Spanish also had influence). There are many similar layered dishes in this part of the world, one of which uses potatoes and squid. The double carbohydrate occurs further north too: in Liguria there is a dish of potato, green beans, pesto and *trofie* pasta.

750g (1lb 10oz) mussels, cleaned and prepared

3 medium onions, peeled and thinly sliced

4 potatoes, peeled and thinly sliced

150g (5½oz) arborio risotto rice, uncooked

sea salt and freshly ground black pepper

a large handful of fresh flat-leaf parsley leaves, finely chopped

3 garlic cloves, peeled and sliced

extra virgin olive oil

4 ripe tomatoes, cut into strips

600ml (1 pint) water

1 Preheat the oven to 180°C/350°F/gas mark 4.

2 Put the mussels in a large pan and add a little water. Cover and bring to the boil, shaking the pan. As they open, remove from the heat. Cool a little, then extract the flesh from the shells. Discard the shells along with any mussels that remain closed.

3 In a medium baking dish layer half the onions, then half the potatoes, then half the mussels, then all the rice.

Sprinkle with salt and pepper and half the parsley and garlic. Drizzle with some olive oil.

4 Repeat the layering process with the remaining ingredients until the baking dish is full. Lay the tomato strips on top and add 600ml (1 pint) water.

5 Bake for 45 minutes. While baking, add more water if the casserole gets too dry inside. Serve, discarding any mussels that remain closed.

SERVES 4

totani in zimino

stewed cuttlefish with bitter greens in tomato sauce

This Ligurian dish, which found its way to Tuscany, can be served with a side dish of steamed rice. It is said to be of Arab origin. The words '*in zimino*' come from the Arab word '*samin*'. Through the centuries it has come to signify a method of cooking fish in butter or olive oil, and a sauce of green vegetables.

500g (18oz) cuttlefish or the smallest squid available, cleaned and prepared (see page 166)

5 tbsp olive oil

2 garlic cloves, peeled and finely chopped

1/2 onion, peeled and chopped

1 celery stalk, finely minced

1 leek, washed and finely minced

sea salt and freshly ground black pepper

150ml (5fl oz) dry white wine

4-5 ripe plum tomatoes, quartered

750g (1lb 10oz) Swiss chard or spinach

1 tsp chopped fresh chilli

a handful of fresh flat-leaf parsley leaves, chopped

1 Wash and rinse the cleaned cuttlefish. Cut the tentacles into small pieces and the rest into strips 1cm (1/2in) wide.

2 In a heavy-based frying pan, heat 4 tbsp of olive oil over a medium heat. Add half the garlic and sauté until lightly golden. Add the onion, celery and leek and cook until tender but not brown – about 6-8 minutes.

3 Add the cuttlefish, season with salt and pepper, and sauté for 3 minutes. Add the white wine and cook over a medium to high heat until it evaporates. Add the tomato quarters and continue to cook over a medium heat for 20 minutes. (If using squid, reduce this cooking time to about 5 minutes.)

4 Meanwhile, wash and rinse the chard, then blanch in boiling water for 1 minute. Drain and chop coarsely. Place in a frying pan, cover and steam over a high heat for 3-4 minutes, turning often. Wipe the pan, add the remaining olive oil and sauté the chard, remaining garlic and chopped chilli over a medium heat for 5 minutes. Season.

5 Stir the chard into the cuttlefish and continue to cook for a further 5 minutes. Sprinkle with the chopped parsley.

SERVES 4

italian preserved fish and its uses

Despite healthy supplies of both salt- and freshwater fish, the Italians use a lot of preserved fish. This is characteristic of many European cuisines: foods need to be preserved when they come in gluts (tomatoes, tuna etc), for when they are scarcer (such as in winter).

ANCHOVIES AND OTHER CANNED PRESERVED FISH

Anchovies are the most familiar preserved fish, and the best anchovies come from Sicily and Sardinia. Fresh anchovies are layered in coarse sea salt, weighted and left for 3 months to mature. Then they are rinsed, filleted by hand (some salted anchovies are gutted only), and carefully packed into jars with oil, or canned in oil. Although canned anchovy fillets are very useful, I usually prefer salted anchovies; they need to be wiped or rinsed to get rid of excess salt, and filleted if bought whole. You can use anchovies in many ways: in the Piedmontese dip, *bagna cauda*; in sauces; in salad dressings (best with stronger leaves such as members of the chicory family); in salads; and, of course, on pizzas. Anchovy paste can be bought in jars, tins or tubes.

Sardines are also eaten fresh, or preserved in oil or salt and stored in cans.

Tuna are eaten fresh and from cans, but in completely different ways: the canned in *antipasti* and sauces (that for *vitello tonnato*, for instance), and the fresh grilled in the same way as swordfish. The juicy *ventresca*, or belly of tuna, is often salted and canned; and salted and air-dried fillets of tuna fish, or *mosciame*, are occasionally found in good delis here. Tuna roe is dried and salted as bottarga (see below). Tuna are smoke-cured too (as are swordfish and sturgeon).

BOTTARGA

Nearly every Mediterranean region offers some version of *bottarga* (preserved fish eggs). The egg sacs are salted, pressed under heavy weights to draw out the moisture, and dried. Once dried, the salami-like logs can be kept for months. Tuna and grey mullet are the most common, the former in Sicily, the latter (obviously much smaller) in Sardinia. Bottarga can be served as a snack with drinks, or in very thin slices with oil and lemon juice, black pepper and parsley. It is also served grated with pasta or rice or scrambled eggs. The flavour of bottarga is very strong and salty, so it must be grated, or very finely shaved or sliced. It is wonderful in a simple salad.

BACCALÀ AND STOCCAFISSO

Baccalà and *stoccafisso* (stockfish) are both forms of preserved cod: *baccalà* is salted at sea and then dried in large chunks when landed; stockfish are air-dried whole. Both need to be soaked for at least 24 hours, in changes of water, to get rid of the salt and soften the flesh; stockfish then needs beating to tenderise the fibres. Both are made into fritters and used in salads and long-cooked stews. Salt cod, which is found more commonly, is expensive, so if possible buy prime pieces from the middle, rather than from the tail and fin ends. The fish is creamy grey with a fine dusting of sparkling salt. In Italy it is sold ready to cook, and there are many regional recipes, the majority from the Veneto.

baccalá

salt cod with tomatoes and basil

Salt cod is traditionally a poverty food, born of the necessity to preserve gluts and to have food in winter. It's now become quite a delicacy though, and with a tomato sauce it's great for children. My sister gives it to her family every Friday, and her 5 children all love it.

675g (1½lb) dried salt cod, soaked in frequent changes of cold water for 24 hours

olive oil for frying

Italian '00' plain flour

3 garlic cloves, peeled and chopped

700g (1lb 9oz) canned Italian plum tomatoes

1 medium dried chilli (*peperoncino*), crumbled

sea salt and freshly ground black pepper

a handful of fresh basil leaves

1 Dry the cod with paper towel and cut into pieces 8 x 6cm (3¼ x 2½in). Heat 1cm (½in) olive oil in a large skillet over a medium heat. When hot, dredge the fish a piece at a time in the flour. Add several pieces to the hot oil and fry until golden and crisp on each side. Remove from the oil with a slotted spoon and drain on paper towels. Continue in this way until all the fish is fried.

2 Preheat the oven to 200°C/ 400°F/gas mark 6.

3 Heat 2 tbsp of the olive oil in a large sauté pan. Add the garlic and cook until golden. Stir in the tomatoes, chilli and some salt and pepper. Simmer for 15 minutes, breaking up the tomatoes with the back of a wooden spoon. If the sauce becomes too thick, add a little water to slacken it.

4 Arrange the fried salt cod in a single layer in a 33 x 23cm (13 x 9in) baking dish. Pour the sauce over the fish and bake for 20 minutes. Serve immediately, garnished with basil.

SERVES 6

poultry and
game

preparing chicken

Italian chicken doesn't come in trays covered in cling film, containing eight thighs or drumsticks, or four to six skinless, boneless fillets or breasts – it comes whole, sometimes still covered in feathers. So every Italian housewife has to know how to joint her chicken, if she wants to cook it in pieces. You could prepare other poultry in much the same way. Always try to get the best chicken possible, free-range and organic.

JOINTING
Use a very sharp knife, poultry shears, or strong kitchen scissors. This method of jointing a chicken gives you 12 pieces; ideal for chicken casseroles.

1 Remove the legs. With the chicken breast-side up, pull one leg away from the body, and cut through the skin between the body and thigh. Pop the ball of the thighbone out of its socket by pulling, then cut down between the ball and socket to separate the leg from the body. Do the same with the other leg. Then divide the legs into thigh and drumstick simply by cutting through the joint. This gives you four pieces.

2 Remove the wings. Press one wing against the body so that you can see where the shoulder joint is. Cut in-between the ball and socket of the joint, then pull the wing out and cut down through the skin. Do the same with the other wing. Trim the wing pinions if you like. You will have two wings.

3 To split the carcass, place a sharp knife blade inside the cavity and pierce one side between the shoulder and ribcage. Pulling towards you, and parallel to the backbone, slit the ribcage. Repeat on the other side. The back and breast of the bird will still be attached at one end. Cut through the bones and skin to separate the back and breast. Now you could cut the back part into two pieces.

4 The two breasts will now still be in one piece, which is what is used in some recipes (see pages 131 and 138). To separate the breasts, place them skin-side up on the chopping board. Cut down through the breastbone on one side to have two breasts. Cut these in half, to make four pieces. Cut all the pieces off the bone if this is what you want to do.

SPATCHCOCKING
Also known as butterflying, this is useful for smaller birds such as spring chickens and poussins, although you can do it to a full-sized chicken as well. Use poultry shears or strong kitchen scissors.

1 Place the bird on its breast and cut along the length of one side of the backbone. Cut along the other side of the backbone and cut it off entirely.

2 Turn the bird over and open it out as much as possible. Using the heel of your hand, strike the bird firmly on the breast; the object is to break the remaining bones so that the bird lies flat. The bird can now be marinated and cooked – in the oven, on a barbecue, or under the grill.

pollo piccolo alla ricotta ed erbe

spatchcock chicken with ricotta and herbs

This dish will impress your guests, and has the advantage of being simple to prepare. You could get the butcher to spatchcock the chickens for you. You could also cook them on the barbecue in summer, basting them with the wine.

4 x small 450g (1lb) chickens, spatchcocked (see page 178)

2 tbsp olive oil

4 fresh rosemary sprigs

freshly ground black pepper

350ml (12fl oz) dry white wine

STUFFING

150g (5¹/₂oz) ricotta cheese

55g (2oz) fontina cheese, finely grated

55g (2oz) Gorgonzola cheese, crumbled

4 slices *mortadella*, finely chopped (optional)

a handful of fresh flat-leaf parsley leaves

1 tbsp chopped fresh marjoram

1 tbsp chopped fresh sage

25g (1oz) butter, melted

1 Preheat the oven to 220°C/425°F/gas mark 7.

2 To make the stuffing, place the ricotta, fontina, Gorgonzola, *mortadella* (if using), herbs and butter in a bowl and mix. Divide into 4 portions.

3 Gently ease the skin from the breasts of each bird and spoon the stuffing into the pocket. Brush each bird with olive oil and top with a sprig of rosemary and a sprinkle of black pepper.

4 Place the birds on a roasting rack in a baking dish, then pour over the wine. Roast for 25-30 minutes, depending on the size. Reduce the heat to 180°C/ 350°F/gas mark 4 and cook for a further 15 minutes, until the chicken is cooked through, basting frequently with the pan juices.

5 Remove the birds and set aside to keep warm. Place the baking dish over a hot plate and bring the juices to the boil, then pour them over the birds and serve.

SERVES 4

pollo al marsala

chicken marsala

Many families or trattorias would serve something simple like this for Sunday lunch. It is very family friendly.

4 medium chicken breast fillets, pounded and seasoned

Italian '00' plain flour

25g (1oz) unsalted butter

2 tbsp olive oil

175ml (6fl oz) dry Marsala

4 tbsp chicken broth (see page 299)

25g (1oz) butter, softened

sea salt and freshly ground black pepper

1 Coat the chicken in flour and shake off the excess. Heat the butter and oil together in a lidded frying pan until the butter is foaming. Add the chicken and cook for 3 minutes on each side.

2 Stir in the Marsala and bring to the boil. Cover and simmer for 25-30 minutes, or until the chicken is cooked through, turning the meat occasionally.

3 Remove the chicken and set aside to keep warm. Add the stock to the Marsala and bring it to the boil. Boil for 2 minutes. Whisk in the softened butter and season to taste with salt and pepper.

4 To serve, spoon the sauce over the chicken.

SERVES 4

pollo brusco di annamaria

poached chicken in a vinegar sauce

Annamaria de' Pedrini is a fine cook and a generous friend. She gave me the recipe for this excellent dish, which has been served at Christmas in the de' Pedrini household in Lombardy for generations. The chicken forms part of the antipasti, together with lobster, prawns, *pâté de foie gras* and *affettato*, or mixed cured meats. You can often see a similar dish in the windows of the best Milanese *salumerie* (delicatessens). It is an easy dish, ideal for a buffet party or for a dinner in the summer.

1 carrot, scrubbed

1 onion, peeled and stuck with 2 cloves

1 celery stalk, trimmed

2 black peppercorns

2 bay leaves

a few parsley stalks

300ml (10fl oz) dry white wine

sea salt and freshly ground black pepper

1 chicken, about 1.5kg (3lb 5oz)

SAUCE

150ml (5fl oz) extra virgin olive oil

150ml (5fl oz) white wine vinegar

2 tbsp capers, rinsed and dried

4 garlic cloves, peeled

55g (2oz) anchovy fillets

2 tbsp Italian '00' plain flour

175g (6oz) porcini mushrooms (ceps) in oil (from a jar), drained

150g (5½oz) artichokes in oil (from a jar), drained

1 Put the carrot, onion, celery, peppercorns, bay leaves, parsley stalks, wine and a little salt in a stockpot. Add the chicken and fill with cold water up to the top of the chicken. Now remove the chicken from the pan and set aside. Bring the water to the boil, then put the chicken back in the pot. When the water comes back to the boil, turn the heat down so that it just trembles, but does not really boil, and cover with a tightly fitting lid. The secret of successful poaching lies in keeping the water just under simmering point. The temperature of the water should be maintained so that only an occasional bubble breaks slowly to the surface. Cook until the chicken is done, about 1¼ hours. Leave in the broth while you prepare the sauce.

2 Put the oil and vinegar in a small saucepan. Chop together the capers, garlic and anchovies and add them to the pan. Heat the mixture and, when bubbles begin to appear at the edges, throw in all the flour while you whisk hard with a small wire balloon whisk. Cook gently for 2-3 minutes, then add 6 tbsp of the chicken broth. Continue cooking for a further 2-3 minutes, whisking constantly. Draw off the heat.

3 If the porcini pieces are large, cut them into about 2.5cm (1in) pieces; cut the artichokes in half. Mix both into the sauce, which should be quite thick. Taste, add salt and pepper and set aside.

4 Skin the chicken and cut into small portions: 2 pieces from each breast cut across, 2 drumsticks and 2 thighs (see page 178). Put into a container and coat each piece with a little of the sauce, keeping some back for the final coating. Cover the container and refrigerate overnight. Also refrigerate the sauce that has been set aside.

5 The next day, transfer the chicken pieces to a serving dish and spoon the remaining sauce over them to give them a fresh and glossy look.

SERVES 4-6

petti di pollo all'ebraica

chicken breasts Jewish style

I was given this excellent recipe by a Jewish friend in Milan, whose family originally came from Piedmont. Recently I was looking through the best book on Piedmontese cooking I know, **La Cucina del Piemonte** by G. Goria, and there I found a similar recipe, but the poultry used was a turkey breast. Goria writes that the dish originates from the Jewish community of Moncalvo, a lovely town in southern Piedmont. This community fitted happily into the local traditions, as did most Jewish communities in Italy up to the War. And many of their dishes had much in common with the local dishes. The Jewish community was dispersed during the persecutions of 1943-45, but the dishes at least remain witness to their culinary tradition. Goria writes that the turkey was served with a sweet-and-sour relish, which is indeed very Middle Eastern. In my friend's recipe, the chicken breasts were served by themselves. I cannot decide whether they are better with or without the relish. So I am giving you the recipe for the relish, and I leave it to you to decide. You might prefer to serve it as an antipasto, as I do. The onions must be sweet, so use Spanish or red ones.

4 chicken breasts, skinned and boned

sea salt and freshly ground black pepper

1 tbsp chopped fresh sage

2 tbsp olive oil

900g (2lb) onions, peeled and very finely sliced

VEGETABLE RELISH

1 yellow sweet pepper, seeded

115g (4oz) aubergine

100g (3½oz) celery stalks

200ml (7fl oz) red wine vinegar

4 tbsp olive oil

1 tbsp concentrated tomato paste

3 tbsp caster sugar

1 Preheat the oven to 230°C/450°F/gas mark 8.

2 Rub the chicken breasts all over with salt and pepper and sage. Grease a small roasting tin or shallow oven dish with half the oil. Lay the seasoned breasts in the dish and cover with the onion. Sprinkle with salt and pepper and pour over the remaining oil.

3 Bake for half an hour, or until the juices that come out of the thickest part of the breasts when they are pierced with a skewer are pale and clear. The onion should be just tender – crisp on the top and juicy underneath. Serve immediately.

4 To make the relish, cut the vegetables into small dice, about 1cm (½in). Put them in a pan with the vinegar and pour in 200ml (7fl oz) of water; the liquid should be level with the vegetables. Add

1 tsp salt and bring to the boil. Simmer for 10 minutes, then drain.

5 Heat the oil in a frying pan and stir in the tomato paste and sugar. Cook for 5 minutes or so to caramelize the sugar a little, while stirring constantly. Now add the vegetables and turn them over and over to coat them in the caramelized oil. Turn the heat down and cook for a further 15 minutes. You must stir very often because there is a very little liquid and you do not want the vegetables to catch. The vegetables should be just crisp at the end of the cooking. Season with plenty of pepper and check the salt.

6 Serve the chicken hot with hot relish, or the relish warm or at room temperature, as an antipasto.

SERVES 4

spezzatino di pollo

savoy chicken stew

This dish is a classic speciality of the trattorias that surround Trasimeno, the principal lake in land-locked Umbria. But this recipe actually came to me from Ezio and Maria Anghinetti, who ran the Trattoria La Maesta near Parma. Ezio originally hails from Umbria, though, and so would accompany it with an Umbrian **torta al testo**, a crisp flatbread baked on the floor of the hearth. The bread of the tile on page 245 or the ricotta flatbread on page 246 would go well with this instead.

1 tbsp olive oil

1 x 1.5kg (3lb 5oz) chicken, cut into 12 pieces

1 small garlic clove, peeled and finely chopped

½ medium onion, peeled and coarsely chopped

1 small carrot, peeled and coarsely chopped

½ celery stalk, coarsely chopped

½ tsp coarsely chopped fresh rosemary leaves

85ml (3fl oz) extra virgin olive oil

2 small, fresh, hot red chillies, seeded and chopped

sea salt and freshly ground black pepper

175ml (6fl oz) dry white wine

250ml (9fl oz) canned tomatoes, chopped

1 Heat the olive oil in a large, heavy-based sauté pan over a medium to high heat and add the chicken pieces. Cover the pan and cook, turning the pieces from time to time, until the chicken has rendered all of its fat and water and has become golden in colour – about 15 minutes. Remove the chicken, and drain off both the fat and liquid.

2 Meanwhile, combine the garlic, onion, carrot, celery and rosemary in the goblet of your food processor, and process to a coarse purée.

3 Return the chicken to the pan and pour the extra virgin olive oil over it. Add the chillies, season with salt to taste, and spoon the puréed vegetables over the chicken. Simmer, covered, for 20 minutes.

4 Pour in the wine and simmer for 15 minutes more. Stir in the tomatoes and simmer, covered, for 15 minutes more, until the chicken is cooked through. If the mixture appears dry at any time, reduce the heat and add extra water. Taste and season if necessary. Serve the stew with bread.

SERVES 4

tacchino alla cacciatore

braised turkey with vegetables

This hunter-style stew — substantial and delicious — is based on a speciality of Mario at the Montagliari trattoria in Chianti. He serves it with potatoes roasted with rosemary.

25g (1oz) dried porcini mushrooms (ceps)

1.25kg (2¾lb) skinless, boneless turkey breast and thighs

40g (1½oz) unsalted butter

2 tbsp extra virgin olive oil

1 small sprig fresh rosemary

1 garlic clove, peeled and thinly sliced

3 bay leaves

2 medium onions, peeled and cut into 2.5cm (1in) chunks

4 medium carrots, peeled and cut into 2.5cm (1in) chunks

2 celery stalks, cut into 2.5cm (1in) chunks

½ tsp each of chopped fresh marjoram, sage and thyme

sea salt and freshly ground black pepper

2 tbsp Italian '00' plain flour

250ml (9fl oz) dry white wine

1 x 400g can chopped Italian plum tomatoes

250ml (9fl oz) chicken broth (see page 299)

1 Preheat the oven to 200°C/400°F/gas mark 6.

2 Soak the porcini in water for 20 minutes. Lift them out of the soaking liquid, strain (keeping the liquid) and coarsely chop. Cut the turkey into pieces roughly 5 x 7cm (2 x 3in).

3 Melt the butter and oil together in a large, heavy-based ovenproof sauté pan over a medium to high heat. Add the turkey and the sprig of rosemary, and brown the turkey on all sides.

4 Add the garlic and bay leaves and cook until the garlic is golden. Stir in the onions, carrots and celery, sprinkle with the herbs, and season with salt and pepper to taste. Sprinkle in the flour and stir until dissolved. Stir in the wine, tomatoes, chopped porcini and their liquid, and half of the broth.

5 Bring to the boil and transfer the pan to the oven. Bake, uncovered, for 35-40 minutes, or until the turkey is cooked through. If the sauce becomes too thick, stir in some of the remaining broth. Remove the bay leaves and the rosemary sprig before serving.

SERVES 6-8

anitra all'uva

duck with grapes

Muscat grapes are my favourites for this dish, if you can find them. This is based on a recipe from the Agriturismo La Luna e il Falò in Piedmont, in a village called Canelli. The Italian name of the trattoria is taken from the title of a novel by Cesare Pavese, meaning 'the moon and the bonfires'.

1 whole duck, about 1.8kg (4lb)

4 tbsp olive oil

sea salt and freshly ground black pepper

1 medium onion, peeled and cut into small chunks

1 celery stalk, cut into small chunks

3 tbsp chopped mixed fresh herbs, such as oregano, rosemary, sage and thyme

3 small fresh bay leaves

150ml (5fl oz) dry white wine

300g (10½oz) mixed seedless green and black grapes

1 Remove the liver and gizzards from the cavity of the duck and reserve them for another use. Rinse the duck inside and out and dry it well. Heat half the olive oil in a large casserole over a medium to high heat. Add the duck and brown evenly on all sides. Transfer the duck to a platter and drain off the fat in the casserole.

2 When the duck has cooled, season the cavity with salt and pepper and fill it with half of the onion and celery and 2 tsp of the chopped herbs. Rub the surface of the duck with an additional 2 tsp of the herbs, and season with salt and pepper.

3 Heat the remaining olive oil in the casserole over a medium heat. Add the duck and scatter all around it the remaining onion and celery and the bay leaves. Cook, stirring the vegetables often, until they are lightly golden, about 10 minutes. Pour over the wine and bring it to the boil. Partially cover the pan and simmer for 1 hour, turning the duck every 20 minutes.

4 Stir 10 green and 10 red grapes into the casserole and simmer, covered, for another 30 minutes, or until the duck is fully cooked.

5 Transfer the duck from the casserole to a shallow platter and cover it with foil. Discard the bay leaves and purée the contents of the casserole in a food mill or in a food processor. Pour the sauce back into the casserole. Simmer the sauce briskly until it has thickened. Stir in the remaining grapes and herbs. Simmer for 2-3 minutes and season.

6 Cut the duck into small serving pieces, removing the skin if desired. Arrange the duck on a shallow serving plate, spoon the sauce and the grapes over it, and serve immediately.

SERVES 4

fagiano alle olivi

pheasant with olives

Pheasant is a great Italian treat during the hunting season, which runs from September to March. Pheasant must be hung for 2-3 days before it is cleaned. Before cooking, the entrails and all the feathers must be removed.

55g (2oz) pancetta, sliced

1 pheasant, cleaned and prepared

115g (4oz) stoned black olives

1 tbsp fennel seeds, crushed in a pestle and mortar

15g (1/2oz) unsalted butter

2 tbsp olive oil

sea salt and freshly ground black pepper

1 tbsp juniper berries, crushed in a pestle and mortar

125ml (4fl oz) dry white wine

4 tbsp chicken broth (see page 299)

1 Preheat the oven to 190°C/375°F/gas mark 5.

2 Wrap the pancetta slices around the breast of the pheasant. Stuff the bird with the olives and fennel seeds.

3 Heat the butter and oil in an ovenproof casserole over a moderate heat, and brown the pheasant slowly for 20 minutes. Season with salt and pepper and the juniper berries. Add the wine and let it evaporate.

4 Add the broth and place in the oven. Roast for 1 hour, basting frequently with the pan juices, until the bird is cooked through.

5 Cut the bird into serving pieces and arrange the olive stuffing around it. Place the casserole over a moderate heat and add a little water to help scrape up the browned bits for the sauce. Pour this sauce through a sieve over the bird and then serve.

SERVES 2

fagiano con castagne
pheasant with chestnuts

The richness of the chestnuts makes a very good combination with the pheasant, and of course both are in season at the same time.

1 tbsp olive oil

25g (1oz) unsalted butter

1 pheasant, jointed into 4

2 medium onions, peeled and sliced

225g (8oz) peeled chestnuts (you can find them in vacuum packs)

3 tbsp Italian '00' plain flour

450ml (15fl oz) beef broth (see page 299)

150ml (5fl oz) red wine

sea salt and freshly ground black pepper

finely grated rind and juice of 1/2 unwaxed orange

1 fresh bouquet garni (parsley, bay leaf, thyme)

1 tbsp chopped fresh parsley

1 Preheat the oven to 180°C/350°F/gas mark 4.

2 Heat half the oil and half the butter together in a frying pan and fry the pheasant joints for about 5 minutes, until browned. Remove from the pan and put into a casserole.

3 Fry the onion and chestnuts in the remaining oil and butter for a few minutes, until brown, then add them to the pheasant.

4 Stir the flour into the fat in the pan, and cook for 2-3 minutes. Remove the pan from the heat, then add the stock and wine gradually, stirring until smooth. Bring to the boil, stirring until it thickens. Season with salt and pepper and pour over the pheasant. Add the orange rind and juice and the bouquet garni.

5 Cover the casserole and bake for about 1½ hours, until the pheasant is cooked through. Serve sprinkled with the chopped parsley.

SERVES 4

piccione con vino rosso
pigeon with red wine

Pigeon is very popular in Umbria and Tuscany. This recipe comes from a family friend who, although now in her seventies, still shoots her own game.

4 pigeons

2 tbsp olive oil

2 tbsp finely grated rind from an unwaxed lemon

2 tbsp chopped fresh flat-leaf parsley

4 fresh sage leaves, chopped

2 garlic cloves, peeled and crushed

2 tbsp capers, rinsed and chopped

6 anchovy fillets, chopped

250ml (9fl oz) dry red wine

sea salt and freshly ground black pepper

1 Joint the pigeons, cutting off the legs and wings, but leaving the breasts whole. Take the breats off the bone (your butcher will do this for you); you will have two breasts per person. (Use the pigeon trimmings to make a delicious stock for another dish, or a soup.)

2 Heat the oil in a casserole, and sauté the pigeon breasts with the lemon rind for 3-4 minutes on each side, or until brown. Add the parsley, sage, garlic, capers and anchovies, and cook, stirring, for 2 minutes.

3 Stir in the wine and bring to the boil. Cover and simmer for 1 hour or until the pigeon is tender. Season with black pepper and salt if necessary.

SERVES 4

coniggio a-a carlonn-a
rabbit fricassée with herbs, pine nuts, olives and white wine

The dialect term '*a-a carlonn-a*' means, in essence, that even an idiot can make this simple dish successfully! This recipe can alternatively be made with free-range chicken.

1 medium onion, peeled

about 20 green olives, stoned

4¹/₂ tbsp pine nuts

2 garlic cloves, peeled

6 sprigs fresh thyme or rosemary

2 tbsp olive oil

1 x 1kg (2¹/₄lb) rabbit (or free-range chicken), cut into 8 pieces

150ml (5fl oz) dry white wine

about 250ml chicken broth (see page 299) or hot water

20 black olives, stoned

sea salt and freshly ground black pepper

1 Finely chop the onion, green olives, 3½ tbsp of the pine nuts, the garlic and herbs. Combine.

2 Pour the oil into a deep sauté pan or shallow heatproof casserole over a medium to high heat. Add the rabbit and brown it on all sides. Remove the rabbit from the casserole and cover to keep the meat warm.

3 Add the chopped onion mixture to the casserole and brown, stirring. When the onion is golden, return the rabbit to the casserole, add the wine and let it evaporate, stirring.

4 Add about 200ml of the broth, bring to the boil, then reduce the heat to maintain a simmer. Cook, covered, for 1½ hours.

5 Add the black olives and enough broth, probably about 2-3 tbsp, to make a sauce. Season to taste with salt and pepper, and sprinkle with the remaining whole pine nuts. Simmer for 10-15 minutes, until the rabbit is cooked through, and serve.

SERVES 4

quaglia in umido
stewed quail

Quail are hunted in winter and spring and the wild ones are much tastier than those bred domestically. My grandfather always served his quail on a bed of polenta.

200g (7oz) diced pancetta

12 quail, cleaned and trussed

125ml (4fl oz) dry white wine

150ml chicken broth (see page 299)

2 garlic cloves, peeled and finely chopped

a handful of chopped fresh flat-leaf parsley

12 ripe tomatoes (preferably plum), skinned and chopped

sea salt and freshly ground black pepper

2kg (4½lb) broad beans in pod, podded

1 Brown half the pancetta in a large saucepan. Add the quail, pour the wine over them, and allow it to evaporate over heat.

2 Add the broth, garlic, parsley and tomatoes, and season with salt and pepper. Cover and cook over a low to medium heat for 30 minutes.

3 While the birds are cooking, fry the remaining pancetta in another saucepan.

4 Add the podded broad beans to the quail pan, cover and cook over a low heat for a few minutes, until the beans are almost tender.

5 Tip the fried pancetta over the quails and continue cooking for 5 minutes, or until the quails are cooked through, to allow the flavours to blend. Transfer to a serving dish and serve.

SERVES 6

meat

polpettone di vitello

veal flat steaks

This is for my sister Gina, who just loves this home-made dish (which changes quite frequently according to whatever takes my fancy).

450g (1lb) minced veal

1 garlic clove, peeled and crushed

a handful of fresh flat-leaf parsley, finely chopped

sea salt and freshly ground black pepper

1 tbsp tomato purée

1 large egg, beaten

4 medium slices bread, crusts removed

90ml (3fl oz) white wine

a handful of fresh breadcrumbs

2 tbsp olive oil

1 Combine the veal, garlic, parsley, salt and pepper to taste, tomato purée and beaten egg.

2 Put the bread in a bowl and pour over the wine. Leave for a few minutes, until the bread has softened. Remove the bread and add it to the meat mixture, then beat well with a wooden spoon.

3 Put the breadcrumbs on a plate. Shape the veal mixture into 6 flat steaks, then dip them in breadcrumbs.

4 Heat the olive oil in a large frying pan and, when it is hot, brown the steaks on both sides. Then cover the frying pan with a lid and cook for 7 minutes, or until the meat is cooked. Serve with a good green salad.

SERVES 6

cotolette alla bolognese

Bolognese veal cutlets

Veal is hugely popular in Italy, in *trattorias*, restaurants, and in the home, particularly in the south of the country.

1 medium egg

sea salt and freshly ground black pepper

8 tbsp fine white breadcrumbs

4 veal cutlets, about 125g (4¹/₂oz) each

55g (2oz) unsalted butter

1 tbsp olive oil

55g (2oz) Parma ham, thinly sliced

55g (2oz) Parmesan cheese, freshly cut into shavings

TOMATO SAUCE

15g (¹/₂oz) unsalted butter

1 tbsp very finely chopped onion

6 tbsp tomato passata

4 tbsp meat or vegetable broth (see page 299)

1 For the sauce, heat the butter in a pan, then add the onion and a pinch of salt and sauté gently for 5 minutes. Add the *passata* and cook gently for 10 minutes. Add the broth, cover, bring to the boil, and then simmer for 5 minutes. Season.

2 In a bowl, beat the egg with 1 tsp of salt. Spread the breadcrumbs on a plate. Coat the veal on both sides in the egg, then in the crumbs, pressing them on to form a thick layer. Chill, covered.

3 In a frying pan big enough to hold the cutlets one next to the other, heat the butter and oil together until the foam subsides. Fry the cutlets until golden, then turn and repeat.

4 Put a quarter of the ham on each steak, and put a quarter of the Parmesan on each piece of ham. Spoon the sauce over the meat. Cover with a lid and cook over a low heat for 7-10 minutes, or until the meat is cooked. Serve.

SERVES 4

making *scallopine*

A *scallopina* (or *piccata*) is the Italian equivalent of what is known elsewhere as *escalope* and *schnitzel*. It consists of a thin piece of prime meat, traditionally veal, which is often made even thinner by beating. Silverside of veal, or the fillet end of the leg (just above the shin, the cut used in *osso buco*) is the usual cut used for *scallopine*, but demand is such that other good, but less prime, cuts are now used, such as best end of neck, and even the shoulder. The best *scallopine* are quickly fried in butter after being dusted with flour, while the *scallopine* from the front of the animal can be rolled around a filling and braised. The thing to remember with veal, though, is that it is a very dry meat (because the animal is so young it contains very little fat), so care must be taken in cooking. This is why in so many European recipes, the veal escalopes are coated in egg and breadcrumbs, or flour, before cooking, as this offers a barrier between heat and meat: think of the breaded *wienerschnitzel* of Austria, for instance.

Nowadays, the *scallopine* technique is applied to many other meats, and you can also make *scallopine* of pork (fillet is best), chicken and turkey (breast).

VEAL SCALLOPINE

Get the butcher to cut these for you. He should cut diagonally across the muscle to get the largest possible slices, cutting across the grain of the meat. The slices should be thin, but not too thin (from 3mm-1cm/^{1}/8-^{3}/8in). You can then divide the pieces into the size of *scallopine* you want. Trim the meat of any fat (there shouldn't be much) and sinew (which you might find in escalopes cut from the front end of the animal).

If you want the pieces to be thinner, you can put them between two pieces of plastic or greaseproof paper and pound them carefully with a rolling pin or cleaver. This also tenderizes the tissues. But don't bang too much, you don't want the *escalope* or *scallopina* to split.

PORK SCALLOPINE

Use the fillet, or tenderloin. Cut thin slices from it, and pound as for veal.

CHICKEN AND TURKEY SCALLOPINE

Remove the breasts from the bone of both chicken and turkey. Remove the skin. With one hand on the meat to steady it, cut the flesh horizontally into escalopes using a very sharp, long knife. You should get about 2-3 from a chicken, depending on size, and about 5 from one side of a turkey breast. Pound as for veal.

rollatine di vitello

braised veal rolls

This recipe comes from the Agriturismo La Viranda, in the Monetferrato zone of Piedmont west of Turin. Veal, the most popular meat in Italy, is often made into rolls – showing the Italian love of 'parcels' – and this classic dish is substantial and delicious.

675g (1¹/₂lb) boned loin of veal

55g (2oz) Parma ham, coarsely chopped

1 small onion, peeled and coarsely chopped

2 small garlic cloves, peeled and coarsely chopped

2 tbsp coarsely chopped fresh flat-leaf parsley leaves

¹/₂ tsp chopped fresh rosemary leaves, plus 1 sprig

3 tbsp olive oil

4 large canned plum tomatoes, drained and finely chopped

125ml (4fl oz) dry white wine

150ml (5¹/₂fl oz) beef broth (see page 299)

8 small sage leaves

sea salt and freshly ground black pepper

1 Cut the veal into thin slices (see page 198, or get the butcher to do it for you) – about 12 *scallopine* – then pound them lightly to make them slightly larger and thinner and to tenderize the fibres.

2 Combine the ham, onion, garlic, parsley and chopped rosemary on a cutting board. Chop until very fine. Arrange the *scallopine* on a work surface and spoon equal amounts of filling on to the centre of each. Roll up, tucking in the sides to enclose the filling. Tie with thin string.

3 Heat the olive oil in a medium-heavy sauté pan over a medium to high heat. Add 6 meat rolls and brown them evenly on all sides. Transfer them to a small platter. Brown the remaining rolls and add these to the platter.

4 Add the tomatoes to the pan and simmer briskly for 2 minutes. Pour in the wine and simmer for 2 minutes. Return the meat rolls to the pan and pour the broth over them. Add the rosemary sprig and sage and season with salt and pepper.

5 Gently simmer the meat rolls, partially covered, stirring occasionally, for 35 minutes, or until tender. Transfer the meat rolls to a shallow serving platter and snip off the string.

6 Simmer the sauce to thicken it slightly. Discard the rosemary, spoon the sauce over the meat rolls, and serve.

SERVES 6

vitello alla crema di funghi

veal with a mushroom cream sauce

This classic veal recipe is based on one from Cibrèo, a ***trattoria*** par excellence in Florence. The recipe uses veal and the seasonal mushrooms that appear from late September onwards. This would, without a shadow of a doubt, be the 'dish of the day' at that time.

1 celery stalk, trimmed and chopped

1 carrot, peeled and chopped

2 whole cloves

3 bay leaves (fresh are stronger)

125ml (4fl oz) dry vermouth or white wine

12 shallots, peeled

500g (18oz) field mushrooms, cleaned and chopped

300ml (10fl oz) chicken broth (see page 299)

2 large egg yolks

4 tbsp double cream

sea salt and freshly ground black pepper

6 veal *scallopine*, cut about 5mm (¼in) thick

2 tbsp Italian '00' plain flour or plain flour

3 tbsp olive oil

chopped fresh flat-leaf parsley (optional)

1 Put the celery, carrot, cloves and bay leaves on a square of muslin and tie into a bag with string. Place this in a casserole dish with the vermouth or wine, bring it to the boil and reduce the liquid by about half.

2 Add the shallot, mushrooms and broth, bring back to the boil, and cover and simmer for 30 minutes. Discard the muslin bag.

3 Whisk together the egg yolks and cream, then whisk in a little of the hot cooking juices. Slowly pour the egg yolk and cream mixture into the casserole, stirring rapidly to prevent lumps forming. Season to taste. Reduce the heat to very low. Cook gently, stirring constantly, until the sauce has thickened. Do not allow to boil. Keep warm.

4 Beat the *scallopine* to tenderize them a little (see page 198). Sprinkle with 1 level tsp salt and ½ level tsp pepper. Coat lightly with flour.

5 Heat a third of the olive oil in a frying pan, and lightly brown the *scallopine* 2 at a time for 3 minutes on each side, or until cooked. Remove from the pan and serve the sauce over the top. Garnish with parsley if desired.

SERVES 6

polpette alla ferrigno

veal and pork meatballs

Meatballs are a family dish and are slightly celebratory in feel – because they take quite a time to make. You must use the best possible meat, and get the butcher to mince it as finely as he can for that melt-in-the-mouth effect. Never use ordinary butcher's mince, as it is too coarse and fatty, and meatballs made with it tend to fall apart.

500g (18oz) minced veal

500g (18oz) minced pork

2 large eggs, beaten

a handful of fresh flat-leaf parsley, chopped

125g (4½oz) Parmesan cheese, freshly grated

2 slices stale bread, soaked in milk and squeezed dry

125g (4½oz) pancetta, diced

sea salt and freshly ground black pepper

TO COOK

2-3 tbsp olive oil

1 medium onion, peeled and finely chopped

2-3 tbsp tomato purée

½ tsp caster sugar

1 Mix all the meatball ingredients together in a large bowl. Shape into about 24 even-sized balls. Using your hands is the easiest method. Flatten each ball slightly into an oval shape about 1cm (½in) thick.

2 Heat the olive oil in a large frying pan and fry the balls until well browned on each side. Transfer to a casserole.

3 Add the onion, tomato purée, sugar and 200ml (7fl oz) water to the frying pan, stirring. Cook for 5-10 minutes, then season with salt and pepper.

4 Pour the sauce over the meatballs, adding enough water to almost cover them. Cover and simmer over a low heat for 1 hour.

SERVES 8

spiedini di maiale, salcicce e prosciutto
pork, sausage and Parma ham skewers

This recipe makes me think of starving Tuscan hunters, coming home or into the *trattoria* after an early morning start, to eat a late breakfast. In fact it would make an ideal brunch recipe here – it's flavorsome, filling and quick.

4 generous herby sausages

2 pork fillet steaks

12 fresh bay leaves

3 lemons, each cut into 4 wedges

12 slices Parma ham

12 x 7.5cm (3in) square thick slices coarse-textured bread

a handful each of fresh sage and thyme leaves, chopped

sea salt and freshly ground black pepper

1 Preheat the oven to 200°C/400°F/gas mark 6, and have ready 4 long skewers.

2 Cut each sausage into 3 equal pieces, and each steak into 6 equal pieces.

3 Arrange all the ingredients on the skewers evenly: first the sausage, then the bay leaf, pork, lemon, ham and bread. Repeat until the ingredients are divided equally between the 4 skewers.

4 Sprinkle with the herbs and salt and pepper, and bake for 10-12 minutes, or until thoroughly cooked. Serve at once.

SERVES 4

lenticchie con salsiccia piccante

sausages with lentils

This is a perfect New Year's dish, as lentils are believed to bring money when eaten at the beginning of the year. *Mostarda di cremona*, a candied fruit chutney in mustard syrup, is available in Italian shops.

2 tbsp olive oil

1 onion, peeled and chopped

1 carrot, peeled and diced

1 celery stalk, chopped

250g (9oz) diced pancetta

300g (10½oz) dried green Italian small lentils (those from Castelluccio are best)

600ml (1 pint) beef broth (see page 299)

1 fresh bouquet garni (2 bay leaves, 2 sprigs rosemary, 3 sprigs thyme, 3 sprigs parsley)

6 fresh Italian sweet sausages

sea salt and freshly ground black pepper

6 tbsp *mostarda di cremona* or other mixed fruit chutney with mustard seeds, coarsely chopped

1 Heat the olive oil in a large frying pan, and sauté the onion over a medium heat until lightly golden. Add the carrot, celery and pancetta and cook for a few minutes, until golden brown.

2 Add the lentils to the pan and sauté for 2 minutes. Add 400ml (14fl oz) of the beef broth and the bouquet garni, cover and bring to the boil. Lower the heat and simmer for 1½ hours. Do keep a check on the liquid, adding more broth if necessary.

3 Heat a grill pan. Butterfly the sausages by slicing them lengthways, but not quite through, and grill on both sides until browned, crisp and cooked.

4 Season the lentils and serve with the grilled sausages and 1 tbsp of candied fruit chutney in its syrup.

SERVES 6

maiale di rostiti in padella

pot-roasted loin of pork

This is rather a grand dish, perfect for a dinner party. It's northern in influence, with Austrian touches such as the juniper berries. The boned and rolled pork loin is pot-roasted in a sauce of wine, grappa and sage, until it is very tender, almost dropping off the bone.

1 boned and rolled loin of pork, about 1.5kg (3lb 5oz)

sea salt and freshly ground black pepper

1 celery stalk

1 onion, peeled

1 small carrot, peeled

1 garlic clove, peeled

6 fresh sage leaves

3 fresh rosemary sprigs

2 tbsp olive oil

150ml (5fl oz) dry white wine

3 tbsp grappa (or vodka)

2 tbsp juniper berries

250ml (9fl oz) vegetable or chicken broth (see page 299)

1 Preheat the oven to 180°C/350°F/gas mark 4.

2 Season the pork loin with salt and pepper all over. Very finely chop the celery, onion, carrot, garlic, sage and the leaves from 1 rosemary sprig.

3 Heat the olive oil in a flameproof casserole, add the pork and brown well on all sides. Lift the pork out and set aside on a large plate.

4 Add the chopped vegetables, garlic, herbs and a little salt to the casserole and sauté for 5 minutes. Place the meat on top. Increase the heat, pour over the wine and grappa and let it all bubble rapidly for a minute or so, turning the meat over once. Then add the juniper berries and half of the broth.

5 Cover the casserole and cook in the oven for 1 1/2 hours, or until tender, turning the meat twice and adding a little more broth if the vegetables appear too dry. To impart extra flavour, lay the other 2 rosemary sprigs on top of the pork about 15 minutes before the end of cooking time.

6 To serve, remove the rind from the pork, then carve the meat into slices. Strain the cooking juices and spoon them over and around the meat.

SERVES 4-6

filetto di maiale e prosciutto in crosta

pork tenderloin baked in pastry

This is a recipe for a special occasion, whether you're cooking at home or eating out. It is the Italian version – a poor man's version perhaps – of Beef Wellington, but it looks very stylish and is perfect for entertaining, as it can be prepared in advance and kept in the wings, ready to go. It would be great for a wedding meal, for instance.

450g (1lb) pork tenderloin

sea salt and freshly ground black pepper

2-3 tsp chopped fresh rosemary

10 slices Parma ham

1 large egg, beaten, for glaze

PASTRY

200g (7oz) Italian '00' plain flour, plus extra for dusting

a pinch of salt

100g (3½oz) unsalted butter, diced

approx. 2 tbsp ice-cold water to bind

1 Preheat the oven to 190°C/375°F/gas mark 5.

2 First make the pastry. Mix the flour and salt together, then rub in the butter until it resembles breadcrumbs. Add enough water to bind into a damp ball. Wrap in cling film and refrigerate for 20 minutes.

3 Lightly season the pork tenderloin, being more generous with pepper than salt, and sprinkle with the rosemary. Wrap the pork in the ham slices, overlapping them. Put it on to a baking sheet.

4 On a floured surface, roll the pastry out to the length of the pork and drape it over the meat, tucking it in under the meat. The pork doesn't need to be completely sealed.

5 Brush with beaten egg and bake for 40 minutes, until the pastry is golden.

6 Allow the meat to rest for about 15 minutes before slicing. Serve without a sauce.

SERVES 6

arista di maiale al finocchio

roast pork with fennel

Fennel seeds are always harvested in the autumn, and the vegetable itself is eaten during the winter months. I am delighted by fennel's growing popularity. Its incredible alkalinity goes perfectly with a fatty meat such as pork. In the south of Italy we eat fennel raw in julienned strips. After a long slow lunch, it aids digestion beautifully.

1 pork loin, about 1.25kg (2¾lb)

1 sprig fresh rosemary, leaves finely chopped

4 garlic cloves, peeled and finely chopped

2½ tsp fennel seeds, bruised

sea salt and freshly ground black pepper

55g (2oz) unsalted butter

1 tbsp olive oil

1 fennel bulb

125ml (4fl oz) milk

250ml (9fl oz) white wine

1 Preheat the oven to 170°C/325°F/gas mark 3.

2 Cut deep holes all over the pork loin. Put the rosemary and garlic in a bowl, then add the fennel seeds and some salt and pepper to taste. Stuff this mixture into the cuts in the pork.

3 Place the meat in a roasting pan with half of the butter and all the olive oil, and roast for about 2 hours.

4 Towards the end of the cooking time, roughly chop the fennel bulb, then cook in a covered pan with the remaining butter and a little water over a low heat until tender. Transfer to a blender, add the milk and blend until smooth.

5 When the meat is cooked, slice it and arrange it on a serving plate. Keep it warm.

6 Pour off the fat from the roasting pan and deglaze with the white wine. Boil for a couple of minutes, then add the fennel mixture. Mix well, and pour over the meat. Serve immediately.

SERVES 6-8

sedano al forno con pancetta
baked celery with pancetta

This is a truly great way to serve celery, whether as the main course of a light lunch, as an accompaniment to meat or poultry, as a **contorno** or vegetable course, or perhaps even as a starter. Baking or parchment paper is ideal, as it looks very attractive when you take the 'parcel' to the table.

2 heads celery

12 shallots

3 tbsp olive oil

4 slices pancetta

2 garlic cloves, peeled

4 sprigs fresh thyme

4 small sprigs fresh rosemary

4 fresh sage leaves

sea salt and freshly ground black pepper

2 dsp white wine vinegar

1 Preheat the oven to 200°C/400°F/gas mark 6.

2 Remove the tough outer layers from the celery, then trim the root but leave the base attached. Now cut across the celery about 9cm (3¹/₂in) from the base, then stand the lower half upright and cut it in half vertically through the centre. Cut each half into 4, to make 8 pieces, keeping them attached to the base. Wash. Peel the shallots; if the bulbs divide, split them.

3 Heat 2 tbsp of the olive oil in a frying pan, then lightly brown the celery and shallots. Keep them moving so they brown evenly. Transfer them to a plate. Increase the heat, add the pancetta and garlic and fry for 2-3 minutes.

4 Lay 4 large sheets of baking paper over an oven tray and lightly grease a 23cm (9in) circle on each. Arrange the celery on the paper, putting the prettiest pieces on the top. Add the shallots, thyme, rosemary and sage, and season.

5 Combine the remaining olive oil with the vinegar and sprinkle all over the vegetables, followed by the pancetta, which drapes over the celery. Fold the paper over and seal each parcel (it is important to keep steam trapped inside). Bake for 40 minutes.

6 Unwrap the paper packages on plates at the table. Serve the vegetable with the juices spooned over.

SERVES 4

carabiniere a cavallo

grilled smoked mozzarella, radicchio and pancetta

This dish translates as 'mounted policeman', so-named because the colour and the fan shape of the radicchio looks like a carabiniere's hat. It makes a deliciously light main course for lunch, but could also be served as a starter or **contorno** (vegetable course).

2 medium heads radicchio

1 tbsp olive oil

8 slices pancetta

4 thick slices smoked mozzarella (scamorza)

2 tbsp fruity extra virgin olive oil

sea salt and freshly ground black pepper

1 Rinse the radicchio and pat it dry. Cut it in quarters. Do not trim the stem as it helps hold the leaves together.

2 Preheat a ridged cast-iron grill pan for 5 minutes. Brush the radicchio with olive oil and place on the grill. Add the pancetta slices and grill together for about 3 minutes on each side, or until the radicchio is tender. (This allows the radicchio to absorb the smoked aroma of the pancetta.) Remove from the grill-pan.

3 Raise the temperature of the grill. Grill the mozzarella slices briefly, until grill marks appear on the surface.

4 On individual plates, fan 2 of the radicchio quarters. Top with 2 pancetta slices and 1 grilled cheese slice. Drizzle with good oil and season with salt and pepper. Serve immediately.

SERVES 4

zucchine ripiene

baked stuffed courgettes

Stuffed courgettes and other stuffed vegetables are a staple of trattoria and home cooking. They are prepared and cooked in advance, probably on a daily basis during the brief courgette season. Try to get really big courgettes for this, because they are easier to handle.

4 large courgettes, about 7-10cm (3-4in) wide and 25-30cm (10-12in) long

100g (3½oz) fresh breadcrumbs

100g (3½oz) Parma ham, diced

85g (3oz) pecorino cheese, grated

85g (3oz) Parmesan cheese, grated

2 slices salami, diced

85g (3oz) provolone cheese, diced

a handful of fresh flat-leaf parsley, chopped

a handful of pine nuts

3 medium tomatoes, skinned, seeded and chopped

sea salt and freshly ground black pepper

olive oil

1 small onion, peeled and thinly sliced

75ml (2½fl oz) dry white wine

55g (2oz) unsalted butter

1 Preheat the oven to 150°C/300°F/gas mark 2.

2 Scrub and wash the courgettes, remove the stem ends and reserve. With the thin blade of a sharp knife, remove the centre pulp from each courgette, working from the cut end, leaving an unbroken shell about 5mm (¼in) thick. Discard the pulp.

3 Put the breadcrumbs in a large bowl and add all the ingredients in the ingredients list up to and including the tomatoes. Season, mix well, then add enough olive oil and a little water to make a stuffing that holds together but isn't wet.

4 Stuff each courgette shell with the stuffing, pushing it inside with your fingers and a wooden spoon end. Replace the end pieces, securing them with wooden toothpicks.

5 Pour enough oil into a frying pan to just cover the bottom, heat, then add the courgettes. Gently cook and roll until golden brown all over. Transfer to a lightly oiled shallow baking dish. In the same pan, cook the onion until golden, then add the wine and butter, and some salt and pepper. Stir and cook for 1 minute.

6 Pour the sauce over the courgettes and bake them for 45 minutes.

7 Remove the courgettes and let them cool. When ready to serve, remove the toothpicks and end pieces and discard. Cut each courgette into small slices and arrange in a clean baking dish. Spoon the sauce over and serve.

SERVES 4

Italian cured and preserved meats

Italy is famous for its cured and preserved meats, and the most favoured animal is the pig. There are two basic types of preserved meat: the whole cured hams and bacon products, and the sausages made from minced meat and fat, such as salami. Meats were once preserved, naturally, to keep them for times when fresh meats were scarce, but now they are an essential characteristic of Italian cuisine, delicious served as an *antipasto*, and used in cooking.

HAMS AND BACONS

'*Prosciutto*' is simply the Italian name for ham, and it covers cooked ham (*prosciutto cotto*) as well as 'raw' ham (*prosciutto crudo*). The most famous cured 'raw' ham is that of Parma, and this meat is made from the hind legs of pigs raised in Emilia-Romagna or Lombardy. The pigs are fed on the sort of whey that is used to make Parmesan cheese, along with other good things, to ensure the meat is tender and full of flavour. To be cured, the legs are massaged with salt for a month, then hung in special well-ventilated rooms to mature for up to 16 months. It is said that the air currents in the Langhirano valley, near Parma, are uniquely perfect, keeping the raw hams in peak condition as they are cured. *Prosciutto crudo* is also produced in other areas, notably in San Daniele in Friuli.

Coppa is sometimes described as a 'poor man's *prosciutto crudo*'. It is made up of parts of the shoulder and quantities of its fat, which are salt-cured, stuffed in a gut casing and then air-dried. It looks like a fatty sausage, but is sliced thinly and served in the same way as cured ham.

Guanciale and *pancetta* are two varieties of Italian bacon. The former, a speciality of Lazio, is made from pigs' cheeks; the latter is made from the belly. Both are salt-cured, often with other flavourings, then air-dried. Both are fattier and much more highly flavoured than British bacon, and are used principally as ingredients in recipes (rather than in a dish such as bacon and eggs).

SAUSAGES

'Salami' is the name given to various, usually pork, sausages that are made with finely or coarsely minced meat, fat and additional flavourings such as spices. These are wrapped in gut, tied, then cured and dried. They are thinly sliced and served cold, usually as part of an *antipasto*. Salami vary from region to region, in texture, flavour and size. *Salami milano* is fairly lean, made with very finely minced meat; *salami napoletano* contains a little chilli; and *salami finocchiona* is made with fennel seeds. *Mortadella*, from Bologna, is the largest of the Italian pork sausages, and is pale pink and studded with fat and occasionally pistachio nuts and peppercorns.

Fresh pork sausages are also available, the most famous probably being the *lucanica* or *luganega*. This is made in a continuous coil, and can be boiled or grilled. *Zampone* are pre-cooked sausages made from pork stuffed into boned pigs' trotters. *Cotechino* is a thick, sometimes pre-cooked pork sausage, which is tender and juicy because it contains gelatinous parts of the pig such as the ear and rind. *Zampone* and *cotechino* are normally cooked to celebrate New Year, and are served accompanied by lentils, which are said to represent money.

tzigonie

grilled beef on a skewer

Mario Gianni owns Trattoria Baffo in the Valtellina region of Piedmont, and his grilled beef on a skewer is an Alpine dish that is seldom seen today. The beef is slightly fiddly to cut, but you could get the butcher to do it for you. The end result is well worth while, as it looks really impressive. He serves it with fried or roasted potatoes and tossed garden salad. You will need 10-12 wooden skewers 22cm (9in) long.

olive oil

350g (12oz) boneless beef sirloin, cut into about 10-12 very thin slices, about 3mm (1/8in) thick

2 tsp fresh rosemary leaves, chopped

sea salt and freshly ground black pepper

1 Preheat a ridged cast-iron stove-top grill or an overhead grill. Rub the skewers with olive oil and allow it to soak into the wood. Do this several times before grilling.

2 Wrap the slices of beef tightly around the sticks, leaving 5-8cm (2-3in) of wood exposed at each end of the skewer. Secure with a wooden toothpick if necessary. Cover the exposed ends of the skewers with foil.

3 Rub the beef with olive oil and sprinkle with chopped rosemary. Place the skewers on or under the hot grill. Brown lightly on all sides, until cooked to your taste, and sprinkle with salt and pepper to taste.

SERVES 5-6

manzo brasato in barolo

beef braised in barolo wine

Piedmont is renowned for its fine aged Barolo, and this is a traditional, robust dish from the region. It's an excellent way of braising beef for a special occasion. If possible, use Barolo that is at least 5 years old, which will give a wonderfully thick, tasty sauce. Otherwise, a good bottle of lesser full-bodied red wine will do.

1kg (2¼lb) joint of braising beef (topside or top rump)

2 carrots, peeled and chopped

1 medium onion, peeled and roughly chopped

2 celery stalks, roughly chopped

a handful of fresh flat-leaf parsley leaves

3 bay leaves

1 tbsp juniper berries

1 tsp black peppercorns

350ml (12fl oz) aged Barolo wine, or other full-bodied red wine

15g (½oz) unsalted butter, in pieces

1 tbsp olive oil

sea salt and freshly ground black pepper

1 Put the meat in a bowl and add the chopped vegetables, herbs, juniper berries and peppercorns. Pour the wine over the meat, cover the bowl and marinate in the fridge for at least 24 hours.

2 Preheat the oven to 180°C/350°F/gas mark 4.

3 Remove the meat from the bowl and dry well, reserving the marinade. Make slits in the surface of the meat and insert the pieces of butter. Strain the marinade, saving the vegetables and flavourings as well as the liquor.

4 Heat the olive oil in a flameproof casserole. Add the meat and brown on all sides over a medium-high heat.

5 Add the vegetables and flavourings to the meat. Add 225ml (8fl oz) of the reserved liquor and some salt. Cover and braise in the oven for about 3 hours, adding more reserved liquor as needed to keep the meat from drying out.

6 When the meat is cooked, lift it out and keep it warm. Discard the bay leaves. Put the vegetables and other flavourings through a food mill with the cooking liquor (or whiz in a food processor). Reheat the sauce, check the seasoning and pour over the meat to serve.

SERVES 6

sugo di carne della fiammetta

chunky meat and vegetable stew

Fiammetta runs the Montagliari Trattoria in Chianti, and this is her husband's favourite recipe. She actually calls it a *sugo*, or sauce, but in reality it is more like a meat stew to be served with potatoes and vegetables (although it would be delicious with pasta too).

4 tbsp olive oil

40g (1½oz) unsalted butter

2 medium onions, peeled and cut into 1cm (½in) dice

1 medium carrot, peeled and cut into 1cm (½in) dice

1½ celery stalks, cut into 1cm (½in) dice

5 sprigs fresh flat-leaf parsley, chopped

450g (1lb) boneless beef sirloin, cut into 1cm (½in) dice

350g (12oz) boneless pork shoulder, cut into 1cm (½in) dice

225g (8oz) sweet Italian sausage, without fennel seeds, casing removed, cut into 1cm (½in) dice

sea salt and freshly ground black pepper

250ml (9fl oz) dry red wine, preferably Chianti

1 tbsp tomato purée

500-750ml (18-26fl oz) beef broth (see page 299)

1 Heat the olive oil and butter together in a large heavy-based flameproof casserole over a medium-to-low heat. Add the vegetables and parsley and cook slowly, tossing occasionally, until very tender, about 20 minutes.

2 Add the meat dice to the casserole and increase the heat to medium. Cook, tossing frequently, until the meat has lost its raw colour. Season well with salt and pepper to taste. Pour in the red wine and simmer briskly until the wine has reduced by half.

3 In a small bowl, blend the tomato purée with 1½ tbsp of the broth. Stir this mixture into the casserole and add an additional 125ml (4fl oz) of the broth. Simmer, covered, for 1½ hours, or until the meat is cooked through, adding broth 125ml (4fl oz) at a time to keep the sauce from becoming too thick and sticking to the bottom. It may not be necessary to use all the broth. Taste and season again if necessary.

SERVES 8

agnello brasato con finocchio e pomodori

lamb braised with fennel and tomatoes

Wild fennel grows prolifically in Sardinia, and the rugged terrain is sheep country, so this combination of lamb and fennel seems natural and almost inevitable. The flavours complement each other well, the fennel helping to cut across the richness of the lamb.

1 boneless shoulder of lamb, about 1.3kg (3lb)

50ml (2fl oz) olive oil

1 onion, peeled and chopped

500g (18oz) canned peeled Italian plum tomatoes

sea salt and freshly ground pepper

2 fennel bulbs, with fronds

1 Trim the lamb of excess fat and cut into pieces, about 2cm (³/₄in) square. Heat the olive oil in a flameproof casserole, add the chopped onion and lamb pieces, and sauté over a medium-high heat until the lamb cubes are browned all over.

2 Add the canned tomatoes to the casserole and season with salt and pepper. Cover and cook over a low heat for 10 minutes.

3 In the meantime, trim the fennel, reserving the feathery fronds, and cut the vegetable into slices. Add these to the lamb and stir well. Cook, uncovered, for about an hour until the meat is tender, adding a little water to keep the meat moist if necessary from time to time.

4 Taste and adjust the seasoning. Finely chop some of the reserved fennel fronds and scatter over the braised lamb and fennel to serve.

SERVES 6

fricassea di agnello e carciofi

fricassée of artichoke and lamb

This delicious lamb recipe is best served with cooked and cooled green beans dressed like a salad with oil, vinegar, salt and pepper.

juice of 2 lemons

2 globe artichokes, tough leaves removed

900g (2lb) boneless leg of lamb

4 tbsp olive oil

2 tbsp fresh flat-leaf parsley, chopped

3 garlic cloves, peeled and thinly sliced

150ml (5fl oz) dry white wine

sea salt and freshly ground black pepper

1 medium egg yolk

1 Pour the juice of 1 lemon into a bowl of cold water. Peel 1 artichoke stem, then cut the top off the artichoke leaves – approximately 5mm (^{1}/4in) from the top. Start peeling the leaves off the artichoke – at least 4 layers – until a pale yellow is revealed. Put the artichoke into the acidulated water and repeat with the other artichoke. Cut the artichokes into quarters and remove the fuzzy chokes and prickly purple leaves at the base. Return the quarters to the acidulated water. Peel off any remaining outside part of the stalks, leaving only the tender marrow. Cut this into rounds and throw into the acidulated water.

2 To prepare the lamb, remove the fat and gristle from the outside of the leg and any nuggets of fat that are lurking on the inside. Cut the meat into 2.5cm (1in) chunks.

3 Preheat the oven to 150°C/300°F/gas mark 2.

4 Heat the oil in a casserole dish. Add the parsley and garlic and sauté. Add the lamb and then the wine and boil for 1 minute.

5 Drain the artichoke pieces and add to the casserole. Season. Cover and bake for 1 hour, or until the meat is cooked through and tender, adding a little hot water if the liquid runs dry.

6 Towards the end of the cooking time, beat together the egg yolk and juice of the remaining lemon, pour over the meat and stir well. Check the seasoning and serve.

SERVES 8

bracio

filled lamb rolls

This is a variation of one of my grandmother's recipes – and is a great example of how meat is served in Italy, either in the *trattoria* or home. The meat is prepared simply and should be of the finest quality. You will need 12 skewers, wooden or metal.

900g (2lb) top round of leg of lamb, cut into 5mm slices

3 tbsp olive oil, plus extra for greasing

sea salt and freshly ground black pepper

18 bay leaves (fresh are best)

2 onions, peeled and cut into 18 small wedges

a handful of fine breadcrumbs

FILLING

4 tbsp olive oil

1 onion, peeled and finely chopped

100g (3½oz) pecorino cheese, cubed

100g (3½oz) diced pancetta

55g (2oz) good bread, cubed

a handful of fresh flat-leaf parsley, chopped

1 large egg, beaten

1 To make the filling, heat the olive oil in a saucepan, then sauté the onion until golden, about 5-8 minutes. Remove from the heat and allow to cool. Add the pecorino, pancetta, bread, parsley and egg and mix well. Season to taste with salt and black pepper.

2 Beat the meat slices to tenderise them. Cut the slices into 7.5cm (3in) squares; you need 18. Put 1 scant tbsp of filling on each slice of meat, near a corner. Roll the corner of meat over the stuffing, tuck in the edges and roll it into a small sausage shape, about 4cm (1½in) thick x 7.5cm (3in) long. Continue until all the meat rolls are done.

3 Preheat the oven to 200°C/ 400°F/gas mark 6.

4 Oil a baking sheet and sprinkle it with salt. Push 2 skewers through the side of a meat roll; add a bay leaf and a wedge of onion. Repeat, alternating the meat, bay and onion, to fill each double-skewer with 3 meat rolls.

5 Pour 3 tbsp olive oil on to a flat plate and put the breadcrumbs on a second plate. Dip each skewer in the oil, then in the breadcrumbs. Arrange in a roasting tin and roast for 20 minutes, turning after 10 minutes.

SERVES 6

fegato alla veneziana

calf's liver venetian-style

Strips of calf's liver are fried very, very quickly in butter, and served with sweet onions braised in wine. This is a classic Venetian dish, and my mother's favourite.

85g (3oz) unsalted butter

400g (14oz) onions, peeled and thinly sliced

125ml (4fl oz) dry white wine

sea salt and freshly ground black pepper

800g (1¾lb) calf's liver, thinly sliced

3 tbsp chopped fresh flat-leaf parsley

1 Heat about half the butter in a lidded frying pan, add the onions and cook for 5 minutes, or until golden. Add the wine and some salt and pepper. Cover and braise the onions over a low heat until very tender, about 25 minutes, stirring every now and again. Remove the onions and keep warm.

2 In the meantime, remove any gristle or membrane from the calf's liver, then cut the liver into strips.

3 When the onions are almost ready, melt the rest of the butter in another frying pan. Add the liver and sauté over a high heat just until cooked through, about 4 minutes. Add salt to taste, then mix with the braised onions.

4 Serve immediately, scattered with the chopped parsley.

SERVES 6

breads and
pizzas

simple doughs

Simple doughs are known in Italy as *'pane semplice'*, and they consist simply of good-quality strong white bread flour, fine sea salt, fresh yeast and water, sometimes a little olive oil – nothing more. **Grissini**, breadsticks and pizza doughs are examples of simple doughs.

Bread-making, however, is never really simple. However precise a recipe might be, other influences can affect your bread dough. The balance of ingredients needs to be perfect to work properly, and sometimes the liquid content is hard to gauge. Different flour types, for instance, will absorb water at different ratios; altitude will affect water absorbency; and the age of the flour and climatic conditions will also vary the liquid content. You actually need to feel your way through the making of bread dough. But don't worry; this comes with practice.

Fresh yeast is best. Crumble it into a bowl, and add a little of your warm water (no more than blood heat or hand-hot, and I think it helps if it is pure, perhaps bottled, water). Cream the yeast into the water with a wooden spoon until it dissolves and becomes smooth. You can use dried yeast in much the same way. Easy-blend yeast should be mixed directly into the flour; it will be activated once the liquid is added.

Sift the flour and fine salt into a bowl or on to the work surface, and make a well in the centre. Put the yeast liquid and oil into the well, then start gently mixing in the flour. The rest of the water specified in the recipe should be added little by little, stirring slowly with a wooden spoon to create a soft, smooth, damp dough. The dampness of the dough is important for success, as it will allow the bread to develop flavour and enable it to rise. If the dough is too dry, it will struggle to rise, and the end result will be heavy.
And you must never underestimate the importance of

kneading. I always feel so happy and positive as soon as I start kneading – the exercise relaxes me. Basically, you use the heel of your working hand to gently push the dough away from you. At the same time, use your other hand to rotate the dough slightly towards you. Continue doing this, so that the dough goes slowly round in a circle. Kneading should be for a maximum of 10 minutes. During this time the dough will change from what is known as a 'raggy' dough to a soft, smooth and silky dough. The dough is ready when you can stretch a small amount across your fingers so you can see through it but it doesn't break (the 'stretch' or 'windowpane' test).

Next you must relax the dough. Leave it in a clean or oiled bowl (glass or plastic, not metal), covered, to rise for about 1½ hours, until doubled in size. The room must be cool to normal, and draught-free.

Knock back the dough – that is, give it a little punch – as this enables the gases to be released. Form the dough into a ball by cupping your hands gently around it, and 'chafe' it by rotating and pressing the sides slightly. Leave it to relax again for 5 minutes.

Shape the dough as indicated in the individual recipes, and leave to prove – the second rise – for the recommended time. Then you can bake your bread.

complex doughs

Complex doughs are bread doughs with a special depth of flavour in crust and crumb. They are basically simple doughs (the combination of yeast, flour, salt and water that I write about on page 228) that have been enriched in some way. Apart from the enriching, the doughs are made, rested, risen, shaped and proved in much the same way as simple doughs.

Fats are the usual enriching ingredients: butter, eggs, olive oil or a light vegetable oil such as sunflower. The fat coats the gluten strands in the flour (gluten is the protein that gives dough its elasticity and strength), and this creates a barrier between the flour and yeast. This has the effect of slowing down the fermentation and rising times, so you must always allow more time to make complex doughs – but this 'slowness' is actually what creates the most interesting flavours and textures. Breads made with enriching fats have a softer, more tender crumb than those made with simple doughs; in fact, some can even become cake-like (see the panettone on page 288; although in the Puddings chapter, it is actually a bread, albeit a sweet one).

Complex doughs can also be created by utilizing a starter. The original sourdough starter of the famous American sourdough bread was a flour-and-water paste left to ferment by wild or airborne yeasts. (Fresh bakers' yeasts are used now.) The Italian version is known as a *biga*. The idea is to prepare the yeast in advance, which will contribute hugely to the ultimate texture and flavour of the bread, giving it an open porous texture, and a lightly fermented flavour. A small amount of flour, water and yeast is left to ferment at room temperature well in advance of the actual bread-baking session – for from 12-24 hours (sometimes up to 36 hours) – and then this starter, or a proportion of it, is mixed in with the flour, water and yeast (and perhaps other ingredients) of the

actual bread dough. There are several versions of *biga* in this chapter: one which you can make and keep (for up to 4 days at room temperature, then refrigerate for a few more days), and a couple that are specific to the individual recipes.

Breads made with a *biga* require more time and more precision than simple doughs, but they are extremely do-able and most enjoyable, as well as slightly challenging. The results are magnificent and will truly make the baker feel a great sense of pride and excitement at their possibilities. When you embark on an enriched dough, you will often have to make the dough over a period of days. Ciabatta, for example, requires many stages, and each stage is vital for the finished result. The dough in fact, which is slightly different to many other enriched bread doughs (see page 238), has to be handled very carefully (like a baby, they say in Italy). However, there is a great sense of anticipation during this process – coupled with a magnificent smell pervading your home!

If you feel you haven't got the time to make bread with a *biga*, you could use what we call a 'sponge', which is basically a junior version of *biga*. It uses the same ingredients and method, but the fermentation time is much shorter (see page 242).

grissini torinese
Italian breadsticks

These crisp sticks of bread, made with a simple dough, are a speciality of Turin, in Piedmont. They are ideal as an accompaniment to an *antipasto* or starter. You could sprinkle them with coarse sea salt, fresh rosemary or dried fennel seeds instead of the sesame seeds suggested here – or indeed leave them plain.

10g (¼oz) dried yeast

325ml (11fl oz) warm water

1 tsp malt extract (optional)

450g (1lb) strong white bread flour, plus extra for dusting

2 tsp fine sea salt

3 tbsp olive oil, plus extra for greasing

2 tbsp fine semolina

egg glaze, made with 1 egg yolk and 1 tbsp water

sesame seeds

1 Sprinkle the yeast into 125ml (4fl oz) of the water in a bowl. Leave the mixture for 5 minutes, then add the malt extract (if using, it adds flavour), and stir to dissolve.

2 Sift the flour and salt together into a large bowl. Make a well in the centre and pour in the yeast liquid and the olive oil. Use a wooden spoon to draw the flour in from the sides. Stir in the remaining warm water, as needed, to form a firm, sticky dough.

3 Turn the dough out on to a well-floured work-surface. Knead the dough until smooth and elastic, about 10 minutes. Cover with a tea-towel and leave to rest for 10 minutes. Knead the dough for a further 10 minutes.

4 Shape the dough into a rectangle, 30 x 20cm (12 x 8in) and 1.5cm (¾in) thick. Cover it with a tea-towel, and leave it to rest for 10 minutes.

5 Preheat the oven to 200°C/400°F/gas mark 6.

6 Lightly oil 2 baking sheets and sprinkle them with the semolina. Cut the dough rectangle lengthways into 4 equal pieces, then cut each piece lengthways into 10 strips. Stretch each strip until it is 25cm (10in) long. Place the strips, about 1cm (½in) apart, on the baking sheets.

7 Brush the strips with the egg glaze and sprinkle with sesame seeds. Bake for 15-20 minutes. Transfer the sticks to a wire rack, then leave to cool.

MAKES ABOUT 40

pane toscano
tuscan bread

This is a recipe I elicited from a Tuscan baker where, for one of my books, we laboured overnight – but the recipe has been considerably scaled down! There is a superstition in Italy that a loaf should always be served right-side-up, and that it is both unlucky and disrespectful to serve it upside-down. My grandfather always made the sign of the Cross on fresh bread with a knife, signifying the importance of bread to him; the staff of life. This is not a simple bread to make, but it is very good, and very Italian.

BIGA STARTER

250ml (9fl oz) warm water

20g (3/4oz) fresh yeast

200g (7oz) strong white bread flour, plus extra for dusting

DOUGH

approx. 250ml (9fl oz) warm water

fine sea salt

625g (1lb 6oz) strong white bread flour, plus extra for dusting

olive oil for greasing

1 To make the *biga* starter, pour the warm water into a large bowl, sprinkle over the yeast and stir until dissolved. Add the flour and blend until the mixture is smooth. Sprinkle over a little extra bread flour and cover with a cloth for 24 hours.

2 To make the dough, stir the warm water and a large pinch of salt into the *biga* starter. Add 125g (4^1/$_2$oz) of flour at a time, blending thoroughly before adding the rest, all except for 125g (4^1/$_2$oz). Sprinkle this retained flour – known as 'bench flour' – on to the work-surface. Turn the dough on to the work-surface and knead in all of the flour; this will take approximately 10 minutes. The dough will be sticky and difficult to handle at first, but after all the flour has been incorporated it should be easier to work with and tender.

3 Transfer the dough to a large oiled bowl. Rub the dough against the bowl to coat it in oil. Cover with a damp cloth and leave to rise for 45-60 minutes in a warm, draught-free place.

4 Punch the dough down to allow the gases to escape, and turn it on to a lightly floured board. Knead it for 5 minutes. Shape the dough into a flat, wide loaf about 35cm (14in) long. Loosely wrap the dough in a towel, leaving enough room in the towel for the dough to rise. Let the dough rest again for 30-45 minutes; it will double in size.

5 Meanwhile, arrange a strong baking sheet, terracotta tiles or a pizza stone on the centre shelf of the oven. Preheat the oven to 200°C/400°F/gas mark 6, allowing a good 30 minutes for the oven to preheat.

6 When the dough is ready, roll it out of the towel directly on to the hot tiles or stone. Make one or more lengthwise slash on the top of the bread using a sharp knife. Bake for 45-50 minutes, until the bread is lightly browned with a thick, hard crust. Turn the bread on its side and knock it on the bottom. If it's done, you'll hear a hollow sound. Leave it to cool.

MAKES 1 LARGE LOAF

bruschetta di finocchio, cipolla e olive
caramelized fennel, onion and olive bruschetta

Fennel has established itself as a deliciously versatile vegetable well beyond the boundaries of its native Italy, where it is eaten raw as a **digestivo**. This is the ideal recipe for converting anyone who remains unconvinced by fennel's charms.

15g (½oz) butter

1 tbsp olive oil

2 onions, peeled and finely sliced

2 fennel bulbs, trimmed, quartered and finely sliced

50ml (2fl oz) white wine

8 black olives, stoned and sliced

sea salt and freshly ground black pepper

4 large slices open-textured bread, cut 1cm (½in) thick

1 Melt the butter and olive oil in a non-stick heavy-bottomed pan. Stir in the sliced onions and fennel, and stew slowly for about 45 minutes, until the vegetables are golden brown and tender, stirring from time to time.

2 Add the wine and olives and continue cooking until the wine has bubbled away completely. Adjust the seasoning and keep the mixture warm.

3 Grill the bread until it is golden brown. Spoon the warm fennel mixture over the bread and serve at once.

SERVES 4

bruschetta con marmellata di cipolle rosse e pecorino

bruschetta with caramelized red onion and young pecorino

This recipe celebrates the young pecorino, which is gloriously sweet, and goes magnificently with the acidity of the onion marmalade. I enjoyed it at Buca San Petronio, a modern trattoria in central Bologna, run by a young couple called Giorgio and Antonia Fini. I loved it, as I did the incredibly memorable pasta served with wild herbs that followed.

3 tbsp fruity extra virgin olive oil, plus extra for serving

3 red onions, peeled and chopped

2 bay leaves

1 sprig fresh rosemary, leaves chopped

2 tbsp red wine vinegar

55g (2oz) soft brown sugar

4 slices open-textured bread, cut 1cm (1/2in) thick

4 handfuls mixed salad leaves

sea salt and freshly ground black pepper

125g (41/2oz) young pecorino cheese

1 Heat 2 tbsp of the olive oil in a frying pan, then add the onions, bay and rosemary. Brown the onions well over a low to medium heat, stirring regularly. Add the vinegar and stir well. Add the sugar and cook over a low heat for 30 minutes. The mixture should be thick, shiny and rich red. Leave to cool.

2 Heat a ridged cast-iron grill pan until hot. Add the bread slices and cook for 1-2 minutes on each side, until lightly toasted and charred at the edges. Put the salad leaves in a bowl and add 1 tbsp olive oil and seasoning to taste. Toss.

3 To serve, spread 1 tbsp of the red onion mixture on each piece of toast and put on to serving plates. Add a handful of leaves and crumble the pecorino on top. Sprinkle with more olive oil and some black pepper.

SERVES 4

crostini con tapenade
crostini with tapenade

Small pieces of baked bread are topped with delicious things and served as appetite-whetters in trattorias all over Italy, but particularly in Umbria and Tuscany, which is where I got this idea. Tapenade is associated with Provence, but politically and culinarily, this region and northern Italy were very close at one point, and many recipes are similar. This tapenade topping is my own, with some ground almonds adding a slightly different taste and texture.

6 slices day-old
coarse-textured bread

3 tbsp fine extra virgin
olive oil

TAPENADE
200g (7oz) stoned,
best-quality black olives

12 sun-dried tomatoes with
2 tbsp oil

a handful of fresh basil leaves

1 garlic clove, peeled

55g (2oz) oil-marinated
anchovies

55g (2oz) salted capers,
rinsed and dried

1 tbsp ground almonds

freshly ground black pepper

1 Place all the tapenade ingredients in a food processor and blend together to a coarse paste. This mixture may be kept in the refrigerator for several days and will get stronger and better.

2 Grill the bread until golden. Brush with oil and top with tapenade just before serving.

SERVES 6

crostini con verdure arrosto e mozzarella

crostini with roasted vegetables and mozzarella

In most trattorias throughout Italy, the bread oven is on permanently, so bread in some form or other will be on offer – plain to accompany the meal, or baked as crostini and topped with some speciality *della casa*.

1 x 55g (2oz) can
oil-marinated anchovies

1 tbsp extra virgin olive oil

1 small, thin, tender
courgette, cut into 1cm
(1/2in) dice

1 small yellow pepper, seeded
and cut into 1cm (1/2in) dice

1 small aubergine, cut into
1cm (1/2in) dice

1 small red onion, halved and
sliced through the root into
half moons

12 cherry tomatoes, skinned

1 garlic clove, peeled and
chopped

sea salt and freshly ground
black pepper

12 thin slices ciabatta bread
(see page 238)

2 x 150g packs mozzarella,
each sliced into 6 pieces

6 large fresh basil leaves,
roughly torn

1 Preheat the oven to 200ºC/400ºF/gas mark 6.

2 Drain the can of anchovies, reserving the oil. Mix this with the extra virgin olive oil. Snip the anchovies into small pieces or leave them whole, whichever you prefer.

3 Place the diced vegetables, onion and tomatoes on a shallow heavy-duty baking tray and add the garlic. Season and drizzle the oil over. Make sure everything gets a good coating. Place on a high shelf in oven for 30 minutes, or until toasted at the edges, then remove from the oven.

4 Place the bread slices on an oven tray and bake at the same temperature for 10 minutes. Remove the bread from the oven and turn the grill on to high. Cut the cheese to fit the bread slices as closely as possible and place on the baked bread. Grill for 2 minutes, until the cheese is just soft.

5 Divide the roasted vegetables and the anchovies between the crostini, pressing lightly into the cheese, and grill for a further 3 minutes, until the cheese just begins to bubble. Garnish with basil and black pepper.

SERVES 6

ciabatta

'slipper' bread

These breads are eye-catching because of their dusty crust and unusual shape, but they are more memorable for their extraordinary open texture and moist and chewy crumb. The Italian dialect word ciabatta translates as 'slipper', which gives you some idea of its shape, which is both flat and slightly puffy at the same time. To make successful ciabatta, you must have a dough that is so wet it is almost unmanageable. But persevere! The *biga* starter used here is different from many others because it relies on a larger volume of flour for its flavour. You will have some *biga* left over, but hopefully this can be passed on to an equally enthusiastic friend to be used.

BIG STARTER (MAKES ABOUT 1KG/2¼LB)

5g (1/8oz) fresh yeast

400ml (14fl oz) water

550-600g (1¼lb-1lb 5oz) strong white bread flour

DOUGH

10g (1/4oz) fresh yeast

500g (18oz) *biga* starter (see above)

15g (1/2oz) fine sea salt

approx. 300ml (10fl oz) warm water

500g (18oz) strong white bread flour, plus extra for dusting

2-3 tbsp olive oil, plus extra for greasing

1 Mix the *biga* ingredients together and beat with a spoon or your hand until a loose dough has formed with no dry flour lumps. You should feel an elastic feeling as the gluten forms. Cover carefully and leave to sit at room temperature for 24 hours. You will use half of it for the ciabatta.

2 For the dough, mix everything together, keeping the olive oil back until the dough is roughly formed and some gluten is beginning to develop. It should be such a wet and sticky dough that it continually adheres to your hand in large elastic lumps. For this reason, many people prefer to make the dough in a mixer or food processor. Persevere with your chosen method of kneading until the gluten is well formed and you have achieved that elasticity and springiness that marks a good dough.

3 Grease a large mixing bowl, bottom and sides, with liberal amounts of olive oil before dropping the dough into it and covering it carefully. The proving dough will be bathed in olive oil. During this rise, the dough will double or even triple its volume, taking 1½-2 hours to get there, perhaps even longer.

4 Ease the oily mass on to a well-floured work-surface, trying not to knock it down, thus keeping its puffiness and gas. With floured hands, divide it into four.

5 Grease two baking trays with olive oil. Gently roll each piece of dough in the flour on the surface and give it a hearty stretch as you pick it up to put it on the greased baking trays. (If you are going to bake it on a tile, put the stretched pieces on floured boards.) With the stretch you render each piece two or three times as long as it is wide. To push them flat, give them a few stabs with your fingertips, but don't be too vigorous or they'll be knocked down and toughened.

6 Cover the loaves loosely with cloths and cling film. Their final proving will take another hour. By the time they are ready to bake they will have risen, but not quite doubled in height. Although they still look oddly flat, don't worry; they will spring up in the oven.

7 Meanwhile, preheat the oven to 200°C/400°F/gas mark 6. Bake the loaves for barely 20 minutes.

MAKES 4 LOAVES

focaccia di olive e rosmarino

olive and rosemary focaccia

This classic Italian bread is flavoured with caramelized onion and garlic, and topped with olives, sea salt and rosemary before being baked. It is made with the usual strong white bread flour, but some wholemeal flour has been added, which gives more character to the dough. The bread is best served warm, drizzled with new season's olive oil. You could also make the bread without the additional flavourings.

2 large fresh rosemary sprigs

2 tbsp olive oil

1 onion, peeled, halved and sliced

2 garlic cloves, peeled and finely chopped

sea salt and coarsely ground black pepper

10 black olives, stoned and halved lengthways

DOUGH

7g (1/4oz) fresh yeast

225ml (8fl oz) warm water

280g (10oz) strong white bread flour, plus extra for dusting

1 tsp fine sea salt

25g (1oz) wholemeal flour

100g (31/2oz) *biga* starter (see page 238)

olive oil for greasing

1 Finely chop a third of the rosemary leaves; keep another third of them whole; divide the rest into tiny sprigs and set aside for the topping.

2 Heat the olive oil in a frying pan and sauté the onion and chopped rosemary for 10 minutes. Add the garlic and cook over a medium heat until the mixture caramelizes. Tip into a bowl and cool.

3 For the dough, dissolve the yeast in the warm water. Mix the white flour with the sea salt on the work-surface, pile into a mound and make a well in the centre. Add the wholemeal flour, *biga* and yeast liquid to the well, then gradually draw in the white flour with your hands and combine into a dough, adding a little extra water if necessary.

4 Knead the dough for 10 minutes until smooth and elastic, then add half the caramelized onion and continue to knead for 10 minutes. Do the stretch test to check that the dough is ready (see page 228). Place in a lightly oiled large bowl and turn the dough to coat it in the oil. Cover with a tea-towel and leave in a warm place for 2 hours, or until almost doubled in bulk.

5 Tip the dough out on to a lightly floured surface and gently knead into a round ball. Place on a well-oiled large baking tray. Cover and allow to rest for 15 minutes, then flatten the dough, using the palm of your hand, to a 20cm (8in) round.

6 Mix the rosemary leaves with the remaining onion mixture and spread it evenly over the surface of the dough. Season generously with pepper. Cover to prevent a skin forming and leave to prove for 2 hours.

7 Preheat the oven to 200°C/400°F/gas mark 6.

8 Stud the dough with the olives and scatter with sea salt. Bake for 15-18 minutes, until golden. Transfer to a wire rack to cool slightly and serve warm, scattered with rosemary.

MAKES 1 LARGE LOAF

impasto per focaccina
basic focaccina

This rich, yeasty bread is a relation of focaccia, but is much thinner, lighter, crisper and crunchier. It can be baked and eaten with soup or by itself, and it is wonderful with a final sprinkling of olive oil and herbs. It is also delicious when stuffed and baked as a sandwich (see opposite). If you ever have any dough left over, wrap it in cling film and store it in the fridge; it will keep for a couple of days. One filled *focaccina* will feed two people.

15g (1/2oz) fresh yeast

225ml (8fl oz) warm water

400g (14oz) strong white bread flour, plus extra for dusting

2 tsp fine sea salt

1 tbsp olive oil, plus extra for brushing

sea salt and freshly ground black pepper

1 tbsp extra virgin olive oil

1 Combine the yeast with a little of the warm water, and stir until dissolved. Put the flour and salt into a large bowl, and make a well in the centre. Add the remaining water, the yeast and the oil, and mix to a dough. Turn it out on to a floured board and knead for 12 minutes, until smooth and elastic. Cover with a damp tea-towel and allow to rest for 12 minutes.

2 Divide the dough into four equal portions and shape each into a ball. Stretch each ball into a 1cm (1/2in) thick x 23cm (9in) diameter circle and place on a baking tray. Cover with a damp tea-towel and allow to rest for $1^1/_2$ hours at room temperature, or until it is doubled in size.

3 Flatten the dough with your hands and use your thumb to form little pockets. Brush the *focaccine* with a little olive oil and sprinkle with sea salt and black pepper. Cover and allow to rise for another hour.

4 Meanwhile, preheat the oven to 200°C/400°F/gas mark 6.

5 Bake the focaccine for 10-12 minutes, until golden. Sprinkle with the extra virgin olive oil as it comes out of the oven. Cool.

MAKES 4

focaccina di caprino e verdure grigliate
goat's cheese and grilled vegetable focaccina

This delicious *focaccina* sandwich is a typical lunchtime dish in many trattorias. Try to find really good extra virgin olive oil for this dish. Use one of the *focaccine* (left) to serve two.

2 fine courgette slices, cut lengthwise

2 fine aubergine slices

1 slice each of red and yellow pepper

a handful of fresh flat-leaf parsley leaves, finely chopped

4 tbsp fine extra virgin olive oil, plus extra for sprinkling

1 *focaccina* (see opposite)

125g (4½oz) fresh tasty goat's cheese

3-4 sun-dried tomatoes, drained and cut into strips

sea salt and freshly ground black pepper

1 Marinate the vegetables and parsley in the olive oil for 1 hour. Meanwhile, preheat the oven to 150°C/300°F/gas mark 2.

2 Grill the vegetables at a medium to hot heat until lightly browned, either under the grill or on a ridged cast-iron grill pan. Turn after 2-3 minutes.

3 Cut the *focaccina* in half horizontally. Spread one-half with goat's cheese, top with grilled vegetables and sun-dried tomatoes, and season. Place on a baking sheet, put the top on and bake for 3-4 minutes only.

4 Sprinkle with extra virgin olive oil and halve or cut into wedges.

focaccia all'olio e salvia

sage and olive oil bread

This version of *focaccia* is made by the sponge method, which is a quicker version of *biga*. The use of the wine may seem unusual, but it acts as an extra ferment, adds a deeper flavour, and helps to give the bread a light, porous texture. The sage crisps on the top in the oven, and looks and tastes marvellous.

SPONGE

20g (³/₄oz) fresh yeast

125ml (4¹/₂fl oz) warm water

150g (5¹/₂oz) strong white bread flour

DOUGH

90ml (3fl oz) dry white wine

90ml (3fl oz) light olive oil

20 fresh sage leaves, chopped

15g (¹/₂oz) fresh yeast

350g (12oz) strong white bread flour, plus extra for dusting

2 tsp fine sea salt

olive oil for greasing

TOPPING

2 tbsp good-flavoured olive oil

1-2 tsp coarse sea salt

4 fresh sage leaves, chopped

1 To make the sponge, sprinkle the yeast over the warm water in a large mixing bowl, whisk it in and let it stand until it is creamy, about 10 minutes. Stir in the flour and beat until smooth. Cover tightly with cling film and leave it to rise until puffy and bubbling, about 30 minutes.

2 To make the dough, add the wine, olive oil, sage and yeast to the sponge mixture, then whisk in the flour and salt, just a little at a time, until the dough is very soft and sticky. Knead on a lightly floured surface, adding more flour if necessary. It should be soft but not wet.

3 Place the dough in a lightly oiled container, cover tightly, and let it rise for 20 minutes.

4 Knock the dough back, and roll it out to a circle about 5mm (¹/₄in) thick. Place it on an oiled baking sheet, cover it and leave it to rise for an hour.

5 At least 30 minutes before you plan to bake, preheat the oven to 200°C/400°F/gas mark 6. Put a baking stone inside the oven if you have one.

6 Dimple the top of the bread. Drizzle over the oil and sprinkle with salt and fresh sage.

7 Place the bread in the well preheated oven (on the baking stone if appropriate). Spray the oven with cold water from a spritzer three times during the first 10 minutes of cooking. Bake for 25-30 minutes, until golden brown. Remove from the oven and cool.

SERVES 4

torta al testo

bread of the tile

The flat, crusty appearance of this age-old peasant bread inspired its name, '***testo***', which means 'tile' in Italian. ***Torta al testo*** is found exclusively in its native Umbria and usually a ***casa***, in the home. This one is stuffed, which adds an extra dimension, and it would be delicious served with the Savoy chicken stew on page 185. You could use Gruyère or Emmental cheese if you can't get hold of fontina: you want a cheese with a high fat content and a low melting point.

15g (1/2oz) fresh yeast

315ml (101/2fl oz) warm water

500g (18oz) strong white bread flour, plus extra for dusting

11/2 tsp fine sea salt

1 tbsp olive oil

FILLING

250g (9oz) fontina cheese

125g (41/2oz) rocket leaves

sea salt and freshly ground black pepper

1 Dissolve the yeast in some of the water. Leave for 5 minutes, then stir to dissolve. Mix the flour and salt together in a large bowl. Make a well in the centre and add the yeasted water and the oil. Mix in the flour and stir in the reserved water as needed to form a firm, moist dough.

2 Turn the dough out on to a lightly floured surface and knead until smooth, shiny and elastic, about 10 minutes.

3 Put the dough in a clean bowl and cover with a tea-towel. Leave to rise until doubled in size, about 30 minutes. Knock back, then leave to rest for 10 minutes.

4 Divide the dough into 8 pieces. On a lightly floured surface, roll out each piece of dough to form a round 20cm (8in) across and 5mm (1/4in) thick. If the dough resists rolling out, leave to rest for 1-2 minutes, then continue.

5 Heat a heavy frying pan or griddle over a medium/low heat until very hot, about 10 minutes. Preheat the oven to 200°C/400°F/gas mark 6.

6 Place one of the dough rounds in the hot pan and prick all over with a fork to prevent air bubbles. Cook until golden on both sides, flipping it over frequently to avoid scorching and to aid even cooking. Repeat with the remaining dough rounds.

7 Stack the rounds on top of each other and cover with a tea-towel to keep them soft. When cool, use a sharp knife to cut around the edge of each bread, and separate it into 2 halves. Top one-half with fontina and rocket and season with salt and pepper.

8 Place the other half on top of the filling and place the stuffed breads on two baking sheets. Bake until hot and the cheese has melted. Cut into wedges and serve warm.

MAKES 8 ROUNDS

schiacciata con ricotta
ricotta flatbread

This is an Umbrian recipe, from a charming *trattoria* owned by Gianfranco Vissani. His bread is memorable, and the *trattoria* is well worth a visit. Any good *trattoria* will make its own bread, of course, and this would be a morning ritual. You could add anything to this bread – crispy bits of pancetta, walnuts, raisins and figs, for instance – but the ricotta is a basic, giving the bread a wonderful texture. In fact this bread can be as interesting as you are!

15g (¹/₂oz) fresh yeast

250ml (9fl oz) warm water

240g (8¹/₂oz) fresh ricotta cheese, at room temperature

3 tsp fine sea salt

a pinch of fennel seeds

400-450g (14-16oz) strong white bread flour, plus extra for dusting

about 2 tbsp olive oil, plus extra for greasing

EGG WASH

1 large egg yolk

1 tsp water

1 To make the bread dough, dissolve the yeast in some of the water in a large bowl. Stir in the ricotta, salt and fennel seeds. Add the flour little by little, using only enough flour to make a soft dough.

2 Turn the dough out on to a lightly floured work-surface, and knead for 10 minutes, incorporating more flour if necessary to keep it from sticking. The dough should be smooth and tender. Transfer to a large bowl and drizzle the olive oil over it. Rub the oil over the dough's surface, cover the bowl with a damp cloth, and leave for 1 hour, until the dough has doubled in size.

3 Preheat the oven to 200°C/400°F/gas mark 6, and oil a large baking sheet.

4 When the dough is ready, turn it out on to a lightly floured work-surface and knead for 2 minutes. Flour the dough lightly, wrap in cling film, and rest it for 5 minutes.

5 Flatten the dough with a rolling pin and shape it into a 33 x 20cm (13 x 8in) oval. Transfer to the greased baking sheet. Cut an 18cm (7in) long slit lengthwise through the centre of the dough to the baking sheet, but do not cut the ends. Spread the split open slightly. Cover the dough with a tea-towel and let it rest for 15 minutes more.

6 Make the egg wash by beating the egg yolk and water in a small bowl. Brush the egg wash over the surface of the dough. Bake the bread on the centre shelf of the oven for 25-30 minutes, or until rich brown and cooked through. Turn the bread on its side and knock on the bottom. If done, the bread will make a hollow sound. Cool the bread on a cooling rack. I break it in half before serving it.

MAKES 2 LOAVES, TO SERVE 8

pane con timo o olive

thyme and olive bread

I found this recipe when I was on a food-tasting trip in Liguria and, of the many olive breads we tried, this was our favourite – perhaps because of the wonderful flavour of the Ligurian thyme. Do use the best olives you can find, preferably ones you have marinated yourself. The bottled water may seem odd here, but it really does improve the flavour.

15g (½oz) fresh yeast

200-250ml (7-9fl oz) bottled water, hand-hot

450g (1lb) strong white bread flour, plus extra for dusting

½ tsp fine sea salt

3 tbsp olive oil, plus extra for greasing

150g (5½oz) black olives, stoned and chopped

6 sprigs fresh thyme, leaves stripped from the stalks

1 Mix the yeast and 50ml (2fl oz) of the warm water. Cover and leave to froth for 15 minutes.

2 Put the flour and salt in a large bowl and make a well in the centre. Add the olive oil and the frothy yeast to the well along with most of the remaining water, and mix together to a stiff, sticky dough. Add the remaining water. Knead on a lightly floured surface for 10 minutes, until smooth and elastic.

3 Add the olives and thyme leaves and knead into the dough. Cover the bowl with a damp cloth and leave in a warm place to rise for 1½ hours.

4 Knead the dough again for a few minutes, then divide it into 4 balls. Place the balls on an oiled baking tray. Press down gently and shape any way you like. Let the dough rise again, covered, for about half an hour.

5 Preheat the oven to 200°C/400°F/gas mark 6.

6 Brush the loaves with water to soften the crust and bake for 30 minutes. Cool on a wire rack.

MAKES 4 SMALL LOAVES

impasto per pizza

basic pizza dough

Pizzas are quintessential *trattoria* fare. This recipe will yield two individual-sized pizzas, approximately 25cm (10in) in diameter. Extra dough balls can be frozen for up to two months.

15g (¹/₂oz) fresh yeast or
1¹/₂ tsp easy-blend dried yeast

50ml (2fl oz) body temperature water

250g (9oz) strong white bread flour, plus extra for dusting

¹/₂ tsp fine sea salt

50ml (2fl oz) olive oil, plus extra for greasing

semolina for sprinkling

1 Blend the yeast with a little water. Sift the flour and salt into a large bowl. Make a well in the centre and add the oil, yeast liquid and some more water. Mix with a wooden spoon, gradually adding the remaining water to form a soft dough. If using easy-blend dried yeast, mix in with the flour, then add the water as above.

2 Turn the dough on to a lightly floured surface and knead for 10 minutes, until it is soft. Don't be afraid of adding flour. Place in a lightly oiled large bowl, then turn the dough around to coat with the oil. Cover the bowl with a clean tea-towel and leave in a warm place for 1¹/₂ hours, or until the dough has doubled in size.

3 Preheat the oven to 200°C/400°F/gas mark 6. In the bottom of the oven, oil and preheat 2 baking sheets.

4 Knock down the dough with your knuckles, then turn on to a lightly floured surface and knead for 2-3 minutes to knock out the air bubbles. Divide the dough in half.

5 On a lightly floured surface, preferably marble, roll out the pieces of dough very, very thinly until 25-30cm (10-12in) in diameter (they should be as thin as a paper napkin folded in four). Lift each pizza on to a rimless cold baking sheet sprinkled generously with semolina. Add your chosen topping, then slide from the rimless baking sheet on to the hot baking sheets or pizza stone. Bake as directed in the individual recipes.

MAKES 2 X 25CM (10IN) PIZZA BASES

salsa di pomodoro crudo

uncooked tomato sauce for pizza

This is one of the most basic sauces in the Italian culinary vocabulary, but the hour's marination is crucial for the development of a full flavour.

750g (1lb 10oz) fresh plum tomatoes

6 fresh basil leaves, torn

sea salt and freshly ground black pepper

1 Skin the tomatoes by cutting a nick in the skin, then plunging them into boiling water for a few seconds. Remove and plunge into cold water. Slip the skins off, then seed and chop the flesh finely.

2 Simply mix the tomato with the basil and some salt and pepper to taste. Set aside for an hour before using.

ENOUGH FOR 2 PIZZAS

calzone di prezzemolo

folded parsley pizza

The literal translation of **calzone** is 'trouser leg', referring to the double thickness of fabric or, in this case, bread dough. The recipe comes from the Bar Mundial in Cassibile, Sicily, so thank you, Gianni Fronterrè. It is lighter than you might expect, not as doughy as many other **calzoni**, and the filling, despite being incredibly simple, is quite delicious. It's also not quite the shape you might imagine, but it's typically Sicilian.

1 quantity basic pizza dough
(see opposite)

olive oil for greasing

plain flour for dusting

FILLING

50ml (2fl oz) olive oil

1 onion, peeled and chopped

a very large handful of fresh
flat-leaf parsley, chopped

freshly ground black pepper

275g (9½oz) mozzarella
cheese, cut into small cubes

1 Preheat the oven to 200°C/400°F/gas mark 6. Prepare the filling by heating the olive oil in a frying pan. Fry the onion until soft, then add the parsley and stir for 2 minutes over a medium heat. Season with pepper and leave to one side. When cool, mix in the cheese.

2 When the dough has doubled in size, knock it back and knead for 4 minutes. Roll out into a rectangle 38 x 20cm (15 x 8in). Spread the onion mixture over the dough, leaving a 1cm (½in) margin all round.

3 Fold the dough lengthways into three, bringing the ends over to enclose the filling, and place on a greased tray. Leave for 10 minutes to rise again and then dust with extra plain flour.

4 Bake for 20 minutes, until light and golden. Cool on a wire rack and then cut into thick or thin slices, for snacks or canapés. Good hot, cold or warm!

MAKES 1 LARGE CALZONE, TO SERVE 2

pizza puttanesca

pizza with spicy tomato, olives and capers

This is my spicy pizza. It gets its zest from the famous southern Italian puttanesca sauce.

2 uncooked basic pizza dough
bases (see opposite)

olive oil for greasing

6 tbsp uncooked tomato sauce
for pizza (see opposite)

15 Ligurian black olives

1 garlic clove, peeled,

4 oil-marinated anchovies

1 tsp salted capers, soaked
and dried

1-2 tsp dried chilli

1 Preheat the oven to the highest it will go, and oil and preheat 2 large baking sheets or preheat a pizza baking stone.

2 Spread the tomato sauce over the pizza dough. Stone the olives and chop the garlic. Arrange the garlic, anchovies, olives, capers and chilli on top.

3 Slide the bases on to the hot baking sheets or baking stone and then into the preheated oven. Bake until the crust is crisp and golden, about 12-15 minutes. Serve with freshly ground black pepper if desired.

SERVES 2

pizza di Sardegna
Sardinian pizza

The pizza was born in Naples, but it has travelled all over mainland Italy and the islands. This one is popular in Sardinia and along the Riviera. The saltiness of the anchovies goes wonderfully with the new season's tomatoes – but don't use any cheese; you don't need it with fish. The traditional Sardinian pizza dough is made with butter, egg and oil, but I haven't had much success with it. It's delicious, though, made using my own pizza dough.

2 uncooked basic pizza dough bases (see page 248)

olive oil for greasing

TOPPING

5 tbsp olive oil

750g (1lb 10oz) onions, peeled and finely sliced

500g (18oz) ripe tomatoes, skinned and roughly chopped

sea salt and freshly ground black pepper

55g (2oz) oil-marinated anchovy fillets

a few black olives, halved and stoned

a handful of fresh oregano leaves

1 To make the topping, heat the olive oil in a heavy pan and fry the onion gently, covered, stirring now and then, until soft, about 20 minutes. Add the tomatoes and seasoning and cook, uncovered, until the sauce is thick. Leave to become cold.

2 Meanwhile, preheat the oven to the highest it will go, and oil and preheat large baking sheets or preheat a pizza baking stone.

3 When the topping is cold, divide it between the pizzas, spreading it evenly. Criss-cross the surface with strips of anchovy and put halves of stoned olives in the spaces. Sprinkle with oregano and bake for 12-15 minutes, until golden brown and bubbling.

SERVES 2

pizza con funghi selvatici

pizza with wild mushrooms

This is a very aromatic and flavoursome pizza, particularly suited to the cold months of the year, when wild mushrooms are in season. I worked once in a ***trattoria*** in Umbria for a while, and noticed that this one, or one very similar, was by far the most popular. The dried porcini mushrooms enrich the texture and flavour.

2 uncooked basic pizza dough bases (see page 248)

olive oil for greasing

TOPPING

1 tbsp olive oil

1/2 garlic clove, peeled and chopped

175g (6oz) fresh wild mushrooms, cleaned and coarsely chopped

15g (1/2oz) dried porcini mushrooms (ceps), soaked in water for 30 minutes

a handful of fresh flat-leaf parsley leaves, roughly chopped

4 tbsp uncooked tomato sauce (see page 248)

150g (51/2oz) mozzarella cheese, cubed

freshly ground black pepper

1 Preheat the oven to the highest it will go, and oil and preheat 2 baking sheets or preheat a baking stone.

2 In a frying pan, heat the olive oil, then add the garlic and sauté over a medium heat until lightly golden. Add the mushrooms and drained porcini and sauté for 5-7 minutes over a medium heat. Sprinkle with parsley.

3 Spread the tomato sauce over the pizza dough bases. Top with the mozzarella cheese and a layer of the sautéed mushrooms.

4 Slide the pizzas on to the hot baking sheets or baking stone and bake until bubbly, about 12-15 minutes. Serve with a twist of black pepper.

SERVES 2

pizza ai quattro formaggi

pizza with four cheeses

This is a classic pizza. It does not call for tomato sauce. I like this combination of cheeses because the spicy and sweet flavours are well balanced, but you can substitute any Italian cheeses you like.

2 uncooked basic pizza dough bases (see page 248)

olive oil for greasing

TOPPING

55g (2oz) fontina cheese, cubed

85g (3oz) mozzarella cheese, cubed

55g (2oz) Gorgonzola cheese, cubed

55g (2oz) provolone cheese, shredded

freshly ground black pepper (optional)

1 Preheat the oven to the highest it will go, and oil and preheat 2 large baking sheets or preheat a baking stone.

2 Cover each quarter of each dough base with a different variety of cheese.

3 Slide the pizza on to the heated pizza stone or baking sheets and bake until the crust is golden and the cheeses are bubbly, about 12-15 minutes. Serve with pepper if desired.

SERVES 2

pizza bianca

white pizza

Here I have given a different pizza dough from the classic one on page 248. This one uses a *biga* starter, which contributes to and enhances the flavour of the dough. A typical Roman pizza would have many classic toppings, but this is the poor man's version, relying solely on the flavours of good oil, salt and rosemary. I often serve this when I'm cooking lunch for a large party of my pupils, as it's light, goes so well with so many dishes, and is easy on the digestion. It's actually more like a bread than a pizza.

BIGA STARTER

2.5g (¹/₁₆oz) fresh yeast

150ml (5fl oz) warm water

125g (4¹/₂oz) strong white bread flour

DOUGH

10g (¹/₄oz) fresh yeast

175ml (6fl oz) warm water

1¹/₂ tsp fine sea salt

375g (13oz) strong white bread flour

3 tbsp olive oil, plus extra for greasing

TO FINISH

olive oil

sea salt

fresh rosemary leaves

1 To make the *biga*, dissolve the yeast in the warm water. Add the flour and mix to a smooth, thick batter. Cover and leave to ferment at room temperature for 24 hours, until loose and bubbling.

2 To make the dough, dissolve the fresh yeast in half the warm water.

3 In a large bowl, mix the salt into the flour. Make a well in the centre, then pour in the yeast mixture, olive oil and *biga*, and combine. Add the remaining water, and mix to form a soft, sticky dough, adding extra water if necessary.

4 Turn the dough on to a floured surface and knead until smooth, silky and elastic, about 10 minutes. Place the dough in a clean oiled bowl, cover and leave to rise until doubled in size, about 1¹/₂-2 hours.

5 Knock back and chafe briefly (see page 228), then rest it for 10 minutes.

6 Roll the dough out to a thickness of about 3mm (¹/₈in). Place on an oiled baking sheet, cover and leave to prove until doubled in size, about 30 minutes.

7 Preheat the oven to 200°C/400°F/gas mark 6. Press the top of the dough with your fingers to form dimples. Sprinkle with olive oil, sea salt and rosemary.

8 Bake for 20 minutes, or until crisp and golden. Serve straight from the oven.

SERVES 4

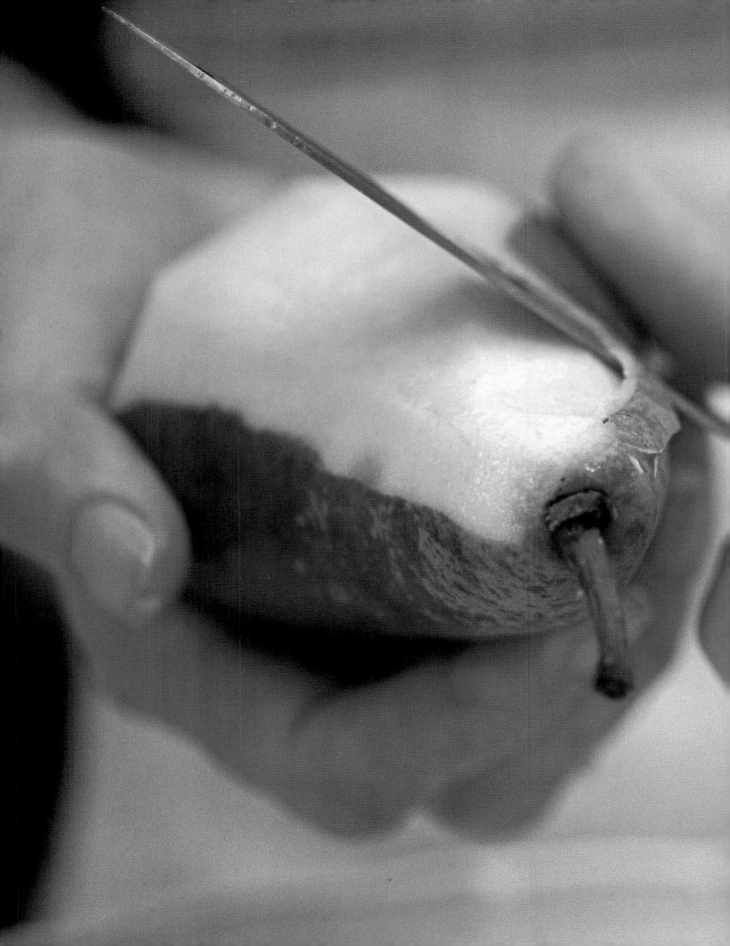

puddings, cakes, biscuits and sweets

torta di cioccolata

chocolate cheesecake

This pudding is for all chocolate and cheesecake lovers, and has a dense, fudgy texture.
I first encountered it in Perugia, in a bar called Sandri. Because the bar was so busy,
I couldn't get any details of the recipe, so I have made it up – but I think I have managed
to capture the richness of that wonderful chocolate experience!

400g (14oz) darkest, best chocolate, with at least 70% cocoa solids, broken into pieces

250g (9oz) unsalted butter

5 large eggs

4 tbsp dark muscovado sugar

125g (4¹/₂oz) ground almonds

125g (4¹/₂oz) Italian '00' plain flour

1 tsp baking powder

2 tsp pure vanilla extract

CHOCOLATE GLAZE

125ml (4fl oz) single cream

125g (4¹/₂oz) darkest, best chocolate as above, chopped

TO SERVE

85g (3oz) mixed berries, chilled

150ml (5fl oz) double cream, whipped

1 Preheat the oven to 160°C/325°F/gas mark 3, and grease and base-line a 23cm (9in) cake tin.

2 Place the chocolate and butter in a bowl over a saucepan of simmering water. Do not let the bottom of the bowl touch the water. Stir until smooth. Set the mixture aside.

3 Place the eggs and sugar in a bowl and beat until light and fluffy, about 6 minutes. Fold in the almonds, flour, baking powder, vanilla and chocolate mixture. Mix well.

4 Pour the mixture into the prepared cake tin and bake for 45 minutes, or until the cake is cooked when tested with a skewer. Cool the cake in the tin.

5 To make the chocolate glaze, heat the cream in a saucepan until almost boiling, then remove from the heat. Stir in the chocolate and continue stirring until the chocolate has melted and is smooth.

6 Spread the cake with the chocolate glaze, cut into wedges and serve with the chilled berries and cream.

SERVES 6

mousse di cioccolato

chocolate mousse

This mousse has an almost chocolate-truffle-type consistency, and is very, very rich. The recipe was given to me by my friend Claudio, who lives in Perugia.

175g (6oz) dark chocolate
with 70% cocoa solids

450ml (16fl oz) whipping
cream

2 large eggs, separated

55g (2oz) shelled hazelnuts,
toasted and chopped

1 Break the chocolate into pieces and put in a heatproof bowl over a saucepan of barely simmering water. Do not let the bottom of the bowl touch the water. As soon as the chocolate has melted, remove the bowl from the heat and leave until it has cooled but is still liquid.

2 Whip the cream until it just holds its shape. Fold in the beaten egg yolks. Whisk the egg whites until they are stiff but not dry.

3 Fold the cream into the chocolate, followed by the chopped hazelnuts. Lastly, fold in the egg whites.

4 Spoon into a serving dish and chill in the fridge for 4 hours before serving.

SERVES 6-8

brutti ma buoni

'bad but good' nutty meringues

In Italy we eat a lot of small cakes or biscuits, particularly after the siesta, to give us a burst of energy. Often they are taken to a friend's house and shared over a cup of coffee and lots of gossip. Wrapped in coloured cellophane, they make wonderful presents.

4 large egg whites

55g (2oz) vanilla sugar

30g (1¼oz) whole almonds, toasted

30g (1¼oz) whole hazelnuts, toasted

1 Preheat the oven to 110°C/225°F/gas mark ¼. Line a baking tray with parchment paper.

2 Whisk the egg whites until fluffy, gradually adding the sugar. Never add the sugar all at once as the egg white mixture will collapse.

3 Roughly chop the nuts, and fold them carefully into the meringue mixture.

4 Spoon 2 tsp for each meringue on to the parchment-lined tray, and bake for 1½ hours, until you get crisp mounds.

5 Leave to cool, then tuck in, or store in airtight tins.

SERVES 6-8

zuppa Inglese
cream and marsala trifle

There are many variations of this popular dessert, which is served in many restaurants throughout Italy. Loosely translated, the Italian name means 'English soup', but in fact it is a rich creamy trifle, which is served mostly at Christmas time.

melted butter for greasing

CAKE
3 eggs
115g (4oz) caster sugar
115g (4oz) plain white or Italian '00' plain flour
1/2 tsp baking powder
3 tbsp Marsala

CRÈME ANGLAISE
450ml (16fl oz) milk
4 egg yolks
85g (3oz) caster sugar
1/2 tsp salt
1 tsp pure vanilla extract
finely grated zest of 1/2 unwaxed lemon

TOPPING
300ml (10fl oz) double cream
a few toasted flaked almonds

1 Preheat the oven to 180°C/350°F/gas mark 4. Brush a 20cm (8in) springform cake tin well with a little melted butter.

2 For the cake, beat together the eggs and sugar for 10-15 minutes, until thick and creamy. Sift the flour and baking powder together then, using a metal spoon, fold into the egg mixture.

3 Spoon the mixture into the prepared tin and bake for 20 minutes, until the cake is golden and has shrunk away from the sides of the tin. Leave it to cool in the tin.

4 When cool, remove the cake from the tin and break it up into bite-sized pieces. Place in a large serving bowl or individual serving dishes. Pour over the Marsala and set aside.

5 Meanwhile, prepare the *crème Anglaise*. In a saucepan, bring the milk to just below boiling point and keep it hot. In a bowl, whisk together the egg yolks, sugar and salt until pale and fluffy. Pour in the hot milk, stirring with a wooden spoon. Return the mixture to a clean pan and heat gently, stirring all the time, until the mixture thickens and coats the back of a wooden spoon. Stir in the vanilla extract and lemon zest and pour over the cake. Leave until cold.

6 When cold, whip the cream until it holds its shape, and then use to cover the *crème Anglaise*. Scatter over the almonds to decorate.

Serves 8

pannacotta

'cooked cream'

This dessert is eaten mainly in the north of Italy, where dairy produce is used to a great extent. It is very rich, so servings are small, and I like to serve it with a purée of apricots that have been soaked in brandy and lemon juice. It isn't cooked at all, despite its Italian name, but set with a setting agent.

300ml (10fl oz) double cream

2 tbsp caster sugar, or more to taste

8 drops pure vanilla extract

2 tsp agar agar or 1 tbsp powdered gelatine

1 Put the cream, sugar and vanilla in a saucepan and simmer for 2-3 minutes.

2 Dissolve the agar agar or gelatine in about 2 tbsp warm water. Beat well into the cream.

3 Pour into a small serving bowl or 4 individual bowls or ramekin dishes. Chill in the fridge for 2-3 hours before serving.

Serves 4

zabaione

zabaglione

This is a most fabulous Sicilian pudding. The delicious foam is so rich, it is best accompanied by fresh fruit. It was once prescribed by Italian doctors as a pick-me-up, and was often eaten for breakfast. It really does produce a good, warm feeling. Be careful when making it, as the egg yolks can so easily be affected by too much heat and not enough stirring (see page 266).

2 large egg yolks

2 tbsp caster sugar

2 tbsp Marsala

1 Put the egg yolks and sugar in a large heatproof bowl, or in the top pan of a double boiler, and whisk together. When the mixture starts to thicken, place the bowl over a saucepan of gently simmering water.

2 Add the Marsala and whisk continuously until the mixture becomes thick, hot and foamy.

3 Spoon the zabaglione into serving dishes and serve at once.

SERVES 2

making custard

The Italian culinary repertoire is rich in custard-based desserts and pastries, which are often bought from the *pasticceria*, in the morning to have with coffee and in the afternoon as a *merenda* (snack), and which are also eaten on special occasions. Ice-creams – the famed *gelati* of Italy – are usually made with a custard base too, and one of the most famous Italian desserts, *zabaione* (zabaglione), is also based on a type of custard.

What unites all the types of sweet custard is the magical chemistry of eggs, which when whisked create a sublime airiness and when heated set in varying degrees. Egg yolks can be transformed into liquid sauces, and they can set into soft baked gels or creams. Egg whites, when whisked with sugar, can turn into light-as-air, crisp meringues (*amaretti*), and they give mousses and soufflés their airy texture and can be whisked into fruit juices and syrups to make sorbets. Indeed, I think the reason why Italian custards are so wonderful is because Italian eggs are so good. If you can't get hold of fresh Italian eggs, try to use the freshest, free-range, possibly organic eggs that you can lay your hands on. When I use Italian eggs, my pasta is richer and yellower, as are my custards.

The Italians don't have a word for custard, unless they call it *crema*, or *crema di uova e latte* (cream of eggs and milk). Neither do the French, but they have deemed it *crème Anglaise*, which perhaps gives a clue as to where they think the sauce originated from! The Italians make a form of *crème Anglaise*, which is an amalgam of milk, egg yolks and sugar. This is their classic sauce for serving hot with hot puddings or cold as an accompaniment for cakes, tarts and other cold desserts, and it is also the basis of what the Italians call *zuppa Inglese* (a trifle, an English influence again). When a basic sauce *Anglaise* is made with cream as well as, or instead of, milk, it is the basis for the best *gelati* (ice-creams).

The Italians also make a *crema pasticciera* (known elsewhere as *crème pâtissière*, pastry cream, or sometimes confectioner's custard). This is a thicker sauce, made using eggs, sugar, and milk and/or cream, as well as some flour or cornflour to act as a thickener. It is used as a filling for crisp pastries, in cakes, or as the soft sweet layer between a pastry case and some sharp fruit.

Custard-making can be quite fraught, as egg yolks are affected so easily by heat. I would advise that you always try to make a custard in a double boiler, which means the heat is not so intense. Always whip your egg yolks with the sugar first: the sugar somehow helps prevent the egg yolks from coagulating (turning into scrambled egg), and makes them better able to withstand heat and thicken in a smooth way. (Sugar has a different effect when you are freezing a custard as ice-cream: it reduces the size of the ice crystals – think of the coarseness of granite, which is low in sugar.) Always have the heat very low – this is especially important when making zabaglione, which is made with only two custard ingredients: egg yolks and sugar, with the addition of Marsala. Keep stirring!

gelato di cioccolato

chocolate ice-cream

This chapter would not be complete without a recipe for chocolate ice-cream, and this one is for chocolate lovers everywhere. My friend Claudio does not freeze the mixture, but serves it as a delicious mousse.

225g (8oz) dark chocolate with 70% cocoa solids

3 tbsp milk

6 large eggs, separated

4 tbsp brandy (optional)

300ml (10fl oz) whipping cream

1 Break the chocolate into a heatproof bowl and add the milk. Stand the bowl over a saucepan of simmering water and heat until the chocolate has melted. Do not let the bottom of the bowl touch the water. Remove from the heat and leave to cool slightly.

2 Beat the egg yolks into the mixture, one at a time, then add the brandy, if using. Leave to cool.

3 Whip the cream until it holds its shape, then fold into the chocolate mixture. Whisk the egg whites until stiff, then fold these into the mixture too.

4 Pour the mixture into an ice-cream machine and freeze according to the manufacturer's instructions. Alternatively, pour the mixture into a shallow freezer container and freeze, covered, for an hour. Turn the mixture into a chilled bowl and whisk until smooth. Return to the container, freeze again until mushy, then whisk again. Return to the freezer to become firm. Cover the container with a lid. Transfer to the fridge 45 minutes before serving.

SERVES 2

spumone di caffé

coffee and cinnamon ice-cream

This is a Neapolitan ice-cream made with cream, custard and ground coffee. A *spumone* is a lighter, softer ice-cream that will never entirely freeze because of its fat content. The use of ground coffee may sound unusual, but I guarantee you'll be delighted by the results. You could serve this with the almond biscuits on page 292.

4 large egg yolks

115g (4oz) caster sugar

1/2 tsp powdered cinnamon

3 tbsp finely ground Italian coffee

750ml (1 pint 7fl oz) double cream

1 Put the egg yolks, sugar, cinnamon and coffee in a heatproof bowl and beat well together.

2 Place the bowl over a saucepan of simmering water – the bowl should not touch the water – and, using an electric whisk, mix until doubled in volume. Remove the bowl from the heat and continue whisking until cool.

3 Whip the cream until it just holds its shape, then fold into the egg mixture.

4 Pour the mixture into an ice-cream machine and freeze according to the manufacturer's instructions. Alternatively pour the mixture into a shallow freezer container and freeze, covered, for an hour. Turn the mixture into a chilled bowl and whisk until smooth. Return to the container, freeze again until mushy, then whisk again. Return to the freezer to become firm. Cover the container with a lid. Transfer to the fridge 45 minutes before serving.

SERVES 6

semifreddo con nocciole e salsa frangelico

hazelnut semifreddo with chocolate and frangelico sauce

Every *trattoria* has a selection of ice-creams on its menu. A *semifreddo* is a more elegant version of a *gelato*.

175g (6oz) caster sugar

2 tbsp water

125g (4½oz) shelled hazelnuts, toasted and finely chopped

275ml (9fl oz) double cream

3 large egg whites

3 tbsp *Frangelico* (a hazelnut liqueur)

SAUCE

25ml (1fl oz) double cream

100g (3½oz) bitter chocolate, with 70% cocoa solids, coarsely chopped

½ tsp pure vanilla extract

a pinch of sea salt

2 tbsp *Frangelico*

1 Line 8 ramekins with cling film, leaving a 7.5cm (3in) overhang.

2 Put half the sugar into a small saucepan, stir in the water and bring to a boil over a moderate heat. Simmer, brushing down the sides of the saucepan with a wet pastry brush, until a deep caramel forms, about 5 minutes. Remove the pan from the heat and, using a wooden spoon, stir in the nuts. Immediately scrape the mixture on to an oiled baking sheet and let it cool until it is hard. Break the praline into small pieces and transfer to a food processor. Grind to a coarse powder.

3 In a stainless-steel bowl, whip the cream until it holds firm peaks, then refrigerate. In a large stainless-steel bowl, beat the egg whites until they hold firm, glossy peaks. Towards the end of the whisking time, whisk in the rest of the sugar little by little. Using a spatula, fold in the praline powder, then the cream and the *Frangelico*.

4 Spoon the *semifreddo* into the ramekins, pressing down to remove any air pockets. Cover with the overhanging clingfilm and then freeze until firm, about 2 hours.

5 In a small saucepan, bring the cream for the sauce to a boil over a moderate heat. Remove the pan from the heat and stir in the chopped chocolate, vanilla, salt and *Frangelico* and let cool. Chill the sauce for 1 hour, then serve it poured over the *semifreddo*.

SERVES 8

sorbetti di clementina

clementine sorbet

Sicily is famous for its sorbets, and indeed for its clementines. The flavour of the fruit is so much stronger and nicer than that of the satsumas you get from Spain. If you can't get hold of clementines or their juice, use blood orange juice instead (blood oranges also come from Sicily). The Vin Santo here actually comes from Tuscany, but it is now found all over the country.

500ml (18fl oz) clementine juice

finely grated zest of 3 clementines, preferably organic and unwaxed

1 tbsp Vin Santo

300ml (10fl oz) water

2 tbsp lemon juice

SYRUP

350ml (12fl oz) water

240g (8½oz) caster sugar

1 Mix together the clementine juice, zest, Vin Santo, water and lemon juice and chill.

2 Make the syrup by bringing the water and sugar to the boil. Quickly lower the heat to a simmer, and simmer for 5 minutes to melt the sugar. Remove from the heat and allow to cool before chilling well.

3 Mix the cold syrup with the cold juices and freeze according to the instructions on page 268. Transfer to the fridge 45 minutes before serving.

SERVES 8

sorbetto di lamponi

raspberry sorbet

Italians love iced food, particularly in the south, where sorbets or ice-creams are wonderfully refreshing in the exhausting heat of the day. *Trattorias* would make *sorbetti* like this, using fruit from the kitchen garden or *orto*, probably grown, tended and made by the *mama della casa* (the house). Loganberries or blackberries may be used instead, in season, for a richer colour and sharper flavour.

225g (8oz) granulated sugar

150ml (5fl oz) water

450g (1lb) fresh raspberries

juice of 1 large lemon

1 Put the sugar in a pan with the water and heat gently until the sugar has dissolved. Boil for 1 minute. Remove from the heat and allow to cool.

2 Press the raspberries through a coarse sieve, or purée in a blender or food processor, then sieve to remove the seeds.

3 Blend the raspberry purée, lemon juice and sugar syrup together, and freeze according to the instructions on page 268. Transfer to the fridge 45 minutes before serving.

SERVES 6-8

making Italian sweet shortcrust pastry

Each region of Italy has its own particular *pasta frolla*, or sweet shortcrust pastry, recipe, and sometimes even a *pasticceria* has its own unique version. The permutations are so endless that it's almost impossible to give a definitive recipe. The basics are flour, butter and sugar, but some pastries can be enriched and enlivened with eggs, ground almonds or other ground nuts, finely grated lemon zest, or pure vanilla extract. And for good pastry, you need good ingredients: Italian '00' plain flour preferably, as it has been milled twice for fineness (thus the double '00'), good unsalted butter and fine sugar (because it blends better). The better your eggs, the fresher your almonds, again the better the end result.

The kind of pastry you make depends on what filling you are going to marry with it and whether that filling is going to be wrapped in it or put into a tart shell. It's a matter of common sense: more liquid ingredients, for instance, need a denser pastry; more condensed ingredients need a lighter pastry. The pastry will always react differently to other ingredients, and I think each pastry is as wonderful as the next.

When you are making pastry, everything should be fairly cold – the room, the utensils, the water, the butter, and even your fingers. This is common sense too: if the room were too warm, the butter would not blend with the flour in the same way, would melt rather than crumble into the desired 'breadcrumb' texture.

Never over-work a pastry, as this would make the gluten in the flour stretch and toughen. Use your fingertips, and a very light technique when blending the flour and butter. Use a round-bladed knife to blend the liquid ingredients in to your dry pastry ingredients; this is lighter than a wooden spoon. And when you have a dough, knead it on a lightly floured surface for a few

seconds until smooth, then wrap it in cling film or greaseproof paper and chill it for 30 minutes. Always let it come back to room temperature before rolling.

Once you have rolled your pastry and cut it into shapes, or used it to line a tart tin, chill it again. If it is not cold, the pastry will shrink in the heat of the oven. Some pastry tart bases are pre-cooked, or blind-baked, while some aren't, and this is another side to the many styles of Italian (and other) pastries. Blind-baking obviously gives a crisper crust, but that is still dependent on what is going to be inside the case. Some pastries are cooked in one go with the filling, without pre- or blind-baking, and this pastry will be denser and less crisp.

Always use greaseproof paper, or foil, plus bought baking beans or some rice or dried pulses that you keep specially for blind-baking. In fact, a great tip for when baking pastry blind is to trim it first, and then put it in the freezer to get really cold. You then put it straight into a hot oven – usually between 180 and 200°C (350-400°F or Gas 4 and 6) so that it doesn't have time to shrink.

Pasta frolla can be savoury, made without sugar obviously. And, to save time, you can often make pastry in the food processor.

tortini di frutta fresca

fresh fruit tarts

Tarts such as this would be made daily in most *trattorias*, using seasonal fruit, often picked from their own *orto* or kitchen garden. The combination of fruit here is not classically Italian, perhaps, but it works very well. You could also try raspberries, strawberries and blueberries, for instance. The *crema pasticciera* is used in celebration cakes and tarts, and in pastries for breakfast. And the almond pastry here is a classic.

ITALIAN ALMOND PASTRY (MAKES ABOUT 400G/14OZ)

150g (5oz) Italian '00' plain flour

a pinch of salt

40g (1½oz) caster sugar

55g (2oz) ground almonds

90g (3¼oz) unsalted butter, cubed

a few drops vanilla extract

1 medium egg, beaten

CREMA PASTICCIERA

3 medium egg yolks

55g (2oz) caster sugar

35g (1¼oz) Italian '00' plain flour

300ml (10fl oz) milk

1 tsp pure vanilla extract

1 medium egg white

150ml (5fl oz) double cream

TOPPING

fruit of choice, eg 115g (4oz) cherries, 115g (4oz) green or black grapes and 2 kiwi fruits

APRICOT GLAZE

225g (8oz) apricot conserve

1 tbsp Kirsch

1 For the pastry, sift the flour, salt and sugar into a bowl, then mix in the almonds. Rub in the butter until the mixture resembles fine breadcrumbs. Make a well in the centre, add the vanilla and egg, and mix with a round-bladed knife to form a dough. Knead on a lightly floured surface for a few seconds until smooth. Wrap in cling film and chill for 30 minutes.

2 For the custard, whisk the egg yolks and 15g (½oz) of the sugar in a bowl until pale and thick. Fold in the flour. Put the milk and vanilla in a pan and bring almost to the boil. Gently whisk the hot milk into the egg and flour, then strain through a sieve back into the pan. Cook the custard over a gentle heat, stirring, until it thickens. Pour the hot custard into a clean bowl, then cover closely with cling film. Allow to cool completely but not to set too firmly.

3 Whisk the egg white until stiff, then gradually whisk in the remaining sugar. Whip the cream until thick. Whisk the cooled custard until smooth, then gradually fold in the egg white followed by the cream. Cover and chill.

4 Roll out the pastry on a lightly floured surface and cut out 12 x 13cm (5in) circles with a round cutter and use to line 12 x 10cm (4in) greased tartlet tins. Trim the edges and prick the base of each tartlet, then place the lined tins on a baking sheet and freeze for at least 15 minutes.

5 Preheat the oven to 200°C/400°F/gas mark 6.

6 Move the pastry cases straight from the freezer into the oven and bake for 15 minutes. Allow to cool a little in their tins, then transfer to a wire rack to cool.

7 Halve and stone the cherries, halve and seed the grapes and peel and slice the kiwi fruits. Mix the conserve and Kirsch in a small pan and heat to melt. Brush over the inside of each pastry case, reserving the leftover glaze. Divide the custard equally between the pastry cases and spread it evenly. Arrange the cherries, grapes and kiwi fruit on top. Reheat the remaining glaze and brush it over. Serve soon.

SERVES 4

crostata di pere a cioccolato

chocolate pear tart

I've been making this tart for ages, and I'm always surprised by how easy it is and by how crisp the pastry is. It comes from a restaurant in Rome, where the proprietress is an Englishwoman married to an Italian. I guess that's where the marmalade comes from! Always use the best dark chocolate, which has a magical affinity with the sweet pears.

ITALIAN CHOCOLATE PASTRY

55g (2oz) unsalted butter

115g (4oz) plain flour or Italian '00' plain flour

25g (1oz) cocoa powder

55g (2oz) caster sugar

1 large egg, beaten

FILLING

3 tbsp orange marmalade

2 ripe pears

115g (4oz) dark chocolate with 70% cocoa solids

55g (2oz) unsalted butter

2 large eggs, separated

115g (4oz) caster sugar

1 To make the pastry, rub the butter into the flour until the mixture resembles breadcrumbs. Sift in the cocoa powder, then add the sugar and enough of the beaten egg to bind the mixture together. Knead lightly, wrap in greaseproof paper and chill in the fridge for 20 minutes.

2 On a lightly floured surface, roll out the pastry and use to line a 20cm (8in) fluted flan tin. Cover the bottom of the pastry case with the marmalade.

3 Peel the pears, cut into quarters and remove the cores. Arrange them in the flan case.

4 Melt the chocolate and butter together in a bowl over a saucepan of simmering water. Do not let the bottom of the bowl touch the water. Set aside to cool.

5 Preheat the oven to 180°C/350°F/gas mark 4.

6 Beat together the egg yolks and sugar until pale and fluffy. Fold in the chocolate mixture. Whisk the egg whites until stiff, then fold into the mixture.

7 Pour the mixture over the pears and bake for 30 minutes, until firm to the touch. Serve hot or cold.

SERVES 8-12

making sponge

Italian cakes are luscious and full of flavour. They are made mainly in *pasticcerie* rather than in restaurants or at home, and most families buy them for special occasions such as Easter or Christmas. These cakes are eaten with coffee in the morning, for *merenda* (at tea time) or after a meal. But one cake is often made at home, and that is the Italian sponge. Light, soft and airy, it can be eaten filled or topped and is used as the basis of many Italian puddings such as trifle (*zuppa Inglese*, see page 263) or *cassata*. Its lightness is an ideal vehicle for alcohols and sugar syrups.

A sponge is a 'whisked' cake – a simple amalgam of eggs, flour and sugar, given lightness by whisking. An Italian sponge, or *pan di spagna* (so-called because it was introduced to Italy by the Spanish invaders of Sicily), is classically a mix of egg yolks and caster sugar, into which beaten egg whites and flour are gradually folded. The classic French Savoy cake (*savoie* or *biscuit*) is made in the same way. Italian sponges are also made by whisking the whole eggs together with the sugar, then folding in the flour, and the French equivalent of this is *Genoise*, also known as Genoese sponge (the name of which rather suggests an Italian influence!). This can sometimes contain butter, making a denser, richer cake, which would last longer than the slightly short-lived classic Italian version. Although we tend to think in Britain that the Victoria sponge is the be-all and end-all of sponges, it is actually not a true sponge, because of its butter content.

Sponges can also be whisked in slightly different ways. One version (as in the *zuppa Inglese*) whisks the eggs and sugar cold: this requires time and effort if being done by hand (but can be achieved in no time with a good mixer). Sometimes a chemical leavening agent is required when the eggs are added whole (the baking powder in the *zuppa Inglese* recipe helps raise the sponge, but is not entirely necessary). The other version (as in my grandmother's *gâteau* on page 284) is whisked over heat, in a bowl over, but not touching, some hot water. By this more traditional method, the heat speeds up the coagulation of protein in the eggs, allowing large

amounts of air to be trapped and so quickly increasing their volume. In both methods the eggs and sugar are whisked to the ribbon stage, or until a little of the mixture, when allowed to fall from the whisk back into the bowl, leaves a ribbon trail on the surface for 2-3 seconds before it disappears.

Sponges are easy to make, and can be very useful indeed. All you need are good ingredients. The eggs must be fresh, because the fresher they are, the more air they will trap when beaten. The sugar must be caster which, because it is finer, blends in more easily. The flour should be plain, soft and sifted (again to trap air): '00' Italian flour is ideal, and should not need sifting, as it has already been double-sifted (thus the '00'). And the oven must be well preheated, the cake tin prepared in advance, and the mixture baked immediately.

BELOW LEFT: A classic Italian sponge is made by first whisking together eggs and caster sugar and then folding in the flour.

ABOVE: the British Victoria sponge is made by first beating together butter and caster sugar, then beating in the eggs, and then folding in the flour. This is not strictly a sponge, as no whisking is required.

torta di cioccolata santini

chocolate cake santini

This chocolate cake is dedicated to my friend Santini, who used to work on my father's farm. It was he that taught me to appreciate combining chocolate and prunes, and the cake is voluptuously rich and indulgent.

unsalted butter for greasing

200g (7oz) prunes

4 tbsp Grand Marnier

1 vanilla pod, split lengthways

8 x 100g (3½oz) blocks dark chocolate with 70% cocoa solids

850ml (1½ pints) double cream

icing sugar to sprinkle

1 Butter a 6cm (2 ½in) deep x 23cm (9in) diameter springform tin, and line with parchment paper, bottom and sides.

2 Reserve 12 prunes to decorate the cake. Halve and stone the rest, roughly chop them and put them in a small bowl with the Grand Marnier and the split vanilla pod. Leave to macerate for 1 hour, stirring occasionally. Remove the pod.

3 Reserve 55g (2oz) of the chocolate, and put the remainder, in small pieces, in a heatproof bowl over a pan of simmering water. Do not let the bottom of the bowl touch the water. Leave for 15-20 minutes, stirring occasionally, until the chocolate has melted.

4 Remove the chocolate from the heat, then gently stir in the cream, soaked prunes and any extra liquid. Pour the mixture into the prepared cake tin, smooth over the surface with a palette knife, cover with cling film and refrigerate the mixture for at least 6 hours, or overnight.

5 When the cake has set, remove it from its tin, discard the parchment paper, and slide it on to a serving plate. Melt the reserved chocolate over a small pan of simmering water for 1 minute, not letting the bottom of the bowl touch the water, and spoon into a small plastic bag. Twist the neck of the bag to push the filling into one corner and, using scissors, snip off a small piece from one corner of the bag. With a zig-zag motion, pipe the chocolate across the cake. Serve chilled, decorated with stoned prunes and some icing sugar.

SERVES 20

torta della mia nonna

my Grandmother's italian gâteau

I have published this recipe before, but I can't resist including it again, as I have wonderful memories of it being served at family gatherings, birthdays and feast days. It can be served as an Italian wedding cake, and it is the sort of thing the local *trattoria* would do for such an occasion, calling it '*torta della casa*'. My grandfather wrote the recipe down in English as my grandmother dictated in Italian. He translated the custard as 'confectioner's custard'.

6 large eggs

175g (6oz) caster sugar

175g (6oz) plain flour or Italian '00' plain flour, plus extra for dusting

CREMA PASTICCIERA

2 tbsp plain flour or Italian '00' plain flour

2 tbsp caster sugar

1 large egg

finely grated zest of 1 unwaxed lemon (optional)

½ tsp pure vanilla extract

300ml (10fl oz) milk

BUTTER CREAM

175g (6oz) unsalted butter

175g (6oz) icing sugar, plus 1 tbsp

1 large egg

100ml (3½fl oz) cold strong black coffee

TOPPING

3 tbsp rum

300ml (10fl oz) double cream

a few drops of pure vanilla extract

5 tbsp toasted flaked almonds or hazelnuts, or a mix of both

seasonal fruit or flowers to decorate (optional)

1 Preheat the oven to 190°C/375°F/gas mark 5. Grease and line a deep 30cm (12in) or 23cm (9in) round cake tin and dust with flour.

2 To make the cake, put the eggs and sugar in a bowl and stand over a saucepan of gently simmering water. Using an electric whisk, whisk until thick and creamy. Gently sift in the flour a little at a time, and fold in. Pour into the prepared tin. Bake the 30cm (12in) cake for 18-20 minutes, or the 23cm (9in) cake for 35-40 minutes, until risen and golden. Turn out and cool on a wire rack.

3 To make the custard, in a small bowl mix together the flour, sugar, egg, lemon zest (if using) and vanilla extract. Gently heat the milk in a saucepan, but do not allow it to boil. Gradually pour the hot milk into the egg and flour mixture. Return to the saucepan and heat gently, stirring constantly with a wooden spoon, until the mixture thickens. Remove from the heat and place a piece of parchment paper over the custard to prevent a skin from forming. Leave to cool.

4 To make the butter cream, in a bowl beat together the butter and the 175g (6oz) icing sugar. In a separate bowl, beat the egg with the remaining tbsp of sugar. Add the egg and sugar mixture to the butter mixture. Using an electric whisk, very gently add the coffee (as it can split) and mix until thick and creamy.

5 To assemble the cake, cut it horizontally into three even layers. Spoon the custard on one layer and spread the butter cream on the second. Sandwich the slices together.

6 Gently pour over the rum to soak into the cake. Whip the cream and vanilla extract until it just holds its shape, then use to cover the top and sides of the cake. Carefully press the nuts on to the sides and decorate with fresh fruit or flowers if desired. Chill before serving.

SERVES 11-12

torta di mele d'maria

apple cake

Maria, who owns San Orsola, where I've spent many happy years teaching, loves this apple cake. The soured cream adds a wonderful acidity to the sweetness of the apple.

1 tbsp demerara sugar

125g (4¹/₂oz) unsalted butter

125g (4¹/₂oz) caster sugar

2 large eggs, separated

2 drops pure vanilla extract

125g (4¹/₂oz) ground almonds

55g (2oz) self-raising flour

150ml (5fl oz) soured cream

175g (6oz) Cox's Orange Pippin apples

whipped cream to serve

1 Preheat the oven to 180°C/350°F/gas mark 4. Grease and line a 20cm (8in) round cake tin with baking parchment, then sprinkle with the demerara sugar.

2 Cream together the butter and caster sugar until light and fluffy. Beat in the egg yolks and vanilla extract, then fold in the almonds, flour and soured cream.

3 Whisk the egg whites until they hold their shape then, using a metal spoon, fold into the creamed mixture.

4 Peel, core and slice the apples, and arrange in the base of the prepared tin. Spoon the creamed mixture over the apples and level the surface. Bake for 45-60 minutes, until golden and firm to the touch.

5 Invert on to a warmed serving plate, and serve warm with whipped cream.

SERVES 6-8

torta alle susine e nocciole

warm plum and hazelnut cake

Fresh, juicy plums, which in Italy are ripe in about the middle of September, give this cake a wonderfully moist texture. It is best eaten warm, with a big dollop of either double cream or crème fraîche.

450g (1lb) ripe plums

100g (3½oz) unsalted butter, diced

85g (3oz) soft brown sugar

2 large eggs

225g (8oz) self-raising flour

55g (2oz) chopped, shelled hazelnuts

icing sugar for dusting

1 Preheat the oven to 190°C /375°F/gas mark 5. Grease and line a 20cm (8in) round cake tin.

2 Cut the plums into quarters, discarding the stones.

3 Cream together the butter and sugar until light and fluffy. Then beat in the eggs one at a time and fold in the flour.

4 Carefully fold in the plums and then pile the mixture into the prepared tin. Sprinkle the hazelnuts on the top, and bake for 45-50 minutes, or until golden brown and firm to the touch.

5 Leave to cool slightly in the tin, then turn out and serve slightly warm, dusted with sifted icing sugar.

SERVES 6

panettone

sweet Christmas bread

Panettone comes from Milan in northern Italy. The breads are exported in attractive tall boxes, which can be seen hanging in Italian delicatessens all over the world. Panettone made at home is not so tall as the commercial varieties, and its texture is not quite so open, but it makes a deliciously light alternative to heavy Christmas cakes.

4 tsp fresh yeast or 2¼ tsp dried yeast

225ml (8fl oz) hand-hot milk

350g (12oz) plain white or Italian '00' plain flour

100g (3½oz) unsalted butter, softened

3 large egg yolks

50g (1¾oz) caster sugar

85g (3oz) chopped candied peel

50g (1¾oz) sultanas

1½ tsp freshly grated nutmeg

icing sugar, for dusting

1 Grease the insides of three clean 400g tomato tin cans or similar. Cut three strips of baking parchment, each measuring 55 x 33cm (22 x 12in). Fold each piece in half lengthways, then use to line the tins. Line the bases with a circle of baking parchment.

2 Blend the fresh yeast with 2 tbsp of the milk until smooth, then stir in the remaining milk. If using dried yeast, sprinkle it into the milk and leave in a warm place for 15 minutes until frothy.

3 Sift the flour into a large bowl and make a well in the centre. Pour the yeast liquid into the well and, using a wooden spoon, gradually draw in the flour from the sides of the bowl until well mixed. Knead on a lightly floured work-surface for 10 minutes until smooth. Form into a ball and place in a lightly oiled bowl. Cover with a clean tea-towel and leave to rise in a warm place for 45 minutes, or until doubled in size.

4 Knead the softened butter into the dough with two of the egg yolks, the sugar, the candied peel, sultanas and nutmeg. Cover and leave to stand, again in a warm place, for a further 45 minutes, or until doubled in size.

5 Divide the dough into three pieces and knead each piece for 2-3 minutes. Form each piece into a smooth ball and place inside the cans. Leave in a warm place for about 30 minutes, or until risen to the top of the cans.

6 Meanwhile, preheat the oven to 200°C/400°F/gas mark 6.

7 Brush the remaining egg yolk over the dough. Bake for 20 minutes, then lower the temperature to 180°C/350°F/gas mark 4 and bake for a further 20 minutes, or until a skewer inserted in the centre comes out clean. Leave to cool in the cans. The panettone can be stored in an airtight tin for up to a week.

MAKES 3 SMALL PANETTONE, TO SERVE 9

biscotti a forma di cuore
heart-shaped biscuits

The Italians are famously passionate and romantic, and making biscuits or other foods in heart shapes is very popular. I think these would be perfect for St Valentine's Day, for someone's birthday, or for part of a special occasion. You can of course make the biscuits any shape. Eat them with ice-cream, dip them into **Vin Santo**, or even eat them with a coffee in the afternoon as a **merenda**, or snack.

125g (4¹/₂oz) unsalted butter, plus extra for greasing

150g (5¹/₂oz) caster sugar, plus extra for sprinkling

1 large egg yolk, beaten

225g (8oz) plain flour or Italian '00' plain flour

finely grated zest of 1 unwaxed lemon

1 large egg white, lightly beaten with 1 tbsp water

1 Preheat the oven to 180°C/350°F/gas mark 4. Grease two large baking sheets.

2 Cream together the butter and sugar until light and fluffy. Add the egg yolk and beat well, then stir in the flour and lemon zest.

3 Knead lightly and shape into a ball. Wrap in cling film and chill slightly to make it firm and easier to roll.

4 Roll out half the mixture at a time, keeping the rest refrigerated. Roll out on a lightly floured surface to about 5mm (¹/₄in) thick. Cut out heart-shaped biscuits. Brush away any excess flour on the biscuits.

5 Put the biscuits on to the prepared baking sheets, spaced apart, and brush with beaten egg white and water to glaze. Sprinkle with sugar.

6 Bake for 15 minutes, until light brown. Remove from the baking sheets and cool on wire racks.

MAKES 20-24

bisquit tortoni

biscuit tortoni

'Biscuit Tortoni' is a creation of a Neapolitan ice-cream maker, one Signor Tortoni. Signor Tortoni was to expand his career, by moving to Paris where he opened the famous Café Napolitaine. His delicious dish is popular throughout Italy, especially in Rome.

300ml (10fl oz) double cream

2 tbsp icing sugar

225g (8oz) chopped almonds, toasted

2 tbsp rum

225g (8oz) amaretti biscuits (almond macaroons)

10 natural glacé or maraschino cherries, or cherries preserved in rum

1 Arrange 10 paper cake cases on a baking tray.

2 Whisk together the cream and icing sugar until stiff. Fold in the almonds, and blend the rum well into the mixture.

3 Crumble the amaretti biscuits into quarters and put pieces in the bottom of the paper cases. Add the cream mixture and top each with a cherry.

4 Place in the freezer for 1-2 hours, until firm. Store in the freezer for up to 2 weeks.

5 Transfer to the fridge 45 minutes before serving.

SERVES 10

fiorentini

italian florentines

There are many variations on this luxurious biscuit, which is said to have originated in Austria, despite its Italian-sounding name.

150g (5¹/₂oz) whole blanched almonds

150g (5¹/₂oz) whole blanched hazelnuts

225g (8oz) natural red glacé cherries

100g (3¹/₂oz) glacé fruits (eg melon, lemon, orange)

55g (2oz) plain flour

¹/₂ tsp ground allspice

¹/₂ tsp freshly grated nutmeg

100g (3¹/₂oz) caster sugar

100g (3¹/₂oz) clear honey

100g (3¹/₂oz) plain chocolate with 70% cocoa solids

1 Preheat the oven to 180°C/350°F/gas mark 4. Grease a 23cm (9 in) round cake tin, and line it with baking parchment.

2 Put the almonds and hazelnuts on a baking tray, and toast in the oven for 10 minutes. Put in a mixing bowl, and leave to cool. Chop roughly.

3 Wash the cherries, then chop all the fruits and add to the nuts. Sift the flour, allspice and nutmeg over the fruits and nuts, and mix well together.

4 In a saucepan, warm the sugar and honey together over a low heat until the sugar has dissolved. Add the honey mixture to the fruit mixture, and then stir together.

5 Turn the mixture into the prepared tin and level the top. Bake for 25 minutes, then leave to cool in the tin.

6 Break the chocolate into small pieces and melt in a pan over boiling water (the water must not touch the bottom of the pan). Spread over the nut mixture in an even layer, then, when set, cut into serving pieces.

MAKES 8 PIECES

germinus

Sardinian macaroons

This recipe was given to me by my friend Antoinette in Umbria, who has a fabulous pastry shop. Her parents come from Sardinia, where wonderful almonds are grown, thus the Sicilian origin of the recipe. Be sure to use fresh almonds for the best results.

2 egg whites

175g (6oz) caster sugar

175g (6oz) flaked almonds

1 tsp lemon juice

1 Preheat the oven to 170°C/325°F/gas mark 3. Cover several large baking trays with baking parchment.

2 Beat the egg whites until stiff. Fold in the sugar, almonds and lemon juice. Place heaped teaspoons of the mixture, well apart, on the baking trays.

3 Bake for about 20 minutes, until lightly coloured. Leave to cool. Store in an airtight container.

MAKES 25-30

biscotti garibaldi

garibaldi biscuits

These biscuits are eaten all over Italy. They are blissfully straightforward to make and children love them.

115g (4oz) plain white or Italian '00' plain flour

85g (3oz) unsalted butter, chilled

55g (2oz) caster sugar, plus a little extra to finish

115g (4oz) currants

1 large egg, beaten

1 Preheat the oven to 180°C/350°F/gas mark 4. Lightly grease a 30 x 20cm (12 x 8in) Swiss roll tin.

2 Sift the flour into a mixing bowl. Dice and rub in the butter until it is evenly distributed and the mixture resembles fine breadcrumbs. Stir in the sugar and currants.

3 Add almost all the beaten egg to bind the ingredients together, and form a soft but not sticky dough.

4 Turn the dough into the prepared tin and roll it out so that the base is evenly covered and the surface is smooth. Brush the remaining egg over the dough and sprinkle with the extra caster sugar.

5 Bake for about 20 minutes, until golden brown. As soon as the pastry is cooked, cut it into 24 rectangles. Transfer to a wire rack and leave to cool.

MAKES 24

torrone di sesamo e mandorle

sesame and almond nougat

This recipe demonstrates the extensive use of honey and almonds in Italian cooking. Sesame seeds are full of calcium, and almonds are good for you, too, so don't feel guilty about enjoying this recipe!

2 tbsp almond or sunflower oil

200g (7oz) fragrant honey

55g (2oz) caster sugar

225g (8oz) sesame seeds

200g (7oz) blanched almonds, toasted and roughly chopped

1 Brush a baking tray and rolling pin generously with oil.

2 Put the honey in a saucepan and heat gently until melted. Add the sugar and slowly bring to the boil. Add the sesame seeds and almonds and heat, stirring all the time, until the mixture thickens.

3 Pour on to the greased baking tray and flatten with the rolling pin into a square of about 28cm (11in) and 5mm (^{1}/4in) thick. Leave to cool slightly.

4 Using a sharp knife, cut into small 4cm (1^{1}/2in) squares. Leave to cool completely. Store in an airtight tin.

MAKES ABOUT 48 SQUARES

tartuffi di cioccolato

chocolate truffles

These are the most scrumptious, wickedly rich truffles, and they really do make the perfect gift at any time of the year. Wrap them in clear cellophane, or splash out on a small gift box for them, and you have a present anyone will welcome.

55g (2oz) petit beurre biscuits

85g (3oz) dark chocolate with 70% cocoa solids

25g (1oz) shelled hazelnuts, finely chopped

35g (1^{1}/4oz) raisins

1 tbsp rum

cocoa powder, for dusting

1 Put the biscuits in a polythene bag and crush with a rolling pin.

2 Break the chocolate into a heatproof bowl over a pan of simmering water (the bowl must not touch the water) and heat until melted. Remove from the heat and mix with the biscuit crumbs. Add the remaining ingredients, except for the cocoa powder, and mix together. Leave to cool for 1 hour.

3 Form the mixture into small balls the size of a cherry, and dust with cocoa powder. Place in little sweet papers, and store in a cool, dry place.

SERVES 12

herbs, spices and flavourings

italian broths or stocks

A good **brodo** – broth or stock – is vital in so many ways in Italian cooking: in the making of soups and savoury sauces, and primarily in the making of risottos (see pages 50-67) and polenta (see pages 68-77). All the ingredients should always be of the very best quality. Three of the four basic recipes below will give you 1.5 litres (2½ pints); the fish broth yields 1.2 litres (2 pints). You could keep the chicken or beef stock for 4-5 days; the fish stock for 1-2 days; and the vegetable stock for 3 days. But all freeze well.

BASIC METHOD

Rinse and prepare your basic ingredients as appropriate. The ingredients for beef and vegetable broths need special treatment (see below). Put the principal ingredients in a large saucepan, add the flavouring ingredients, then pour in the water. Bring to the boil then follow the separate broth instructions. Skim off any scum from time to time. Strain through a fine sieve and cool as quickly as possible. If necessary, remove any solidified fat from the surface.

CHICKEN BROTH

A chicken broth should really be made with a good, whole raw chicken, although you can use a raw carcass or bones, or chicken pieces (chicken wings are available quite cheaply). You can also make broth with a cooked chicken carcass, but this will not be so flavourful. A game stock can be made from game birds in the same way as for chicken stock.

1.4kg (3lb) chicken, 3.4 litres (6 pints) water, 2 onions, peeled, 2 celery stalks, 2 carrots, 10 black peppercorns, 3 bay leaves, and some parsley stalks. Bring to the boil, boil rapidly for about 5 minutes, then reduce to a simmer, uncovered, for 2 hours.

FISH BROTH

Use the bones from white, not oily, fish. When you buy cleaned fish from the fishmonger, ask for the bones – and some extra fish bones or heads too.

1kg (2¼lb) white fish heads and bones, 2 litres (3½ pints) water, 2 peeled onions each stuck with 5 cloves, 2 carrots, 2 celery stalks, 2 bay leaves, 10 black peppercorns, and 500ml (18fl oz) dry white wine. Bring to the boil, then simmer uncovered for 20 minutes until well reduced.

BEEF BROTH

Use raw beef bones and scraps, or beef shin. A lamb, pork or veal stock can be made in the same way.

Roast 1kg (2¼lb) bones or shin first with 2 large peeled and quartered onions, for about 30 minutes in a 200°C/400°F/Gas 6 oven. Pour off any fat. Put onions and beef in a large saucepan, add 3 celery stalks, 1 head garlic, 2 carrots, 2 large tomatoes and 3 bay leaves. After bringing to the boil, boil rapidly for about 5 minutes, then reduce to a simmer, half covered, for 2-3 hours.

VEGETABLE BROTH

Use the most flavourful vegetables you can find.

Firstly fry the vegetables – 3 crushed garlic cloves, 1 large onion, coarsely chopped, 4 leeks, 2 carrots, 2 celery stalks, 1 fennel bulb, halved – in 1 tbsp olive oil and 40g (1½oz) unsalted butter, until softened but not browned. Add a handful of parsley stalks, 4 bay leaves and 4 sprigs fresh thyme, and 3 litres (5 pints) water, and bring to the boil. Reduce the heat, cover and simmer for 1 hour. Strain, and boil rapidly to reduce by half.

italian herbs and spices

THE MOST COMMONLY USED HERBS

Herbs are a cornerstone of Italian cooking. All herbs contain aromatic essential oils in their leaves, and basically, in culinary terms, there are two types: 'hardy' herbs and 'soft' herbs. In hardy herbs these oils are less volatile than in softer herbs because of the climate extremes to which they have been exposed. For instance you could happily add a bay leaf or a sprig of fresh thyme or rosemary – all of them 'hardy' – to a stew, while a sprig of 'soft' basil would lose its unique fragrance very swiftly on being cooked.

The most commonly used Italian hardy herbs (or *erbe robuste*) include bay, thyme, rosemary and sage, all of which grow higher up, or in cooler temperatures than 'soft' herbs (see below). Bay is used in *aromi*, the Italian equivalent of a bouquet garni, and in marinades. Thyme grows wild all over the Mediterranean mountains, and is used in many meat dishes, in *aromi*, and in marinades for olives. Rosemary goes well with roasted meats, and is used all over the country to scent focaccia. Sage is one of the most popular hardy herbs, and is used with white meats (especially pork, a Tuscan speciality, and in a veal saltimbocca), with calf's liver and in stuffed pastas.

The most commonly used Italian soft herbs include basil, parsley, oregano and mint. All of these are softer in leaf and stalk than hardy herbs, and are much more vulnerable to temperature. Basil comes in 2 types: *lattuga* or 'lettuce' has huge leaves, while *genovese* has very small leaves. The former can be added to sauces towards the end of cooking, or in salads; the latter is used to make pesto. I hardly need to describe the uses of parsley, as they are legion (I use it like salt) – but try to get flat-leaf or continental parsley rather than the British curly. Oregano grows wild in the mountains in Italy, and is wonderfully fragrant (more so when dried).

Use it in pasta sauces and on pizzas. Mint is probably my favourite herb, and I use it a lot – doing wonders for courgettes, tomatoes, potatoes, sauces, marinades and fish. It also makes a great mint pesto for pasta, gnocchi and risotto (see page 47).

THE MOST COMMONLY USED SPICES

Spices are not nearly so appreciated as herbs in Italian cooking. Salt and pepper (black usually) are the most basic, and they are used in almost everything. Saffron is now grown in Italy, although it is not native; its spicy, bitter taste is the classic flavouring of a risotto Milanese, and is also used in fish sauces and soups. Cloves add flavour to meat dishes, broths, cooked and preserved fruits, while juniper lends its wonderful tang to game and other meat dishes. Nutmeg is used in potato dishes, stews, stuffings for ravioli, and with spinach. Chillies are the most widely used of all, especially in the south of the country, where fresh chillies and dried – *peperoncino* and *diavolillo* – are added to almost every dish, whether meat, fish or vegetable. And of course, vanilla – the pod itself and its black sweet seeds – is used in many desserts, and especially in *gelati* or ice-creams.

italian piquant ingredients

By 'piquants', I mean those strongly flavoured ingredients that are uniquely characteristic of Italian cooking, which lend savour, piquancy and a special 'roundness' to many Italian dishes. They include Parmesan cheese, anchovies, garlic, capers, lemons and dried porcini mushrooms (*ceps*).

PARMESAN CHEESE

This famous Italian cheese is like no other, in that it is used as an intrinsic flavouring in many dishes. Made with semi-skimmed, unpasteurized cow's milk, the cheese is straw-coloured with a brittle, grainy texture and a fruity, fragrant flavour. At 1-2 years, it is pale, supple and crumbly, when it is good for use in desserts, especially with pears, apples, grapes or nuts. It is also served grated into olive oil, as a dressing. At 3-4 years it is darker, drier and very hard, and is the classic grating and flavouring cheese for pasta, risottos, polentas and other dishes.

ANCHOVIES

These are probably the best-loved of all Italian fish, and although they are eaten fresh, they are usually eaten preserved, either marinated in oil, or salted. See page 172 for further details.

GARLIC

Whether classified as a herb, spice or vegetable, garlic is one of the foundation stones of Italian cooking. It appears in virtually every sauce for pasta, and indeed one of the most basic spaghetti sauces consists only of garlic and olive oil: *spaghetti con aglio e olio* is eaten at least once a fortnight in most homes, and has a similar place in the nation's life as they say beans on toast (which I hate) has in Britain. Garlic enhances vegetables, salads, dressings, soups, dips/sauces such as tapenade and pesto, and roasted it can be spread like toothpaste on to *bruschetta* or *crostini*.

CAPERS

Capers are the buds of a plant grown mostly in the islands of Lipari and Pantelleria near Sicily. They need to be cured before they can be eaten, in vinegar, brine or dry salt. The salted are best, but need to be washed well before use; the capers brined in jars should be rinsed. The unique flavour of capers is added to dishes towards the end of cooking: to sauces, particularly those accompanying fish, to salads, tapenade, and to cooked vegetables. They're good on pizzas too.

LEMONS

The lemon is the fruit of a tropical tree, but is now grown all over the south of Italy, primarily in Campania, my native region. Lemons are rich in Vitamin C, but it is in cooking that they are most useful, their acidity lending flavour and enhancing flavour, whether the juice or powerful zest is used. Lemon juice can be added to almost anything – dressings, sauces, gravies, salads; and the zest adds zing to anything from salads to cakes, ice-cream, liqueurs and pastry. Lemons are like medicine to sweet and savoury foods.

DRIED PORCINI MUSHROOMS (CEPS)

Wild mushrooms are a passion for most Italians, and in season you will see hunters all over the forests, and market stalls laden with a glorious harvest. They are eaten fresh, but the *cep* or *porcino* ('little pig') is dried, when it becomes one of the primary sources of flavour in many Italian dishes. Dried porcini need to be rehydrated before use: soak them in water to cover for about 20 minutes until they soften (and strain and keep the soaking water for stock, it retains much of the flavour). Use in pasta, polenta and meat sauces, with vegetables (great with potatoes), and on pizzas.

italian oils and vinegars

Oils and vinegars are hugely important in Italian cooking, and I truly believe that the best of both of them come from Italy.

OLIVES AND OLIVE OIL

Olive oil, for me, is the bottled essence of Italy, and the silvery green of the olive tree is the most characteristic colour of the country. Every housewife in Italy, whether from Tuscany, Umbria, Liguria or Calabria, will have good stores of a variety of olive oils in her kitchen. And she will also have some olives themselves, which she will have preserved from the tree (by brining or salting), plain or with other aromatics. She will use these in cooking, or simply serve them to eat in the hand. The olives from Ascoli Piceno in the Marches, which borders on Umbria, are so huge that they can be stuffed (with capers, garlic, breadcrumbs, herbs). Olives are also used in bread doughs, on top of pizzas, in salads, as an *aperitivo*, in tapenade and on *bruschetta*.

The quality of olive oils depends on the type of tree, the ripeness of the fruit, the climate, the location and the soil. Most oil is pressed from unripe green olives (they become purple and black as they mature). Tuscan oil is considered precious because the olives are picked early, yielding an oil that is high in flavour but low in volume. Conversely the Ligurian Taggiasca olives (also eaten in the hand) are picked and pressed when almost ripe.

There are three grades of olive oil: extra virgin oil, virgin oil and olive oil, and all are high in monounsaturates. Extra virgin comes from the first pressing of the olives (from September to November); the fresh oil is often too peppery to enjoy straightaway, and needs to mellow in the bottle for a few weeks. Extra virgin is the one you should use in dressings, or as the last delicious drizzle on top of a soup or vegetable Do not cook with it, as heat damages the proteins. Virgin oil is usually produced from more mature olives, and this is the oil to use (because of its higher acidity) for light cooking or in dressings such as mayonnaise. Plain olive oil is the one to use for cooking, preserving vegetables and for making a flavoured oil (with chillies, garlic, herbs). Never ever be without some good olive oil if you want to cook Italian.

VINEGARS

Every Italian kitchen will also display a variety of vinegars. We won't have raspberry, sherry or Champagne (or the horror that is the British malt vinegar), but we will have red, white and, our favourite, balsamic vinegars. All three are used in cooking and in salad dressings, but balsamic is always the most highly prized. It is produced in Modena in the region of Emilia-Romagna. The Trebbiano grape is used exclusively, and it is the must of the grape that is used in the acidification. The must is transferred to an oak barrel for a length of time and then transferred to other barrels to vary its flavour over a period of 5 years, during which it develops its character. Sometimes the maturation takes even longer – up to 30 years – which is why balsamics labelled '*tradizionale*' are so expensive. There are available, however, good balsamic vinegars aged from 5 to 20 years. Use a good balsamic as a flavour enhancer, in marinades and dressings, brushing on foods before cooking, in good olive oil for dipping your bread into, and sprinkled in a miserly fashion on some grilled or steamed vegetables.

index